CATEGORIES IN TEXT AND TALK

INTRODUCING QUALITATIVE METHODS provides a series of volumes which introduce qualitative research to the student and beginning researcher. The approach is interdisciplinary and international. A distinctive feature of these volumes is the helpful student exercises.

One stream of the series provides texts on the key methodologies used in qualitative research. The other stream contains books on qualitative research for different disciplines or occupations. Both streams cover the basic literature in a clear and accessible style, but also cover the 'cutting edge' issues in the area.

CATEGORIES IN TEXT AND TALK

*A Practical Introduction to
Categorization Analysis*

Georgia Lepper

SAGE Publications
London · Thousand Oaks · New Delhi

© Georgia Lepper 2000

First published 2000

SAGE Publications Ltd
6 Bonhill Street
London EC2A 4PU

SAGE Publications Inc.
2455 Teller Road
Thousand Oaks, California 91320

SAGE Publications India Pvt Ltd
32, M-Block Market
Greater Kailash - I
New Delhi 110 048

British Library Cataloguing in Publication data

A catalogue record for this book is available from the British Library

ISBN 0 7619 5666 2
ISBN 0 7619 5667 0 (pbk)

Library of Congress catalog card number 131532

Typeset by Type Study, Scarborough, North Yorkshire
Printed in Great Britain by Athenaeum Press, Gateshead

Contents

Preface

This book is the product of a career which crosses several disciplines. I am about the same age as Sacks would have been had he lived. I am also American, and was educated in a similar milieu. In those days, I encountered social science, and turned away from it, with much the same feeling Sacks describes – a disappointment with its failure to address an 'understanding of the way humans do things'. It was many years later, having returned to academic study in Britain, that I first encountered his work. I felt immediately 'back home' in the company of his wide interests combined with the discipline of his methods. The book reflects that appreciation in taking a multi-disciplinary approach. It is my hope that its readers will find in it some of the same excitement in encountering the open space of analytic enquiry which Categorization Analysis, practised with the discipline and restraint which Sacks imposed on himself, can bring.

When I first started doing the analysis, I remember, faced with some mundane text, struggling with the feeling, 'there's nothing there'. There were marvellous studies by those few researchers who were practising categorization analysis, and the examples of Sacks' own analyses from his lectures. It was hard to get from where I was, to where they were. One of the things which helped me was my professional training in analytic psychotherapy, which had taught me to listen closely to the talk in the consulting room, even when I didn't know what was going on. With faith built on that experience, I persevered, and soon found that concentrated attention to seemingly trivial details in the texts I was studying was rewarded by deepening awareness, not only when I was analysing data, but even when I was practising my craft of psychotherapy. In writing this book, I hoped to provide a guide to the beginning researcher to find a way into the text or talk under study, by building an 'analytic attitude': an attitude of deep attention to the details of talk and text.

It follows from the nature of my personal and intellectual development, that I have had the privilege of a wide variety of formative experiences with teachers and colleagues. Colleagues within the profession of analytic psychotherapy who support my allegiance to empirical method; colleagues in sociology who tolerate my psychoanalytic formation and training; friends and family who put up with my flights of intellectual energy and excitement; students who get interested in the process with me, and push my thinking ahead with their own: I thank them all.

Most of all, I have to thank David Silverman, who introduced me to categorization analysis, and helped me to develop my practice of the discipline in a grounded and rigorous way. He has supported every phase of the writing of this book. Thanks are also owed to those who have helped with the analysis and some of the data used in the examples – the 'MCD Group': Moira Kelly, Kay Fensom, Sally Hunt and Tim Rapley. They also read and commented on drafts of some of these chapters, as did my students at the University of Kent. They made me make it simpler and better. Thanks also to Charlotte, who crafted the photo-image.

1

Introducing Categorization Analysis

CONTENTS

What is categorization analysis?

Data extract (Sacks, 1992a: 144)

```
1   Joe:     (cough) We were in an automobile discussion,
2   Henry:   discussing the psychological motives for
3   Mel:     drag-racing in the streets
```

With this co-produced sentence, three young teenagers, members of a therapy group, greet a new arrival who has just been introduced to them. It comes from an 8 minute segment of data, drawn from the opening of the session, which Sacks studied intensively over a period of several years. Here are some of the things he was interested in:

- *how* the speakers demonstrated their collaborative interest in a topic ('automobile discussion'), and through it, their identity as a unit;
- *how* the syntactic 'we' is employed in the context to render as an observable, 'we are a unit';
- *how* the participle 'drag-racing' provides for a hearable description of who they are, and how they want to be identified.

Sacks comments:

> We get, then, a kind of extraordinary tie between syntactic possibilities and phenomena like social organization. That is, an extremely strong way that these kids go about demonstrating that, for one, there is a group here, is their getting together to put this sentence together, collaboratively.
> It's hard to figure out how they could do that right off, in anything like as sharp a way as they picked. (1992a: 145)

Sacks goes on to demonstrate how the construction of the sentence – its grammatical features, and the way the speakers are able to draw upon those features – provides the evidence for an alternative understanding of how to study language:

> About the third part [Mel's 'drag racing on the streets' – line 3] there is no question that it collaborates with the second in making of the first, the 'independent clause'. Neither the second or third alone are sentences, and the two together do not make a sentence. Only with the first is it all a sentence. So that particular choice of participle is to be accounted for by reference to some task of social organization, solved by reference to syntactical features. The participle, then, becomes an object in the technology of social structures, I suppose. (1992a: 146)

The subsequent development of the technique of categorization analysis is built on the kind of examination to which Sacks subjected this data. It is the attempt to answer some of those questions by taking categorization as an object in the technology of social structures, and examining how it is that ordinary speakers employ formal features of language as a resource in order to 'do that right off, in anything like as sharp a way as they picked'.

Sacks' primary concerns were not about language as such, but about social processes. His aim was to develop a natural observational method of studying social interaction, using:

> methods [which] will be reproducible descriptions in the sense that any scientific description might be, such that the natural occurrences that we're describing can yield abstract or general phenomena which need not rely on statistical observability for their abstractness or generality. (1992a: 11)

Sacks and his work

Sacks delivered much of his thinking in oral form, in the context of lectures to his students at UCLA, and later at UCIrvine. Here are some of the titles of the lectures in which Sacks worked on the data from this therapy group over a period of five years:

'Hotrodders' as a revolutionary category
Tying rules, insult sequences

Invitations, identification, category bound activities
Clausal construction: hot-rodding as a test
Pervasive, inexhaustible topics
'Patients with observers' as 'performers with audience'
The dirty joke as technical object

A hall mark of Sacks' method was the intense scrutiny to which he subjected naturally occurring data – talk and text drawn from a variety of sources. He did not approach the data in the manner of classical sociological analysis, with 'operational definitions' of social phenomena, such as 'power' or 'class' or 'role', seeking to identify the causes of the phenomena. Indeed he was very critical of this approach. Instead, he asked of his data these questions: What kind of social object is this utterance/communication? What interactional work does it do in the context in which it was employed? *How* does it achieve the task it seeks to do? His method was 'bottom up', within the tradition of **analytic induction**. He returned to the same data over and over again, gradually uncovering the complexity of what is happening at each moment in ongoing everyday interaction through relentless analytic attention to the detail of the talk or text.

Sacks completed graduate training in law at Yale, where, influenced by the teaching of Harold Lasswell, he began to think about how the law actually *worked* (Schegloff, 1992: xii). As we will see, how social life works was to be the primary focus for all his later work. On Laswell's advice, he then went to the University of California at Berkeley to continue his graduate studies in research, rather than pursuing the practice of law for which he had formally trained. There he encountered Erving Goffman. Later he collaborated with Harold Garfinkel, whom he had already met. It is from this collaboration that much of the suicide helpline data comes which forms an important source for the early analyses. The systematic study of everyday life, initiated by Goffman and Garfinkel – under the titles the 'interaction order' and 'ethnomethodology' – was the major influence on Sacks' work. Other important strands of influence were contemporary developments in philosophy and linguistics: 'ordinary language philosophy', and particularly Wittgenstein; and the theory of generative grammar being developed by Chomsky. Sacks combined the two disciplines – the study of everyday interaction, and the study of ordinary language – into a new discipline: the study of naturally occurring conversation.

In the first lecture he gave to students in UCLA, he drew on work from his PhD thesis based on recorded data from telephone helpline conversations between suicidal callers and telephone counsellors. He introduces some considerations on conversational sequencing from the opening exchange of a 'call for help'. In the manner which would characterize all his analyses, he remarks that he 'was very puzzled by "I don't know" in return to "May I help you". I couldn't figure out what they were doing with it.' He then makes some observations about this exchange, and in conclusion, he makes an important point about his method:

As a general matter, then, one can begin to look for kinds of objects that have a base environment, that, when they get used in that environment perform a rather simple task, but that can be used in quite different environments to do quite other tasks. (1992a: 8)

In the second lecture, Sacks moves on to another way of considering his suicide helpline data: he considers the classes of persons to whom the suicidal caller might turn for help, as evidenced in the conversations he is studying. He shows how 'ceremonial relationships' can be understood in relation to the way talk is constructed around everyday social interaction. Here is evidence both of the influence of Erving Goffman, who supervised his PhD research, and of his move away from Goffman's model. For Goffman, the ceremonial order precedes and makes possible everyday interaction. For Sacks, the situated organization of the interaction, including both the sequencing of the talk, and the deployment of 'membership' categories – the classes of persons and actions – precedes and makes possible the ceremonial, and, by extension, the social order. Out of this insight, the study of categorization developed into a systematic analysis of the ways in which classes of persons – membership categories – and their activities – category bound activities – are employed within a 'base environment' – a membership categorization device – to assemble the 'inference rich', recognizable actions and descriptions which, Sacks proposed, form the foundations of social order.

If the influence of Goffman can be seen in Sacks' initial approach to his data, so also the influence of Garfinkel is evident in the core focus of Sacks' method: its concentration on the situated nature of the talk under study. Garfinkel introduced into his study of everyday social interaction the concept of indexicality – the notion that in everyday life, the meaning of words is dependent on the context of their use. Sacks extended this concept by applying it in a systematic way to the study of naturally occurring talk.

So the work I am doing is about talk. It is about the details of talk. In some sense it is about how conversations work. The specific aim is, in the first instance, to see whether actual single events are studiable and how they might be studiable, and then what an explanation of them might look like.

Thus it is not any particular conversation, as an object, that we are primarily interested in. Our aim is to get into a position to transform in an almost literal, physical sense, our view of 'what happened' from a matter of a particular interaction done by particular people, to a matter of interactions as a product of machinery. We are trying to find the machinery. In order to do so we have to get access to its products. At this point, it is conversation that provides us such access. (Sacks, 1984a: 26–7)

Sacks' methods and generalizability

In his later work, Sacks widened his focus of attention from the study of single examples of situated talk, and began to consider how to treat aggregates of data. In his introduction to the second set of lectures, which contain the lectures delivered after Sacks' move to UCIrvine, Schegloff (1992: xi) characterizes this shift to:

- *an order of organization,* rather than a particular practice of talking;
- *a class of places in an aggregate of data,* rather than an excerpt;
- *an organizationally characterized problem or form of interactional work,* rather than an individually designed outcome;
- *invariances of features* rather than context specified practices.

It could be said that this shift of analytic attention follows the practice of what Kuhn (1970) calls 'normal science', in moving from a natural observational method, in which Sacks was at first engaged, to a more generalizing phase of theoretical formulation, during which observations are tested across increasingly large samples. Sacks grounded his method in science by arguing that an important aspect of science is that 'findings' are not simply things found, but the end product of a set of procedures. The basic rule of scientific method is the reproducibility of findings, and reproducibility depends on agreed and public procedures which can be followed by anyone to produce the same findings. It follows, he argued, that the procedures followed in scientific analysis are as important a part of science as the findings, and that the study of procedures is therefore no more, and no less, a legitimate object of study than any other object of scientific enquiry.

Subsequent developments

Sacks published very little in his lifetime, and many of his papers were only published after his premature death in an accident in 1975. The complete *Lectures in conversation* were assembled from the notes and recordings of former students, and published in 1992. Sacks' oeuvre is, therefore, 'unfinished' work, in the sense that when he died he was still very much in the process of developing what he expected to be a general theory of conversational interaction. Publications which would have set out his ideas in a systematic way were planned, but were not completed before he died. The consequence is that his colleagues were left with a framework theory, which they then took the responsibility for taking forward. His closest collaborators, Schegloff and Jefferson, have been the most important figures in that development. Primarily under their influence, the analysis of conversational sequencing – which became known as Conversation Analysis, or CA, as I will term it in this volume – has developed over the last 25 years into an important research discipline which is used in many branches of social science. A large corpus of work now stands, incorporating two distinct strands of development: further development of 'the machinery of talk' – the general theory of conversation; and extensive applications of sequential analysis across a wide variety of social science disciplines. Slowly, CA has gained acceptance in sociology departments. It has also been an important contributor to other areas of social science – anthropology, ethnography, linguistics, and more recently, psychology.

Categorization analysis – the second strand of analysis which Sacks undertook – has had a slower and more restrained development. Schegloff and Jefferson continued to develop theory and method of sequential analysis, but very little work on categorization was done in the post-1975 development of Sacks' work in the USA. However, in the UK, interest in membership categorization analysis continued at the University of Manchester, and it was from there, in the late 1970s and early 1980s that new developments in the theory and application of categorization analysis flourished, under the influence of Cuff, Watson, Drew, McHoul and others.

Cuff's work (1980/1993) addressed the notion of 'multiple realities' proposed by Schutz and popularized in constructionist sociological theory (Berger and Luckman, 1967). Using Sacks' theory of membership categorization, Cuff shows how issues of 'multiple realities' can be treated as what Sacks called 'members' issues' – an everyday accomplishment of ordinary interaction which happens in an orderly and rule-governed way. At the same time, Cuff showed that the basic rules of categorization which Sacks developed must be refined and extended in order to accommodate the reality of everyday discourse, in which competing and conflicting versions are negotiated in the context of the talk.

Cuff's work touches on another aspect of Sacks' work, referred to in Schegloff's introduction to the lectures:

> [Sacks'] observations about control of categorization structures and deployments and the problem-type addressed to the ordering of cognitive or psycholinguistic or interpretive operations are theoretically central to the responsibilities of a sociological, or more generally interactional, sector of what are now called the cognitive sciences. And ... [in] the understanding of how linguistic and category terms work, indeed can work, their import goes well beyond the interactional domain which is their initial locus. (Schegloff, 1992: xxxix)

The study of how conceptual understanding – versions of reality, for example – is organized and employed in everyday talk laid the groundwork for the most important single contribution to the theoretical development of categorization analysis, made by Lena Jayyusi, in her book, *Categorization and the moral order* (1984). In this study, Jayyusi brings together the analytic techniques which had been developed by her colleagues in Manchester into a consistent explanatory framework. She links the empirical method of categorization analysis with the notion of 'procedural knowledge' to show how categorization analysis can be used to study the situated rationality of the moral precepts which underpin social and cultural order.

The work of the 'Manchester School', as it became known, inspired new and growing interest in the application of categorization analysis to the study of talk and text. Schegloff, however, has argued (Sacks, 1992a: xlii) that analysis of membership categories risks the kind of analytic 'promiscuity' of the common sense attribution of theoretical categories to naturally occurring data which Sacks was so critical of in the work of other sociologists. Schegloff warns against the danger of the researcher importing his or her own categories and interpretations into the analysis, and claims that it was because of this looseness that Sacks stopped working on membership categorization in the last couple of years of his life.

A careful study of the later lectures does not, however, altogether support Schegloff's argument. Sacks' interest in the empirical issues of sequential analysis continued and developed throughout the lectures, without doubt, but he also continued to explore his conceptual model of social structure-in-action. From the Spring 1968 lectures right through to the final lectures, he turned his attention to story-telling, possibly influenced by the work of Labov, whose work was being published at that time. In the early lectures, it was the analysis of children's stories which provided the first impetus to his study of the relationship between categorization and culture. I believe his wider focus on the phenomenon of story-telling must be seen as continuation of this analytic concern. Sacks' analytic work on story-telling, though not a strong feature of CA literature, has been highly influential in the development of the study of narrative and life stories. Some of that development is discussed in Part III of this volume.

Rod Watson has strongly argued against Schegloff's position, making the case for the conceptual, as well as empirical, commitment to the study of *social structure-in-action*, to which Sacks remained committed throughout the Lectures:

1. Sacks was always concerned with social *activities*: 'categorization was to be analyzed as a culturally methodic (procedural activity rather than in terms of an inert cultural grid)'.
2. For Sacks, categories came to have meaning in specific *contexts*: he did not see categories as 'storehouses' of decontextualized meaning.
3. Sacks made it clear that category use did not reflect psychological processes (such as information processing) but depended on 'cultural resources [which are] public, shared and transparent'.
4. Above all, the issue for Sacks was not the content of categories, but the procedures through which they are invoked and understood. (quoted in Silverman, 1998: 129–30)

Watson argues (Silverman, 1998) that both categorization and sequential analysis are essential if the development of a comprehensive theory of structure-in-action, which was Sacks' aim, is to be achieved. The development of both empirical and conceptual analysis is also the guiding principle of this introduction to doing categorization analysis.

How to use this book

This book is intended as a practical introduction to the empirical analysis of talk and text through the application of membership categorization analysis, or categorization analysis, as I shall refer to it throughout. Its aim is to remain faithful to Sacks' inductive analytic method, building conceptual understanding of the tools of categorization analysis, and how they can be applied, through the detailed analysis of naturally occurring talk and text. Most of the chapters are therefore arranged around a series of exercises, and discussions of examples drawn from the work of Sacks and those who followed him in developing the theory and practice of categorization analysis. By starting at the beginning, the novice researcher can build skills in the practice of categorization analysis, and a conceptual understanding of the method, in a systematic way.

The book also provides a practical introduction to the variety of applications of categorization analysis in social science. Parts II–IV introduce three fields of enquiry to which categorization analysis can be fruitfully applied, with examples of analyses and exercises to introduce the reader to the practice of the method. Readers who already have an acquaintance with CA may want to go directly to those chapters which apply directly to their research interests.

In Part I, all the major tools of categorization analysis are introduced. In my own experience, and that of my students, it is sometimes difficult to see how to get from the concepts to the practice of analysing talk and text. To help the reader to work with the concepts in a practical way, I have introduced exercises, many based on Sacks' original data samples, throughout the text. By the time you have worked through Part I, you should begin to have some sense of what it is that categorization analysis is attempting to do, and how to go about setting up your own project.

Having introduced some of the basic tools, Part II then introduces Sacks' thinking on the relationship between talk, context and culture. In this Part, the conceptual case for the use of categorization analysis in the study of culture and its institutions is made, using empirical analysis to demonstrate how categorization analysis can be employed to analyse talk and text from a variety of sources. In addition to its general discussion of the analysis of context, the content of Part II will be of particular interest to students of cultural studies, ethnography and anthropology seeking an empirical method for the study of cultural phenomena.

Part III introduces the reader to the empirical study of story-telling which occupied Sacks' attention in the later lectures. It traces subsequent developments in the application of Sacks' method to the growing discipline of the analysis of narrative and life stories in a variety of social science disciplines, ranging from ethnography and anthropology, to discursive and developmental psychology, and psychotherapy. It demonstrates the principles of analysing stories from a variety of perspectives, using examples and exercises to develop practice competence.

Part IV develops a model for the use of categorization analysis in the study of organizations. After outlining the growth of the development of the 'action model of organization', examples and practical exercises demonstrate how categorization analysis can be applied to a variety of empirical questions. Finally, an extended case study illustrates the use of a variety of categorization analytic techniques and concepts, demonstrating how they can be applied and generalized.

Part V introduces the reader to some essential technical and professional considerations in the practice of research: issues of validity and reliability; the use of technology in the collection, management and analysis of data; and the practice of ethical research.

At the end of the text, you will find a glossary of the core concepts of categorization analysis which are introduced in the text, to which you can refer for quick reference as you are reading. Terms which appear in the Glossary are indicated in bold type in the text. Appendix A is the transcription notation developed by Gail Jefferson. Appendix B is a sample consent form, which can be adapted as appropriate should you need to obtain consent to use recorded data.

In whatever way you use this book to approach the study of categorization analysis, I would recommend that you stop to apply the concepts in the exercises which are provided as you are working through the chapters. In addition to developing your understanding of the concepts, and how they can be applied, they will help ground your thinking in the data, and develop the habit, essential to the method, of *saturating* the data with your analytic attention to the details of the talk or text.

The assumption that categorization analysis is complementary to sequential analysis is basic to my understanding of the method. In many of the examples reference will be made to sequential features of talk. This volume should be read as a companion to *Doing conversation analysis: a practical guide*, by Paul ten Have (1998), to which you should turn for an introduction to the principles of sequential analysis. It may also be helpful to you to refer to the CA/Ethno News Website, maintained by ten Have, for up to the minute information about developments in the field: pscw: uva.nl/emca/dca/index.htm

Recommended reading

Have, P. ten (1998) *Doing conversation analysis: a practical guide*. London: Sage.
   The companion piece to this volume, ten Have's introduction to conversation analysis provides a thorough and clear introduction to the concepts and practice of the sequential analysis of talk.

Sacks, H. (1984a) 'Notes on methodology'. In J.M. Atkinson and J. Heritage (eds), *Structures of social action: studies in conversation analysis*. Cambridge: Cambridge University Press.

Sacks, H. (1984b) 'On doing "being ordinary" '. In J.M. Atkinson and J. Heritage (eds), *Structures of social action: studies in conversation analysis*. Cambridge: Cambridge University Press.

Two articles published posthumously, were compiled by Gail Jefferson from the lectures, in order to bring together some of Sacks' thinking on key issues of method.

Schegloff, E.A. (1992) Introduction. In H. Sacks, *Lectures in conversation*, vols I and II. Oxford: Basil Blackwell.
Schegloff provides a wide-ranging account of the development of conversation analysis and its place in the intellectual developments of its time.

Silverman, D. (1998) *Harvey Sacks and conversation analysis*. Key Contemporary Thinkers. Cambridge: Polity Press.
Silverman introduces Sacks and his work, placing it within its intellectual origins, and outlining its development.

Part I

PRACTISING THE ART OF CATEGORIZATION ANALYSIS

2

First Principles

CONTENTS

*In this chapter, the fundamental conceptual tools of the methodology of categorization analysis will be introduced, using examples to demonstrate how the concepts are applied in practice. Learning to do categorization analysis involves developing what I call an 'analytic attitude'. By this I mean that the researcher must acquire the habit of suspending normal intuitive judgement about the meaning of talk, or text, and open up his/her analytic attention to details which normally pass unnoticed. If we were to think about how we are riding a bicycle, we would probably fall off; if we were to analyse how we understand what someone has just said, there would be no conversation. Nevertheless, just as we **do** rely on an embodied knowledge of how to balance a bicycle, we also do employ systematic procedures to understand the import of what someone has just said. The objective of categorization analysis is to demonstrate what those procedures are and how they are employed. Developing skill as a categorization analyst – like learning to ride a bicycle – involves practice. To help you, exercises will be introduced throughout the chapters which follow, so that you can practice in a systematic way. Try not to cheat – practice as you go along.*

The baby cried

Let us start with the first example Sacks used in his early lectures.

EXERCISE 2.1

The x cried. The y picked it up.

Complete the sentences.

The example comes from a story told by a child, aged 2 years and 9 months, and Sacks concentrated on the first line of the story: 'The baby cried, the mommy picked it up'.

Most speakers of English will be able to complete this puzzle without difficulty because it embeds some rules about 'what goes together'. These 'rules of use' exhibit regularities, which can be generalized and studied empirically. In this case, the ordinary hearer will identify *x* as 'mother' (the child's word was 'mommy' which in itself gives us information about the speaker). You will almost certainly have identified the *y* as 'baby'. How were you able to do this?

Categorization analysis studies how categories are employed in naturally occurring talk and texts. It studies the pragmatic use of words – that is, how the 'dictionary' meanings are employed in situated use. The focus of attention is on the procedures by which interactants (or readers) decide on an ongoing basis about what meaning is relevant in the context of the utterance. Sacks used this example extensively to show how a child even as young as 2 years and 9 months has enough knowledge of 'what goes with what' to construct a meaningful – and by 'meaningful', what we mean here is 'hearable' – description.

You were able to solve this puzzle because of the categories 'cried' and 'picked up'. These are activities commonly bound to mothers and babies. The 'picked up' doesn't need further explanation, in the context of 'cried'. You used the categories 'cried' and 'picked up' in order to infer who the 'subjects' *x* and *y* were. Sacks termed this class of categories 'category bound activities' (CBAs).

> **Category bound activities** are action words which link 'subjects' and 'objects'.

As action words, they normally appear in one of the verb forms. In searching for words to put in the place of *x* and *y* you were 'searching' for nouns

– probably common nouns, given 'the'. Sacks called this class of categories 'Members'. In starting to analyse a text, it is often helpful to start your search by searching for action words, identifying CBAs; and then, because actions require actors, you can link them to the membership categories which they invoke. Those 'Members' may appear as actors or as subjects in the text or talk, or they may be implicit. That is, a turn of talk, or a strip of text, may tell you which membership category is to be heard, or it may require you to make an *inference* about what membership category is relevant.

One of the important phenomena of naturally occurring talk which interested Sacks, was how inferences about what is going on are made by the parties to the talk. Categorization analysis is 'a study in the method-ology and relevance of Member's activities of categorizing Members' (Sacks, 1972b).

> **'members'** in its lower case form refers to the actual speakers and hearers who are the parties to the talk. They, as participants, are also **'Members'** – that is, for the purposes of the talk they may occupy one, or more, membership categories within the talk.

For example, the narrator of the 'baby cried' story is a member address-ing another member (the author of the book *Children Tell Stories*, who elicited stories from young children for just that purpose.) S/he is also an incumbent of the category 'Child', and for the purposes of the book rep-resents that category. That was the principle of selection. When you saw the completed text of the story as it was told, you may have realized that this was the story of a child even though I did not make the context of the original telling of the story explicit. You will have made your inference from the narrator's use of the membership category 'mommy'. In (Ameri-can) English, it is 'children' who have 'mommies' – not adults. It is in this way that we make that inference about the category incumbency of the Member who is addressing us through the story.

This simple example shows the complex nesting of inferences which emerge from even the most minimal text. This child did not have a com-plete grammar at her disposal – a more 'mature' version would probably have been, 'The baby cried. Its mommy picked it up.' Nevertheless, this young child has already grasped a complex set of rules of use for com-municating her understanding of the expectable relations of 'members' and 'Members' in her world. And we hear it that way.

Sacks called these rules of use an 'inferencing machine'. Categorization analysis studies the underlying rules of inference in naturally occurring interaction by examining how speakers and hearers make inferences about what is going on, and how they provide for inferences to be made from what they say or do. These rules of use are organized within what Sacks termed Membership Categorization Devices (MCDs).

> **Membership Categorization Device:** 'That **collection** of membership categories, containing at least a category, that may be applied to some population, containing at least a Member, so as to provide, by the use of some rules of application, for the pairing of at least a population Member and categorization device member. A device is then a collection plus rules of application.' (Sacks 1972b: 32)

Sacks developed the concept of the MCD as a means of defining context formally, as an object of empirical enquiry, without reference to specific content. It defines context in terms of a **Collection** of categories demonstrably in use in spoken language which are understandable according to their belonging to a collection of words that 'go together'. It borrows from the formal logic of set theory in the sense of describing members of a set, by virtue of which other members of other collections are excluded from that set. However, it differs from set theory in that it addresses categories-in-use in the context of spoken language, rather than theoretical entities. *When in use, the 'collection' to which categories belong has to be established in the setting of the actual speech, by the application of pragmatic rules of use.*

EXERCISE 2.2

The baby cried. The mommy picked it up.

The categories 'baby' and 'mommy' belong to a collection. How would you identify that collection?
    If you were then to consider what rules of application might apply to that collection, by examining the child's story, at least one rule is evident. Can you describe it?

The categories 'baby' and 'mommy' are part of a collection of 'Members' about whom certain things can be pragmatically understood. They are adequate descriptions in themselves – Sacks used the term 'referentially adequate' – but in the context of the utterance, they are linked, and will be heard as members of a collection. In the English-speaking culture – and this would be true of probably all cultures – babies and mommies would be part of the collection 'family'. There could be a culture where babies and mommies are separated and do not have any relationship at all. In that culture, the collection 'family' would contain different categories, or might even be non-existent. *Collections are dependent on context; they are 'situated'.* For the English-speaking hearers of this story, one of the rules of application relevant to the collection 'family', is that when babies cry, they may well be picked up; and that mommies will typically do the picking up. In applying that rule of application, the child narrator is invoking the

MCD, 'family'. So, even though s/he doesn't use a referential pronoun, we are likely to hear that the baby is the baby of the mommy, and that the baby and the mommy are linked by rules of application such that we infer that it is she who picked the baby up.

Membership categorization devices

A membership categorization device is a collection plus rules of application: this story fragment demonstrates the minimum condition within which MCDs function as an organizing principle for the management of inferences and the possibility of understanding of utterances. Sacks, however, continued to work with this fragment over several years and was able to show still more rules of application embedded in its structure. The kind of attention to microprocess which Sacks practised is an important part of developing the analytic attitude of which I spoke at the beginning of this chapter. So let us continue with these two sentences, seeing what other treasures were mined from them.

>   The **baby** cried. The **mommy** picked it up.

One of the things that might be noticed about this particular membership pair is that the two elements make a pair which typically go together. Sacks noticed that this kind of pairing is common in all kinds of culturally describable situations, and so he included among the rules of application, the Standardized Relational Pair (SRP).

>   **Standardized Relational Pair:** A pairing of Members such that the relation between them constitutes a locus for rights and obligations. Examples abound: 'Husband' and 'Wife', 'Mother' and 'Baby', 'Lecturer' and 'Student', and 'Doctor' and 'Patient'.

Consider the following example from Sacks' data on telephone calls recorded on a telephone suicide helpline.

Data Sample 1 (Sacks, 1972b)

1   S1:   Have you ever been married, Miss G . . .?
2   C1:   No.
3   S2:   And you're out here kind of on your own and things not going well?
4   C2:   That's it.
5   S3:   You've no one out here?
6   C3:   Well, I have cousins, but you know, they're cousins. They're third or fourth cousins . . .

EXERCISE 2.3

Examine this data extract closely.

- Identify the standardized relationship pairs which are invoked in the text.
- What locus of rights and obligations is invoked?
- What inferences can we make about the relevant categorization device?

In this data extract, the staff member's question 'Have you ever been married, Miss G?' (line 1) invokes the SRP Husband/Wife. In the case of married persons, the locus of rights and obligations constituted by the SRP Husband/Wife provides for the first step in a search procedure for a potential helper to be called upon. The important thing about SRPs, Sacks noted, is that by invoking such a pairing, the speaker draws upon culturally shared inferences about what might be expected of the incumbents of those membership categories. Sacks argued that these shared inferences provide, at the unit level of interaction, for the culturally-provided-for orderliness of conversational interaction.

Notice now what follows this question and answer sequence: the caller's negative reply then creates the need for a further search. The counsellor clarifies the situation with the inference that the caller 'is out here kind of on your own', and, receiving confirmation, follows with the next question – 'You've no one out here'. The counsellor continues the search for relevant Members who could be called upon to help through use of the 'indexical' term 'no one', to which the caller's reply is: 'Well, I have cousins . . .' (line 6). The caller hears, and responds to the counsellor's query 'You've *no one*' with a reply within the device 'Family'. The important point to note here, is that *as categorization analyst I am relying on the evidence of the hearing within the text to identify the categorization device which is being invoked*. It is not my interpretation, but the speakers' understanding of each other's utterances which constitutes the necessary evidence for the analysis. Sacks demonstrated that indexical terms – usually definite or indefinite pronouns, but also some verbs – play an important role in the collaborative construction of categorization devices. We will explore the use of these terms further in Chapter 3.

Here in this data extract, as in the story, 'The baby cried. The mommy picked it up', we have established that the relevant membership categorization device is 'Family'. How we recognize that, as hearers, embeds another rule of application:

Consistency rule: If a population of persons is being categorized, and a category from a membership categorization device has been used to characterize a first member of that population, then hear subsequent categorizations as coming from that device.

This is the importance of the consistency rule: if a population of at least two members is being categorized, it is possible that more than one MCD may be used. For example, a 'baby' may be heard as part of the collection 'family', or might be heard as belonging to the collection 'stages of life' – for example, 'that baby has become a toddler since I last saw her'. In a hearable utterance, one or more membership categorizations may be relevant. In the data extract, the consistency rule was applied by the caller in her response to the question, 'You've no one out here?' (line 5) – the question is heard as referring to the categorization device 'family', and the response offers membership categories relevant to that device – 'cousins'.

In the case of 'The baby cried', a single categorization for each of the two characters was adequate. It is often the case, whether there is one speaker, or more than one speaker, that a single categorization will be relevant and sufficient. This is provided for by the economy rule:

> **Economy rule:** For any population of Members being categorized, whether the consistency rule, or combining rules, are being applied, it may be sufficient to apply only one category to each member.

The economy rule can be demonstrated by looking at some further examples of children's' stories:

Data extract (Sacks, 1972b: 34–5)

1 Once there was a baby pig. He played with his Mommy. He went to Mommy. Mommy went to Daddy.
2 The Daddy works in the bank. And Mommy cooks breakfast. Then we get up and get dressed. And the baby eats breakfast and honey. We go to the school and we get dressed like that. I put coat on and I go in the car . . .

These children have grasped the essentials of constructing a hearable story. They know what must be added to 'Mommy', 'Daddy' and 'baby', in order to invoke the MCD 'family', within the constraints of the consistency rule: each member is categorized once within the Device. These stories are (minimally) referentially adequate as potential descriptions of the family and its activities.

The child's story tells us something about how categories may be combined in order to create a referentially adequate utterance. Either consistency, or combining rules, must be applied to produce hearability. At the core of competent talk is the capacity to combine categories in recognizable ways, and this capacity involves both knowledge about how things go together, and the transmission of that knowledge. The children's stories interested Sacks because in them were clear examples of how, through the application of the 'consistency rule', children learn to order their world into culturally recognizable form. This leads to one of Sacks' most important claims:

> Note then the character of the consistency rule; on the one hand it is used to generate the terms, given a first, and on the other, it is used to detect the relation of the generated term. These parallels shall turn out to be deeply important. A culture is an apparatus for generating recognizable actions; if the same procedures are used for generating as for detecting, that is perhaps as simple a solution to the problem of recognizability as is formulatable. (Sacks, 1992a: 226)

It is important to remember that Sacks was not simply developing an empirical method for the study of social interaction, although conversation/categorization analysis is certainly that. He was also addressing some of the fundamental methodological and epistemological problems of social science. So even in a chapter on the analytic technique, it is also important to keep an eye on what fundamentals are being addressed by the method, as Sacks did in his lectures. The two are inseparable.

This repertoire of three fundamental rules of application then allows us to account for several more features of the story, 'The baby cried'. How do we account for the child's use of 'the mommy'. S/he probably hasn't heard 'the mommy' presented as the proper form by an adult speaker, who would have said, 'its mommy', even though in the story as it stands it is hearable as the 'baby of the mommy'. Or, an adult could have said, perhaps in reporting to a child, 'The baby cried. Mommy picked it up.' So what, asked Sacks, is the significance of the child's use of the indefinite article, in a sentence such as this (and many more examples from children's talk can be shown)?

To address this issue, Sacks described a further refinement of the consistency rule, which he termed, duplicative organization.

> **Duplicative organization:** A collection of membership categories treated as a unit. When categorizing a population, potential members are then treated as a unit, not as countable individuals. When one category from that collection is used, then it will be inferred that any other category from that device can be used to construct an adequate description simply by virtue of occupying a position within that device.

For example, the relative relations of 'mommies' and 'babies', and the activities that apply to them, can be applied over an indefinite number of possible descriptions. A 'family' is an example of a duplicatively organized device. In the case of the story, 'The baby cried. The mommy picked it up', we hear the baby as the baby of the mother according to the rule of duplicative organization. Another way of describing such organization is a 'team', where the production of any category within the team will automatically invoke inferences about who else might be expectably present. The presence and absence of incumbents of any position would then constitute a matter to be explained.

The child author of 'the baby cried' has at her disposal one important collection: the collection 'Family'. In searching for potentially correct descriptions of her relevant world she will make extensive use of it. Adults may help her to do this by referring to other members of her world within the 'family' collection. Here is an example:

A: ((a little girl)) Who's that?
B: ((her mother)) That's Rita. Remember when you went to the party last week and met Una? Well that's Una's mother. (Sacks, 1992a: 326)

It could be argued that this is just a trivial example of the child's limited repertoire of a single device. However, when she discovers that by employing the device 'Family', with its expectable set of relations of which she has singular experience, she can also construct other potentially adequate descriptions, she has extended her range of participation in the communicative culture into which she is being socialized. The child has then seen that a device contains categories which can be generalized over a variety of situations, and used to generate descriptions, and culturally relevant stories with which to enter into story-telling engagement with other people in her developing social world. Story books written for children exploit the phenomenon, by building on the device children know best and generalizing it into the wider world (Baker and Freebody, 1987).

Let's look again at the data sample from Sacks' telephone helpline:

Data sample 1 (Sacks, 1972b: 64)

1   S1:   Have you ever been married, Miss G . . .?
2   C1:   No.
3   S2:   And you're out here kind of on your own and things not going well?
4   C2:   That's it.
5   S3:   You've no one out here?
6   C3:   Well, I have cousins, but you know, they're cousins. They're third or fourth cousins . . .

We've noted that the counsellor first searches for a relevant description of members who might be turned to by someone in need of help. The first search involves the SRP husband/wife. This leads, by extension, to the MCD 'family' ('You've no one out here?', line 5) and the negation of the search for member of 'Family' to whom the caller can turn. What I am interested in now, is the third turn of the caller – line 6: 'Well I have cousins, but you know, they're cousins. They're third or fourth cousins . . .'.

This fragment illustrates another important aspect of duplicative organization. One of the things noticed in this exchange is that the counsellor first searches for a relevant standardized relational pair within which 'help' might be ordinarily expected. If the caller is married, then an immediate inference could be made that a husband would be the first person to turn to for help. In the absence of an incumbent of this category, the search is widened to include the device 'Family', within which other potential members with rights and obligations to help might be found. This procedure leads to a further rule of categorization:

> **Programmatic relevance:** If a pair of categories with the features of standardized relational pairs is relevant, then the non-incumbency of any of its pair positions is an observable, that is, it can proposedly be a fact. Furthermore, various uses may be made of the facts of the presence or absence of persons to fill the potential pair positions.

In the case of Miss G, there is a progressive search on the part of the counsellor to discover a member of 'Family' who could be describable as a person who could reasonably be expected to help. In Turn C3, Miss G provides her evidence for the non-incumbency of this position: she only has 'cousins', and they are 'third and fourth cousins'. With this, she effectively ends the search procedure, by replying within the MCD 'Family' and demonstrating that there are no available members who can fill the potential description of family members who ought to help, by downgrading even those family members who she is able to produce from (by implication, first) 'cousins' to 'third' and 'fourth' class relevance.

In this exchange, the search for help turns upon the search for a relevant membership category. For Sacks, this search procedure was evidence of the more general kinds of procedures used in any conversation for deciding what is relevant. Through that analytic process he sought to discover more general rules of relevance which provide for the observability and describability of social phenomena. Here is how he characterizes his analytic procedure:

> Now I've introduced the term 'category-bound activities'. I want to propose a relevance rule and that is: If someone names – as for example what they were doing – a category-bound activity that provides, first, for the relevance of the category to which the category is bound. Then, by use of the consistency rule, the collection of which the category is a member is made relevant. So that by naming as the thing you were doing, some activity which is category bound, you provide the relevance of some collection of which it's at least the case that some particular activity is bound to a category of that collection. (Sacks, 1992a: 301)

Here is another longer data extract which demonstrates some of Sacks' provision for rules of relevance:

Data sample 2 (Sacks, 1972b: 65)

```
1   S1:  Well I understand what these pressures are on you. Is there anyone you
2         trust, anyone who can take care of you, because right now, you need
3         some taking care of. You need somebody to move in and take over.
4   C1:  The only people I know are people just like myself. I don't have any
5         regular friends.
6   S2:  Well what about people just like yourself.
7   C2:  They give me all kinds of things and they . . .
8   S3:  Well what about your doctor?
9   C3:  I don't have a family doctor.
10  S4:  Well somebody prescribed those pills.
11  C4:  Well he's just a doctor. I only called him up.
12  S5:  You never saw him?
13  C5:  A long time ago, for a little thing. I don't know him that well.
14  S6:  You think he'd take over?
15  C6:  I don't know.
16  S7:  What about your parents?
17  C7:  I can't tell them. I'd rather kill myself than tell them.
18  S8:  You can't tell them what?
19  C8:  Anything.
20  S9:  Not even that you're suffering and need to be in a hospital?
21  C9:  No.
```

EXERCISE 2.4

Examine this second extract from Sacks' telephone helpline. It also involves a search for help.

- What CBAs do the speakers employ?
- What membership categories are generated through them?
- What SRPs are invoked in the text?
- Can you identify how the consistency and economy rules are applied?
- What 'facts' are generated by the application of the rule of pro-grammatic relevance?

This is a complex strip of talk. In it, all the rules I have introduced are nested within each other, and it shows how speakers and hearers use the rules to 'collaborate' in the production of meaningful talk. I've chosen this example because it shows how collaboration generates meaningful interaction, but does not necessarily generate helpful co-operation. Non-co-operation, disagreement and obstruction in conversation are also rule-governed. The rules of categorization can be used by participants to all kinds of interactional ends.

Category bound activities

Consider the following extract, in which three speakers collaborate to produce a sentence.

Data extract from a group discussion (Sacks, 1992a: 136)

```
1   Ken:     We were in an automobile discussion
2   Roger:   discussing the psychological motives for
3   (    ):  hhhhh
4   Al:      drag racing on the street.
```

EXERCISE 2.5

- What category bound activity is evoked by this collaboratively produced sentence?
- What is the likely membership category collection linked to the CBA?
- Can you make an inference about who the speakers might be?

You probably realized that, given the CBA 'drag-racing', the likely collection of members was 'teenagers'. The context of the talk is a discussion between the teenage members of a therapy group, and it follows the introduction by the therapist of a new member – another teenager – to the other group members. Sacks used data from this therapy group extensively in his lectures.

One of the things Sacks hoped to be able to achieve with his method of analysing conversation was a rigorous way of recognizing and predicting members' activities. In the case of this group therapy session, it may well have been a matter of importance to all concerned to tell whether this new member was being 'invited' or 'rejected' by the group. As Sacks pointed out, when analysing this segment:

> since invitations stand in alternation to rejection, what we would like is to discriminate between the two. We want to provide for the recognizability of 'invitation' for some cases, and for the recognizability of 'rejection' for some. And if we get a method, then we ought to be able to use it to generate other cases than this one, where, then the ones that we generate ought to be equally recognizable as invitations or rejections. With that we have some idea of the tasks involved. (Sacks, 1992a: 300)

Sacks viewed this co-produced sentence as an event of great interest, and one which functioned in a highly particular way in the context of this discussion. He demonstrates that by co-producing the sentence, the group members act as though they are a unit – and create the conditions in which the newcomer is 'invited' to join in a group whose activities properly include discussion of both 'psychological motives' and 'automobile discussions'. Sacks also goes on to sugggest that an 'automobile discussion' can act as a 'cover' for all kinds of other discussions which the teenagers might be inclined to have.

To complete this introduction to the basic tools of categorization, let's look to another segment from these group therapy sessions which interested Sacks:

```
1  Ken:        Did Louise call or anything this morning?
2  Therapist:  Why, did you expect her to call?
3  Ken:        No. I was just kind of hoping that she might be able to figure
4              out some way of coming to the meetings. She did seem like
5              she wanted to come back.
6  Therapist:  Do you miss her?
7  Patient:    Oh in some ways, yes. It was nice having the opposite sex in
8              the room, ya know, having a chick in the room. (1992a: 461)
```

Sacks was interested in the way place categories are used to formulate descriptions which may not have to do with the location at all. In this case, he demonstrates, the choice of the category 'in the room' (line 8) replaces the possible description 'in the group' in the way 'going to bed' replaces 'having sex' (also a topic of interest in the group!). Sacks argues that by downgrading the location from 'the group' to 'the room', the speaker is able to allude to the SRP male/female ('the opposite sex', lines 7–8) and the category bound activities that might be implied (i.e., being interested in a girl), while he weakens the force of the utterance, which could be heard as implying a 'compliment'. In the case of this question and answer exchange from the group therapy session, Sacks shows how the group member's choice of categories allows for a 'safe' reply – yes, I do miss her, but it could be anyone of the opposite sex, in any place.

Location categories

One of the first important papers to build on Sacks' formulation of rules of categorization was a paper written by Schegloff, entitled 'Notes on a conversational practice: formulating place' (1972). Taking this observation of Sacks as a starting point, Schegloff analysed many sequences of talk in which speakers use place to do the interactional work of conversation. Out of this study, came a new group of category-concepts which came to be called location categories.

> **Location categories:** For any location to which reference is made, there is
> a set of terms each of which, by a correspondence test, is a correct way to
> refer to it. On any actual occasion of use, however, not any member of the
> set is 'right'. (Schegloff, 1972: 81)

Schegloff demonstrated that location categories, like membership categories, and category bound activities, are situated in the context of their
use. The problem, as Schegloff characterized it, is 'How is it that on particular occasions of use some term from the set is selected and other terms
are rejected?' (1972: 81).

This empirical question Schegloff then set out to analyse. He demonstrated that in all kinds of activities whose topic included location – reporting travels, giving directions – speakers are not providing a map which will
correspond to the map printed on a page, but rather that the speaker will
typically assess and address the common sense geography shared by the
hearer, and fashion a 'map' tailormade for the occasion. This empirical
work of analysing actual conversational data led to the realization/recog-
nition that location categories do not only designate 'places in the world',
but also function to generate distinctions and provide for inferences on the
part of speakers/writers and hearers/readers. He goes on to discuss three
cases of categorial practices which are organized through the management
of location categories: location analysis, membership analysis and topic or
activity analysis.

Location analysis

The common sense geography employed by interactants may be used for
a variety of sense-making purposes. It may be organized into a concentric
or a hierarchic structure which is generated for the purpose of the talk. For
example, the chosen geography may be organized according to nearness
or farness (concentric) or into orders of importance. To talk about France
from the perspective of America may be 'far', or may be part of the hierarchy 'Europe' then 'France', then 'parts of France'. Or it may be organized into the more general, indexicals like 'here' and 'there', or relational
terms, such as 'back there' or 'in front', allowing for the context to be built
as the exchange proceeds. Another important location category is 'home',
which, depending on the context, could be my living room, my street
address, my town, or even, my country (on arriving at the airport, for
example). How the common sense geography is employed is an empirical
matter for the analyst. In whatever way location categories are employed,
it will be part of the work of the analyst to show how the location is
formulated for the purposes of the conversational task in hand. Typical
situations which might arise occur in the giving of directions, or making

arrangements to meet; or, very commonly, in the telling of a story. Here's an example:

> A: En' I couldn't remember what I did with it so I said to Joan, 'Go ahead an' I'll run *back*'. An I ran back and when I came down, uh, I, uh, they said 'you've missed all the ex*cite*ment . . .' (Schegloff, 1972: 88)

In this turn, the speaker tells a story, the point of which is non-presence at a reportable event. These relational location categories formulate an indefinite, but very local place, which provides for inferences about the speaker's absence. The point of the story is about absence, not about location, but location categories do the work.

Membership analysis

A second consideration in the analysis of a location formulation is the work it is doing with respect to the membership analysis of the speaker and hearer. By identifying the membership category of the hearer, speakers anticipate and respond to each other's shared or common sense geography, and orient to hearings and mis-hearings on an ongoing basis, in generating an inference rich exchange. Here's another example from Schegloff's data:

> D: . . . They're setting up emergency at uh uh the cattle barn. Y'know where that is?
> C: Yeah: I live on 38th about 10 blocks east. (1972: 93)

In this exchange, the response offers a location category which is not necessary in terms of the content of its information, but is interactionally relevant as confirmation of the hearer's claim to know.

Topic or activity analysis

Another potential site for the analysis of location categories is the topic, or activity formulated by reference to locations which carry inference rich implications. The location of an activity – as Sacks points out in the example 'go to bed with' – may suggest an interpretation without naming the activity in ways which can be very useful to speakers and hearers. Location categories are an important means of doing discriminations and disavowals. Here's an example from some research of my own:

> DW: BTEC First Bus&Fin OSD came to see. [Principal] to report harassment by Security Staff. This arose because she has broken her pass and asked to come into the building to go to the Library (6pm). She queried whether any rule stating f/t student cannot enter college in the evenings.

EXERCISE 2.6

- Can you identify the location categories embedded in this text?
- How do they relate to CBAs?
- What membership categories can you identify?
- Can you make any inferences about what the import of the story might be?

There are a variety of location categories deployed in these two sentences. There are the physical locations – the door of the building, the Library within the building, the kind of building itself, a college, which gives information about the kinds of activities which might be expected to happen there. These seem to be in contrast to the activities which are actually registered – harassment, reporting, complaining about the issue of entering. Did you notice the time in parenthesis? Time can also act as a location category, imparting information about what inferences are to be made from the text. In this case it was very important. The membership categories involved – Security Guard, Student and Principal – suggest that the import of the story is to do with matters of discipline and control. A lot more about this report will be analysed in Chapter 6. It forms part of an extended story about DW.

It may have taken you quite some time to work your way into this text – it is very inference rich. What about the issue of who is 'right' and who 'wrong', or 'good' or 'bad' which this story is manifestly about? Sacks noticed this factor in some of his work on the children's stories:

Pussy scratched. He cried. He's a *bad* boy. He banged. He stopped crying. He's a *good* boy. He cried again.

Sacks goes on to comment on this story in relation to the application of the economy rule. He says that:

While the economy rule does not preclude the use of combinations of membership categories for single population Members, its presence does mean that the task of being socialized to doing adequate reference does not involve having to learn combinatorial possibilities for each pair. . . . The combinatorial problems are between classes of modifiers, of which (good, bad) are prototypes. (1992a: 35)

This child has mastered a combinatory categorization: *good boy, bad boy*. The same 'boy' can occupy two categories, with referential adequacy and hearability. Having learned the prototype categorization devices, membership categorization and classes of modifiers (good and bad), the basic principles of combination are demonstrably available to this young speaker. Each new case does not have to be learned, because the fundamental rules – economy, consistency and combinatory – are applied.

Though Sacks was clearly aware of the issue of combinatorial possibilities – which includes the problem of versions of categorizations – he made a claim that his 'overbuilt machinery' based upon 'the baby cried' story would be found to be generalizable to more complex utterances. Was it? In later developments in the study of categorization, Cuff and his colleagues at the University of Manchester argued that the Sacks 'machinery' was in need of further development and refinement before it would be adequate to meet the combinatorial tasks presented in contests of versions in the context of multi-dimensional talk. In the following chapter, we will follow some of those developments.

Summary

In this section, the basic tools of categorization analysis, first presented by Sacks in his Lectures, have been introduced. Sacks worked hard in his lectures, developing principles of analysis by example, demonstrating the process by which he arrived at those principles by showing what he did and how he did it. He did not present complete and unassailable 'results', but invited his students to join in a process with him, frankly indicating how time-consuming and difficult it could be. Though conversation analysis has been dominated, since Sacks' death, by **sequential analysis**, the lectures show that Sacks continued to be interested in the way in which categorization rules underpin meaningful interaction, and ultimately social structure. Working back and forth from empirical example to rules of inference, and from rules of inference to the way in which shared understandings of social and cultural reality are systematically constructed on a turn by turn basis through the application of those rules, is the core of the theory and practice of conversation/categorization analysis.

Recommended reading

Sacks, H. (1972b) 'An initial investigation of the usability of conversational data for doing sociology'. In D. Sudnow (ed.), *Studies in social interaction*. New York: Free Press.
  This is the paper in which Sacks put forward the most complete statement of his theory of rules of categorization. It is difficult to read and very dense. It shows the comprehensiveness of the theory which Sacks was trying to build. Essential reading if you intend to study categorization analysis at any depth.

Sacks, H. (1979) 'Hotrodder: a revolutionary category'. In G. Psathas (ed.), *Everyday language: studies in ethnomethodology*. New York: Earlbaum.
  In this paper, Sacks uses his method of analysing categorization to address a traditional domain of sociological enquiry.

Schegloff, E.A. (1972) 'Notes on a conversational practice: formulating place'. In D. Sudnow (ed.), *Studies in social interaction*. New York: Free Press.
This early analysis stands as an example of best practice.

Schegloff, E.A. (1992) Introduction. In H. Sacks, *Lectures on conversation*, Vol I. Oxford, Blackwell.
Schegloff's introduction to the Lectures provides an analytic overview of Sacks' work and its wide-ranging applicability.

3

Practising the Art of Categorization Analysis: Further Developments

CONTENTS

In Chapter 2, I introduced some of the early work in the analysis of categorization. After Sacks' death, the analysis of conversational sequencing became the primary focus of interest in the USA, and categorization analysis was left behind. However, in the UK, a group of researchers at the University of Manchester continued to work with categorization analysis, and to develop the basic framework developed by Sacks in his lectures. In this chapter, we will see how those developments of the basic rules addressed both technical and substantive analytic issues about the bases of social interaction, whether spoken or written.

Versions

In Manchester, a group of researchers continued to work on and develop Sacks' original work on categorization analysis. Cuff (1980/1993) employed data from a radio talk show, which, like the telephone helpline data of Sacks' original work, invited callers to present problems for solution. In this case the problems were family problems. In this monograph, he laid the groundwork for extending the study of categorization into the analysis of predicates – qualifying conditions which identify differences between versions of the basic category collections. There are not only families. There are 'good' families and 'bad' families, and in the work of conversation, making those distinctions, and establishing the identity of members and the propriety of actions is of paramount importance. Cuff argued that it was necessary to extend the concept of the 'machinery' of categorization which Sacks developed through 'the baby cried' story, to the wider domain of naturally occurring social interaction, where issues of 'rightness' and 'wrongness', and 'goodness' and 'badness' become important components of the inferences to be made by speakers and hearers.

In order to accommodate the expansion of the method, Cuff introduced an extension of the notion of the SRP, and an accompanying notation. The SRP, he argued, was not a single entity to be 'found', but rather is assembled by speakers on a turn by turn basis in the context of the talk, during which modified versions may be created through the use of predicate modifiers. We do not just have an SRP Parent/Child. In the actual work of determining which version of the facts shall prevail, we find differing descriptions which can be held to be the case. In his example from the radio talk show, the problem teenager of a caller is the subject under discussion. Cuff demonstrated that the nature of the problem can and often will be debated between alternative versions: in this case, it was a matter of deciding whether the problem was one of worried parent/difficult teenager, or possibly an overanxious mother/normal teenager. The same SRP can generate two versions. Let's call them SRPa and SRPb. And these do not exhaust the possibilities of versions which might arise in the context of talk about difficult teenagers. We might also discover, SRPc – frustrated mother/scapegoated son – or SPRd – demanding father/pressurized son – and so on. This observation raises an important issue: it is not the facts which are in dispute, but the way in which the interactants employ the facts to do descriptions.

The work of speakers is not to establish 'identity' in the global understanding of that term, but to produce specific identifications tied to recognizable activities out of the possible categorizations available to speakers of the language. The work of hearers is to employ those same categorizations in order to make sense of the descriptions of actions and activities being produced.

Let's look again at the report on D.W., which you already worked on in Exercise 2.6.

DW: BTEC First Bus&Fin OSD came to see [Principal] to report harassment by Security Staff. This arose because she has broken her pass and asked to come into the building to go to the Library (6pm). She queried whether any rule stating f/t student cannot enter college in the evenings.

EXERCISE 3.1

Can you identify alternative possible versions of the SRP which is constituted in the report on DW?

These two sentences embed two possible versions of the SRP security guard/student, which turn on the two CBAs 'harassment' and 'complaining'. What is the import of the first two lines of this report? One version could provide for the inference that security guards are exercising undue power in the discharge of their duties, and that a student is legitimately complaining. Call that SRPa – security guards/innocent victim. Another version might provide for the inference that legitimate authority is being exercised by security guards, and a student is defying that authority. Call that SRPb – security guards/troublemaker. We shall see later on in this chapter how the rest of the report develops this conflict of versions.

These developments in the analysis of predicates place Sacks' central analytic concern about the recognizability of actions at the heart of this more developed project of categorization analysis. The group of researchers working in Manchester throughout the 1970s and early 1980s developed the techniques of categorization analysis into a wider domain of enquiry than that which Sacks had developed in his original work, and provided the basis for using categorization analysis as a tool for investigating interactional phenomena at the society and institutional level. Payne and Hustler (see Payne, 1976; Payne and Hustler, 1980) were exploring categorization work in classroom teaching, and addressed methodological issues relevant to educational research; Watson (1978, 1983) studied the categories of 'victim' and 'offender' in routine police work; Atkinson, Cuff and Lee (1978) studied the interactional accomplishment of a meeting; and the early work of Sharrock (1974) laid the groundwork for the study of knowledge as categorial procedures, to be taken up in far greater detail by Coulter in later work (1979, 1989).

Predicates

In her book, *Categorization and the Moral Order* (1984) Jayyusi gathered all this work together and provided an enlarged framework for the practice of categorization analysis. She introduced several important new concepts.

Clusters:
(a) Categories . . . conventionally carry with them a *cluster* of expectable features – i.e. the constitutive trait . . . carries with it a cluster of related possible actions, traits, preferences, haunts, appearances, places times, etc. . . . The use of categorizations is not only descriptive of persons, but it is through and through an *ascriptive* matter.
(b) this cluster is itself embedded in the logico-grammatical relationship between concepts. (1984: 26–7)

In the practice of categorization analysis, and especially when tackling larger amounts of text, the search for these clusters, and the identification of their ascriptive properties, involves a search for the clusters on which the talk draws in order to produce its descriptions, and even more importantly, its ascriptions. The problem for the researcher becomes: how do I identify the clusters of related categories?

Jayyusi distinguishes between two methods which speakers and hearers may employ in the production and recognition of the categories in use:

category generated features are 'systematically produced [in the talk] through their tie to some category'.

category bound activities are 'formulated, implicitly or explicitly, as conventionally accompanying some category'. (1984: 36–7)

One important feature of the analytic work of the researcher is to discover, and distinguish, these two phenomena. In the one case, the speakers and hearers build the relevant categories in order to establish a particular categorization; in the other, they employ a particular category in order to bind the description to a particular categorization.

Let me illustrate this with the case of the report on DW. What is the effect of the use of the word 'harassment'? In this case, the use of the word binds the description which follows to the categorization device 'control', with its relevant activities – reporting, stopping, – and Members – security guards and students. It is a category bound description. Here is the next part of the text:

R and M [security guards] reported that (a) she has been in and out of B . . . all of the term, (b) she is rude and aggressive, (c) spends her time in the refectory and not in the library and (d) she was involved in some of the troubles last term.

In the second part of this report, a second description is assembled, and it provides evidence for one of the versions embedded in the first two lines of the report. Here, the reporter (all the time using the 'facts') assembles a description, which constitutes an ascription (on the part of the security guards) that the student is a 'troublemaker'.

EXERCISE 3.2

Using the principles of the consistency and economy rules, and the rule of duplicative organization, along with the basic concepts in the CA toolkit – category bound activities, membership categories, location categories – can you discover how the ascription 'troublemaker' is generated by the reporter?

If you have succeeded in carrying out some of this analytic task, you are well on your way to mastering the basic techniques of categorization analysis. You will have noticed how the increasing size of the text both enriches the possibilities of analysis, and makes it far more complex. Important issues of validity arise from this increasing complexity. (Issues of validity and reliability will be discussed in Chapter 14.) These later developments of categorization analysis extend far beyond the initial 'apparatus' described by Sacks. SRPs no longer pertain to the one locus of rights and obligations studied in detail by Sacks – the giving of help – but can be extended to the study of all kinds of category pairs which involve rights and obligations. Not only are the 'activities' studied by Sacks subject to empirical scrutiny, but also, the deployment of knowledge, and the construction of motive are seen to be category bound and available for analysis as procedures for arriving at meaning.

You will remember from Chapter 2 that conversation analysis, as Sacks conceived it, is not an interpretative method of analysing talk. It is an empirical method whose aim is to identify the observable procedural features by which meaning is arrived at. Sacks' claim was that these procedures are invariant. By moving into greater levels of complexity, how is the categorization analyst able to demonstrate the invariant from the idiosyncratic in any given text? Jayyusi addresses this as follows:

> The issue, then, is not a mechanical application of the consistency rule where one *decides* what device these two categorizations (or any co-selected categories) are drawn from, but rather to see what device-category they could, strictly or conventionally, imply for the task or **relevance** at hand that is displayed in the talk within which this category is embedded. . . . The device then is not so much presupposed as implicated in the selections. (1984: 83)

In the practice of categorization analysis, the task for the analyst is to demonstrate that:

> the activities of categorization are not only describably methodical but also that the activities are done methodically is quite essential to the ways that they are seen as graspable by Members. (Sacks, 1972b: 37)

One of the properties of category-bound activities and category- pairs systematized by Jayyusi is the production of disjunctive categories.

> **Disjunctive categories:** Asymmetric category pairings which generate conflicting characterizations of the same person.

In the following section, I will discuss applications of the notion of 'disjunctive accounts', generated by disjunctive categorization, and how it has been applied in sociology, in anthropology and in psychology. This wider sampling from the CA corpus will give you some idea of the flexibility of categorization analysis as a method.

Analysing disjunctive categories

Disjunctive categories which have been of interest to practitioners of CA are policeman/offender; doctor/patient; judge/defendant; politicians/members of the public. Much CA research has focused on these kinds of pairings to explore how disjunctive accounts are managed in the everyday practices of those persons going about their everyday activities in settings which have long been of interest to sociologists – crime and the law, medical practices and the political order. Rod Watson initiated an important study of one important group of categorizations with his study 'Categorization, authorization and blame negotiation in conversation' (1978). He draws attention to the links between categorization work and sequential structure of talk which was being studied in great detail in the USA, arguing that the two aspects of conversational structuration are mutually constructed. The data he employs are again taken from a telephone helpline. He compares his findings with those of Paul Drew (1978) and Dorothy Smith (1978).

Here's one exchange of the talk being analysed:

1	Caller:	can't even have that in this country, there's black people come
2		in this country and get more than what (I), than what white
3		people get (no good) I am not against blacks everybody's got
4		to live but I've never in my life known how hard it was till I
5		(tried it) it's disgusting (how the country is run) disgusting,
6		I'm only one in a million but I'll spread it about what the
7		church can do for you it can do nothing, the Catholic do more
8		*everyday* in the week than the Protestants do I think it's
9		disgusting I do really and truly.
10	Counsellor:	do you – have you spoken to your vicar or anyone at
11		Church? Do – do they know that you're infirm?
12	Client:	(I am not needy) I am not one of them types that come
13		screaming (Watson, 1978: 105)

In this example, notice how the 'search for help' is not organized within the device 'family', and the 'rights and obligations' which obtain within that device. What is constituted is 'the country' (line 5), and in this turn of talk, the caller links a description of her personal state to the state of 'the country', through the ascription of moral blame/responsibility in the production of racial, and later, religious groups. In this way she ties the category bound description 'entitlement' to her present predicament – others get 'better looked after than her' (CBA). Notice the applications of the consistency rule: the membership category 'black people' is invoked to attach blame within the device 'race' and (by implication – 'black people come here' – immigrants) as a means of assembling the (blaming) version of society – 'it's disgusting (how the country is run) disgusting'. By invoking one category, a collection is implicated (the 'economy rule') – a rule of application which has implications for the construction of any moral account/moral blame: once one member of a device is implicated, the categorization of that member may be generalized to all the members of the device ('race' or 'immigrants'). Still within the device 'the country', she then ties in 'the church', assembling a second 'blaming' version of 'society' – 'it [the church] can do nothing' (line 7). This description is then further qualified by the production of the competing categorizations 'Catholic' (who 'do more *everyday*', line 8) and 'Protestants' (who by implication, 'do nothing'). These situated applications of the rules of categorization, reveal not only how knowledge and reasoning about social structures or states of affairs are constructed and deployed for local, contexted interactional purposes, but also how social structures or states of affairs are sustained in everyday interaction.

The reply of the counsellor demonstrates a further application of the rules: according to the rules of duplicative organization, the device 'Church' may be taken as a device which includes Catholic, Protestant, and so on – that is, a type of faith – or alternatively, as a device in itself which includes the possible members 'vicar', 'parishioners', 'curates', and so on. Note how the counsellor takes advantage of this rule of application to shift the topic from 'Church' ('types of faith') to 'church' (members) who might be (category bound) to 'help': a 'search for help', and away from 'blaming'.

Now note the reply of the client:

Client: (I am not needy) I am not one of them type that come screaming

Here is a demonstration of the co-concurrence of 'preference organization', a principle of sequential analysis, and a categorial device, which together establish the caller's rejection of the counsellor's version. She observably hears the 'blame' implicit in the counsellor's response ('you haven't told them you need help') when she responds 'I'm not needy. I'm not one of them types'. In rejecting the 'search for help' version for the 'blaming' version she has presented, the 'blaming' takes a reflexive turn, and a counter-accusation on the part of the counsellor is observably heard by the caller. Now we have what Jayyusi would later term a 'disjunctive account': on the one hand, the caller whose preference is for an account of 'blaming' within the overall device 'the country', and on the other, the counsellor, whose preference is for an account of 'search for help'. The effect of the counsellor's disjunctive account of the facts is the generation of a disjunctive pairing of the SRP counsellor/client: it becomes SRP accuser/accused.

Jayyusi later demonstrated that the distinction generated here between personal and category bound rights and obligations is seen to:

> provide some of the tools by which members orient to and resolve issues of the relationship between individual and collectivity in occasioned and varied ways. These are issues that social scientists have long, and largely to little avail, been concerned to solve; they turn out to be members' issues that are organized in fine-grained and complex ways. (1984: 46)

In a much later study of the disjunctive accuser/accused pair, I compared the written reporting on DW with another reporting – this time, a talk interview on the *Today* programme – an early morning news programme on BBC Radio (Lepper, 1995). The topic is the activities of protesters against a new road-building scheme, which have been subject to a court injunction. I was seeking to identify what differences in the production of the category 'troublemaker' might be observable in these two very different reporting sites. Here is a short excerpt from the first part of the interview. The speakers are the programme presenter, and Mr M, the local Conservative MP, and Dr G, a protester:

1	Presenter:	Mr M. First, do you approve of this injunction?
2	Mr M:	Yes. Good. Let's not forget it's not peaceful demonstrators
3		that are being injuncted. It's those that have caused trouble,
4		those that have made a situation very dangerous from time to
5		time, and I just hope that kind of demonstrator will now go
6		home.
7	Presenter:	So you're saying that every one of those fifty is a known
8		troublemaker?
9	Mr M:	Well, I'm saying that the court has looked at this matter, it's
10		taken its decision, and I back that thoroughly.
11	Presenter (to Dr G):	Are you a troublemaker, Dr G?

EXERCISE 3.3

Examine this extract. See if you can identify how category devices are managed to create the disjunctive category pair accuser/accused.

Can you demonstrate how category boundness and category assembly are used to evoke authorization and apportion blame?

How very different is the immediate production of the category 'troublemaker' in this interview report, from that of the report on DW, where the categorization is carefully assembled and a matter of inference. However, as is clearly observable in the text, being heard openly accusing someone of being a 'troublemaker' is no more attractive to Mr M than it is to the report writer in the college. The authorization for his assertion about 'troublemakers' is referred out (and up) to 'the courts' (line 9). In both cases, occasions for blame and authorization are reportably lodged in a hierarchy of agency and responsibility – as indeed are the complaints of the caller in the data extract on page 36. Jayyusi showed how these deployments of categories in a hierarchical system of relations (**hierarchies of relevance**) are used to generate, manage and interpret the social order as a moral order which is *methodically* grounded in the everyday practical activities of individuals contesting and defending disjunctive versions.

This implies that 'the very act of interpretation, the evoking of some specific frame of context, is an act of power whereby participants try to establish what is acceptable evidence or truth, and what could be meant at any given time' (Duranti and Goodwin, 1992: 18).

Indexicals, or 'pro-terms'

In previous sections I have made reference to indexicals. In the following section, we will explore how the study of indexical expressions has been undertaken by categorization analysts. First, a definition:

> **Indexical:** A type of expression whose semantic value is in part determined by features of the context of utterance, and hence may vary with that context. Among indexicals are the personal pronouns, such as 'I', 'you', 'he', 'she' and 'it'; demonstratives, such as 'this' and 'that'; temporal expressions, such as 'now', 'today', 'yesterday'; and locative expressions such as 'here', 'there', etc. (Audi, 1995)

Sacks was very interested in the operation of indexicals in the deployment of categorization devices. Indexicals implicate devices. In his analysis, the 'problem' of indexicals – how they acquire their meaning in the context of an utterance – becomes an empirical one: 'What we have to do is try to construct what a procedure might be for determining what it is that's being referred to when somebody says "you", "we", etc.' (1992a: 333).

Here's a complex use of personal pronouns in the telephone helpline data extract we looked at above:

Client: I'm not needy. I'm not one of them types that come screaming
Counsellor: Well, no, I, we, you don't have to go screaming ... if they just know, I, I mean people do care but they've got to know before they can care, don't they? (Watson, 1978: 106)

In the client's denial of her neediness – we have already seen how this exchange between counsellor and client generated the disjunctive pairing accuser/accused – she employs the complex indexical 'them type' to all those (non-specific) persons who 'come screaming'. In his response, the counsellor clearly has heard the problem which is posed. How is the breach to be repaired? Watson demonstrates how the counsellor's use of the personal pronoun 'we' works to do that repair. Sacks observed that the use of 'we' can substitute for 'anyone' in a 'warmer' sort of way, and Watson draws on this observation to show that by altering the 'I' to 'we', the counsellor includes himself, and everyone, in a warmer sort of way, such that the idea that 'anyone', indexed by the 'we' (even 'you' and 'me') might have the right to care.

Here's another example of the role that indexicals play from the group therapy data: the location-category 'here'. 'Ken', the young man in the therapy group from the example on page 24, is talking about how well he is doing at his military school. One of the others says to him, 'What are you doing here?' The apparent place term 'here' functions in this utterance to index a whole range of implications about what kinds of people might find themselves in a therapy group.

Hierarchies of relevance

As we have seen, Jayyusi greatly enriched the possibilities of application of categorization analysis by extending the technique into the study of predication – the methods by which ascriptions about membership are accomplished. She showed how the generation of disjunctive categories frequently leads to the possibility of disputes about which ascription will prevail. The resolution of these kinds of disputed ascriptions typically depends on the practical situation at hand, and appeal is made to what Jayyusi termed a **'hierarchy of relevance** or consequence'. By this she means, the parties to the interactional work invoke public criteria about which categorization should take precedence in the matter at hand. These criteria, she emphasizes, must not be invoked programmatically by the researcher, but need to be demonstrated as relevant with respect to the text or talk under study. In her study she gives two examples: in *this* culture we would not ordinarily doubt the order of relevance of the obligations of a man who is both a chess club member and a doctor, or the order of relevance of the obligations of a woman who is both socialite and mother. Both would be held accountable in respect of the second category over the first, should a conflict arise between them. However, as Jayyusi notes, conflict between category incumbency such as 'doctor' and 'father' might provoke a much more noteworthy dilemma for resolution. Suppose the man as 'doctor' is treating the critically wounded when he comes across his son among them. Such a conflict of categories, which is of necesssity situated, forms the basis of much social story-telling in fiction and drama.

Let's look at the rest of the exchange between the radio interviewer and his interviewee to see how this phenomenon is manifested in the news media:

1	Presenter:	Are you a troublemaker, Dr G. Hello, Dr G. [The phone
2		connection to the second interviewee has been lost.] We
3		have a problem there – that's a shame. He's just been called
4		a troublemaker and he can't defend himself . . . Let's see if
5		[we can
6	Mr M:	[it was the court that called him a troublemaker.
7	Presenter:	Indeed indeed. But I dare say that if he were there he
8		would . . . but look, Mr M, surely people ought to be
9		allowed to demonstrate and it's a question of defining what
10		a troublemaker is, isn't it?

EXERCISE 3.4

- How is a hierarchy of relevance invoked in this text?
- Can you identify *how* the interviewer demonstrates his hearing of that hierarchy of relevance and attends to its consequences?

This little strip of talk demonstrates very markedly how the hierarchy of relevance is employed by the interactants in the complex moves of 'defining what a troublemaker is'. The 'Member of Parliament' implicitly places himself under the direction of the 'courts', when challenged for blaming Dr G of being a 'troublemaker' – the presenter's re-ascription of his phrase 'those that have caused trouble'. He is merely backing the court of law. The presenter, for his part, demonstrates his hearing of this hierarchy ('Indeed indeed', line 7), before reasserting his control of the interview with the direct question, 'but . . . surely people ought to be allowed to demonstrate' (lines 8–9). Note that though the ascription 'troublemaker' is actually that of the presenter, not the court, invocation of the 'court' by the interviewee must be attended to, *and takes precedence over the category incumbency of both speakers*.

Wider applications of categorization analysis

Hester and Eglin conclude their review of Jayyusi's work on MCD analysis by noting that membership categorization analysis, as she developed it, has the potential to extend into wider domains than that of traditional sociological enquiry. They cite the sociologies of law, deviance, politics and media, history and moral and legal philosophy as example. They conclude by claiming that:

the scope of MCD inquiry may extend beyond these traditional sociological domains. Is there any scholarly activity, indeed any human activity carried out in language, that does not entail describing, judging and inferring, to which membership categorization (extended to things other than persons) is not applicable? (1992: 264)

Without attempting to address that rather large claim, the rest of this section seeks to suggest some applications of categorization analysis to other scholarly and practical disciplines outside the traditional domains of sociology. As noted in Chapter 1, in the early years of its development, conversation analysis quickly crossed the boundaries of anthropology, ethnography and sociology. Recent developments have seen the applications of conversation and categorization analysis employed in social and individual psychology.

The psychology of the individual

Sacks was an early reader of Vygotsky, the highly influential Soviet psychologist whose major work, *Thought and language,* was first published in English in 1962. In a reaction to the behaviourist psychology of the day, Vygotsky developed a theory of human psychology, and a method for empirical research, which was based on the premise that culturally produced sign systems of thought and language are transmitted through the mediation of social interaction, and that it is through this process of mediation that the human being has the capacity to act on the social and natural world, and transform it. He applied this theoretical stance to place observation at the heart of his method. He sought to make visible the orderly learning processes underlying the apparently banal and habitual everyday activities of children's play. Sacks' study of data from children's talk and stories gives us a clue that in addition to adult conversation, the developmental aspects of language in the socialization of the child were issues that concerned him, and which he saw as having relevance for the development of conversation analysis.

In his 1997 study of the competing models of mind and language in psychology and sociology, Derek Edwards notes the following:

Although Sacks did not take it up as a serious empirical project, he saw it as necessary and insightful to consider how any kind of adult competence could possibly be acquired, and was *designed to be acquired,* and how such a developmentally relevant interactional design was a built-in feature of the public, 'visible' nature of conversational competence. (1997: 297)

The important point here is that adult competence is *'designed to be acquired'.* This proposition is a corollary of the already noted core statement of Sacks' method: that the rules governing the methods of production of an utterance are the same rules used in the methods of hearing an utterance. The situated application of the rules of production and hearing, through which adults teach, and children acquire, the sense of there being a society is therefore a potential object of enquiry through the application of conversation and categorization analysis.

Sacks provides an interesting example of this in an early lecture on 'Accountable Actions':

> It's rather well known that very young children have, from the perspective of adults, a rather poor notion of causation. They don't know how things happen to happen. Now, among the ways that adults go about formulating rules for children are two which it's important to distinguish. Call them Class 1 and Class 2. A prototype of Class 1 is 'Don't stick your hand on the stove'. Prototypic of Class 2 is 'honor thy father and mother' – and such things as 'If you want people to love you, you should love them, be thoughtful to them etc.' belong in that class. (1992a: 77–8)

Sacks goes on to argue that distinguishing these two rules has to be learned by children case by case, with the result that they need a lot of assistance from adults. At the same time, parents frequently conflate the two in an attempt to restrain children's activity. 'If you go out in the woods, the wolf will come and eat you' would be an example of a famous version. That is, Class 2 propositions may be represented, and heard, as Class 1 propositions – that is, what are contingent relationships between events from the adult perspective, may be presented as materially causal relationships in order to achieve what are social goals – 'Do as I say or else'. And, as Sacks goes on to argue, in the process of development, children may assimilate the two classes of propositions in ways which persist into adulthood – that is, the rules for assigning causality learned in childhood may become the rules by which they interpret events in the adult world, often with inappropriate consequences.

Social psychology

These rules of causality are one case of a variety of rules which form the basis for inferences about events in the social world, and about other people's motives and intentions in the context of social activities and events. In the lecture which follows, entitled 'On exchanging glances' (1992a), Sacks continues to develop his theme in a similar vein, exploring the ways in which we understand, and make use of our understanding of, other people's minds, in order to accomplish practical social action. The point he is making, is that the predication of intentionality, and the interpretation of intentionality, is a member's accomplishment, and observable as such. He sets his students an exercise, which is stated as follows:

> I want you to be watching others watching each other. You can add personal remembrances if you want, or you can begin to record the encounters happening to yourself, but as the assignment, you're to be watching others looking at

each other. . . . Put down the place and the time. The more detail the better. (1992a: 82–3)

EXERCISE 3.5

Set Sacks' assignment for yourself. Develop the habit of observing interaction in all kinds of public settings as you go about your own ordinary activities. Try to see if you can infer what classes – that is, what categories – the watchers are seeing. You may be able to make this inference by observing what the watchers do next.

Sacks was concerned to demonstrate that social order is dependent, on a moment to moment basis, on the kinds of inferences people make about what is happening. They do this through interpretations of others' intentions and actions in the context of the available categorial resources. He gives the example of a verbal fight on the street between an older man and a younger woman which ends with the slapping of the girl. People have stopped to watch, and potentially to intervene, in the event that this is a case of kidnap, or an unprovoked attack by a stranger. When the situation is assessed as 'father and daughter', the people disperse. The relevant category bound activity would then be 'interference' rather than 'rescue'. In the case of James Bulger, two older boys kidnapped a young child from a shopping mall in the UK, and subsequently beat him to death. In the later enquiry, several people reported that they had observed the crying child being pulled along by the older boys. As in the case of the 'father and daughter', they read it within the device 'family' as 'older brothers looking after a younger brother'. One woman who actually stopped the children was told this by the older boys. The adults passed by, failing to intervene, with dire consequences.

Story-telling and narrative analysis

As we have already seen, Sacks was interested in story-telling as an example of social-order-in-practice, and viewed the analysability of stories as an important source of data in the empirical study of situated action. In Part III, we will undertake a detailed study of the analysis of stories. In the context of this chapter, it remains important to note the general applicability of the analysis of stories as an important potential application of conversation and categorization analysis across all the social sciences, where the analysis of narrative generally is increasingly seen as an important analytic tool.

Summary

In this chapter, the later developments in categorization analysis which have added substantially to its explanatory and analytical power have been introduced. You will see that the link between theory and method is very close: unlike many forms of research, where the technique happens 'behind closed doors', the analysis of texts should be as transparent as possible; it should 'saturate' the text, leaving no part of the data unexplained. Its conclusions should be observable; they should emerge from the process of analysing the data, not be 'proved' by the data.

If you have practised some of the techniques, using the exercises, you should be beginning to be able to apply the method to different kinds of talk and text. You will have begun to get a sense of the uncertainty of the process, the feeling 'there's nothing there', which slowly gives way to the recognition of patterns and regularities in the phenomenon under study. Sacks worked continuously, over periods of months and even years, on small data extracts, mining more from them with each return. It's a demanding, but rewarding, process, and one which works better if you can find colleagues to share your puzzles and ideas with.

Recommended reading

The key theoretical texts which have been referred to in this chapter are:

Hester, P. and Eglin, S. (1992) 'Category, predicate and task: the pragmatics of practical action', *Semiotica*, 88(3/4): 243–68.
Hestor and Eglin provide a critical review of Jayyusi's work, adding to it with more recent findings.

Jayyusi, L. (1984) *Categorization and the moral order*. London: Routledge and Kegan Paul.
Jayyusi's book is difficult to read, but is the seminal text in developing the potential of categorization analysis beyond the point where Sacks left it.

Key empirical studies to begin to explore:

Baker, C.D. (1984) 'The search for adultness: membership work in adolescent–adult talk', *Human Studies*, 7(3/4): 301–23.

Baker, C.D. and Freebody, P. (1987) 'Constituting the child in beginning school reading books', *British Journal of Sociology of Education*, 8(1): 55–74.

Baruch, G. (1981) 'Moral tales: parents' stories of encounters with the health professions', *Sociology of Health and Illness*, 3(3): 275–96.

Cuff, E.C. (1993) *Problems of versions in everyday situations*. Washington DC: International Institute for Ethnomethodology and Conversation Analysis. University Press of America.

Drew, P. (1978) 'Accusations: the occasioned use of member's knowledge of "religious geography" in describing events', *Sociology*, 12: 1–22.

McHoul, A.W. and Watson, D.R. (1984) 'Two axes for the analysis of "commonsense" and "formal" geographical knowledge and classroom talk', *British Journal of the Sociology of Education*, 5: 281–302.

Mehan, H. (1979) *Learning lessons: social organization in the classroom*. Cambridge, MA: Harvard University Press.

Sacks, H. (1979) 'Hotrodder: a revolutionary category'. In G. Psathas (ed.), *Everyday language: studies in ethnomethodology*. New York: Earlbaum.

Watson, D.R. (1978) 'Categorization, authorization and blame negotiation in conversation', *Sociology*, 12: 105–13.

For applications of CA to other disciplines, see:

Duranti, A. and Goodwin, C. (eds) (1992) *Rethinking context: language as an interactive phenomenon*. Cambridge: Cambridge University Press.
A collection of empirically grounded articles on applications of the analysis of interaction to the study of context and culture.

Edwards, D. (1997) *Discourse and cognition*. London: Sage.
Edwards provides a comprehensive introduction to the use of CA in the field of psychology.

Givon, T. (1997) *Conversation: cognitive, communicative and social perspectives*. Amsterdam: John Benjamins Publishing Company.
A collection of empirical studies of talk from a variety of disciplinary perspectives.

Part II

ANALYSING CULTURE USING TALK, TEXT AND IMAGE

4

Analysing Context

CONTENTS

The concept of context and its relationship to the study of culture has become an important focus for contemporary social science research. The chapters in Part II explore the contribution that categorization analysis can make to that study. Examples and exercises are taken from key sites of culture – the newspaper, radio, posters and reports – to show how the analysis of both talk and text can be tackled using the tools of categorization analysis.

A newspaper headline

Pregnant mum stabbed and sister threatened
DRUG PUSHERS IN CROSS BORDER TERROR

One of the interesting things about headlines is the way in which they draw upon categorizations to attract the interest of readers, and to inform them about the story which follows, in very few words. Here's a story which would certainly always be 'newsworthy' – two women, one pregnant, stabbed and threatened. This fact, however, is not the main point of the story, as is indicated by its secondary relation to the main headline: 'Drug pushers in cross border terror'. Well, I wonder, what is the relationship between these two facts? Shall I read the story?

EXERCISE 4.1

Examine this headline. As an ordinary newspaper reader, what kind of story do you expect to follow?
   Using the basic tools of categorization analysis introduced in Part I, what can you now show about *how* it sets up your expectations?

As a reader of this headline I might expect two stories. First, a story about a mother (she is a *pregnant mum*) and her sister. By employing a duplicatively organized set of categories, the writer sets the scene for a story about an extended family, and people who have expectable relations within the categorization device 'family', including the SRP 'sister/sister', and the SRP 'mother/child' – implicating a network of responsibilities for the young and dependent. It is also a story about a pregnant woman, who was stabbed: stabbing is category-bound to violence, but may have a variety of implications. The stabbing of a gang member would carry less moral weight than the stabbing of a pregnant woman, let alone mother. So we can see how just three words, through application of the consistency rule, can embed some complex relations, along with inferences about what is happening. CBA 'stabbed' confirms that the story is one of violence. Including three more words 'and sister threatened', on application of the consistency rule, tells still more:

- that a mother and a sister were the victims of an attack, not parties to a brawl;
- that the sister was the sister of the mother (assume that a second membership category belongs to the same device as the first);
- that I can expect a story about violence, and probably one about 'innocent victims'.[1]

Turning to the main part of the headline, further inferences can now be made. The second aspect of the story is that it is a story not only about violence, but also about terror: *Drug pushers in cross border terror.* This is no commonplace domestic violence, no incident between people known to each other, but – and perhaps this is the main point – it is a story about 'ordinary' people, members of the collection 'family', being threatened by drug pushers – members of the collection 'criminals'. Implications of terror extend beyond the recognizable experiences of violence 'family' members might have – rows between members of the family; rows with neighbours. 'Terror' as CBA implicates a kind of impersonality which is not commensurate with the ordinary world of families.

What, then, do I make of the modifier 'cross border'? What does this suggest about the story which is to follow? If the CBA 'terror' generates an expectation of something unpredictable, and from outside the ordinary world of 'family', then 'cross border', as an ascription, might seem redundant. What, then, is its function in this headline?

The answer is one of *context*: this headline appeared in the *Derry* (Northern Ireland) *Journal*, in February 1995. It follows, therefore, that the main point of the story may rather be about terrorism, and perhaps about related criminal activities, and therefore about an attack on the readers' society, as much as about an attack on a particular family.

I think I'll read it.

Context and culture

In the Chapters 5 and 6, we will explore how Sacks' understanding of the relationship between categories and context generates a robust empirical method for the study of coherent social action, from the level of the individual speaker to the level of **culture**. In order to do that, we must be very precise about what is meant by those terms. First, I want to show how the terms '**context**' and '**culture**' can be understood as aspects of a continuous process, which may be called a '**field** of relations'. In the rest of this chapter I will show how the method of categorization analysis can be applied to a variety of kinds of data, and for a variety of analytic purposes, in the empirical analysis of culture.

What is context?

The term 'context' is used in various ways in the social science and the arts, and appears often to be employed for the purposes of the analysis to hand, without any clear definition of the term. This fact may seem to suggest that the term is, therefore, conceptually weak. However, to dismiss it on this evidence would be to miss rich opportunities for analysis. All those engaged in the study of social interaction over the past 30 years have had to recognize the importance of taking into account the situated nature of the phenomena they have been studying. Once social phenomena, including language, are no longer studied as an abstract, formalized system, but rather, as a set of practices, the aspect of temporality cannot be ignored. 'Context' is the concept which acknowledges temporality as an active constituent aspect of meaningful social interaction.

In philosophy, 'context' has been of interest to those thinkers who were interested in practices, rather than laws, of inference and justification. The concept of context first became important in the work of Dewey, and was subsequently developed in the American school of 'pragmatism'. According to Dewey, categories of knowledge, or concepts, are the product of mediating experience, rather than 'representations' which correspond to antecedent facts. Dewey collaborated closely with the social theorist,

George Herbert Mead, at the University of Chicago in the 1920s and 1930s. They were followed in the 1950s by the 'Chicago School' of sociology. Their perspective on the nature of knowledge and reality had a powerful influence on the development of the strand of American social thought through which we traced the evolution of Sacks' work in the introduction to this book (Chapter 1).

The concept of 'context' also provides the basis for the 'ordinary language' philosophy of Wittgenstein, and for subsequent developments in the empirical studies of language commonly known as 'pragmatics'. For Wittgenstein, as for Dewey, the great epistemological error of traditional philosophy lay in the notion that knowledge is a process of inspection of the world to discover what is 'in' it. Both held that our thoughts and concepts are, rather, processes through which we discover it. For Dewey, knowing is doing. Wittgenstein took this notion one step further: knowing is doing things with language. If we want to discover what the nature of knowledge is, we need look no further than how language is used in ordinary ways. Philosophy becomes an analytic, descriptive practice, grounded in a naturalistic understanding of human action.

In current social science research, uses of the term 'context' abound. For many social scientists within this tradition, the term 'context' signifies the presence of background against which the interpretation of the meaning of human action and culture may be achieved. The distinction is echoed in the technical terms 'emic' (near) and 'etic' (far), borrowed from linguistics to describe the distinction between the 'internal' features of a culture, set against universalized aspects of culture. Sometimes the 'figure/ground' distinction is borrowed from the vocabulary of visual arts. In this use of the term, what moves forward (conceptually) must be viewed against what is then generalized, or backgrounded. 'Context', in this analysis, means the interpretation of meaning. It is the sense of 'context' commonly employed in the method of analysis known as 'social constructionism'.

In the field of sociology, interest in context, informed by the tradition of 'pragmatism', produced an increasing interest in micro-studies of the everyday social world. Goffman's study of everyday interaction, which produced the concept of **frames** as an object of study (1974), first attracted Sacks to the University of California. Goffman, through his study of face to face interaction, drew serious and systematic attention to the pervasive influence of context in the organization of human interaction, and its relationship to cultural practices. However, his focus was descriptive, rather than empirical. When Sacks, having encountered Garfinkel and ethnomethodology, began to look systematically at the micro-processes of actual conversations, he proposed that context be conceived as actively generated on a turn by turn basis by speakers, rather than as a pre-existing 'frame' within which interaction takes place according to independent rules. It was this difference which led to a split between Goffman and Sacks. Goffman could not accept that phenomena at the level of turn-by-turn talk could provide an adequate explanation of what happens in, for example, an exchange of greetings, when, for him, the analyst of interaction must take account of rituals which explain the wide cultural variations of the same basic human interaction. Sacks argued that the procedures by which ritual interactions such as exchanges of greetings are generated and recognized constitute a necessary and sufficient description of the means by which context, and by extension, cultural rituals, are generated and sustained. Goffman accused conversation analysis of empty formalism.

The disagreement between Sacks and Goffman goes to the heart of the problem of the relationship between interaction, context and culture. Goffman correctly identified Sacks' model as one of 'system constraints' (Silverman, 1985). Systems theory turns out to be relevant to any consideration of the development of the concept of 'context' as a site of enquiry. The anthropological work of Gregory Bateson (1972) which provided the basis for a theory of human communication based on the notion of interaction as a system of relations, was a strong influence on the work of Goffman, and informed his thinking about the centrality of ritual in the organization of human culture. The issue embedded here is: what relationship can be discovered between the actions of speaking subjects, and the 'form of life' (Wittgenstein) within which that interaction takes place? The first major text which attempted to tackle this problem was *Directions in sociolinguistics: the ethnography of speaking* (Gumperz and Hymes, 1972), which provided the impetus to a wide range of studies in a new discipline – the empirical study of the phenomenon of context. Conversation analysis was one of them. In the years since, a group of related, but separate, disciplines have emerged, most of which will have been referred to at some point in this volume. Often they are unaware of each others' findings, to their detriment. One of the arguments put forward here, is that the method of categorization analysis offers an empirical tool across a wide range of potential sites of investigation of the phenomenon of 'context'.

It is important to recognize that within the tradition of pragmatism and ordinary language philosophy, in which Sacks' work is properly placed, the sense of 'context' is not to be understood as implying a relativist, or 'social constructivist', position. The notion of context as proposed by Dewey and Wittgenstein is one in which the conceptual structure of knowledge and thought are held to be shaped by the forms and processes of the natural world. Sacks' understanding of his project clearly follows within this tradition. However, unlike the philosophers, Sacks' achievement was to develop an empirical method which used naturally occurring data rather than invented example. His claim was very strong:

- The detailed ways in which actual, naturally occurring social activities occur are subjectable to formal description.
- Social activities – actual, singular sequences of them – are methodical

occurrences. That is, their description consists of the descriptions of sets of formal procedures persons employ.

- The methods persons employ to produce their activities permit formal description of singular occurrences that are generalizable in intuitively non-apparent ways and are highly reproducibly usable.
- Such findings have significance for what it is that sociology can aim to do, and of how it can proceed. In brief, sociology can be a natural observational science. (Sacks, 1984a)

How can categorization analysis contribute to the empirical analysis of context?

A first approach to operationalizing the study of 'context' might best be a descriptive one: what are the aspects of context which its study must take into account? First is the important distinction between 'figure' and 'ground'. In practice, human actors foreground some acts and activities, while backgrounding others, in order to achieve both perceptual and communicative coherence. The term 'context' derives from the Latin 'con-textus' – 'a joining together'. An important aspect of the study of context, therefore, concerns the analysis of how foreground and background join up – that is, how a focal activity relates to, invokes, and is rendered meaningful in relation to backgrounded features. Central to Garfinkel's study of everyday interaction, of major concern to Sacks, and to many of those who have developed conversation analysis, is the concept of indexi-cality. The term was employed by Garfinkel to specify the basic premise of ethnomethodology: 'Members' accounts are reflexively and essentially tied for their rationality to the socially organized conditions of their use' (1967: 4). He proposed that this basic condition of human sociality is the locus for objective social enquiry.

As seen from the perspective of the phenomenon of indexicality, the analysis of context necessarily implies a two-way traffic between focal activities and the environment within which they occur. Three aspects of context must be taken into account:

- *first*, approaching context from the perspective of an actor actively operating on the world within which he or she finds him- or herself embedded;
- *second*, tying the analysis of context to the indigenous activities that participants use to constitute the culturally and historically organized social worlds that they inhabit; and
- *third*, recognizing that participants are situated within multiple con-texts which are capable of rapid and dynamic change as the events they are engaged in unfold. (Duranti and Goodwin, 1992: 5)

In addition to the factors of the 'external' world they inhabit, there is the additional element of the reactions, plans and intentions (the 'internal' worlds) of others. People themselves 'become environments for one another' (McDermott, 1976, quoted in Duranti and Goodwin, 1992). The dynamic play of contextual forces in the temporal and spatial **field** of human interaction is apparently unlimited in its complexity. What means of bringing this complexity under some kind of rigorous discipline can be brought to bear on the wide range of data which might be relevant? Duranti and Goodwin propose several levels of analysis, all of which bear on each other, but which, for the purposes of analysis, may be tackled variously by different methods. The relationship between the 'focal activity' and the environment in which it occurs, as the object of study, generates some specific empirical questions:

- *How* does the setting become a resource for the interactants?
- *How* do the postures, gestures, giving and withdrawal of attention – the behavioural aspects of the context of interaction – contribute to the formation of a recognizable 'focal event'?
- *How* do the sequences, the **relevant category environment**, the resources of 'genre' in talk or in text work to constitute the relevant context for those engaged in communicating with each other?
- *How* are collective phenomena, the 'discursive practices' characteristic of the culture in which the activity takes place, the systems of knowledge (what counts as true or false), deployed in setting specific ways, to achieve interactional ends – to gain the attention or validation of others, or to win arguments, for example?

It will be clear already that Sacks' methods were aimed at addressing some of these concerns. In a lecture to the American Anthropological Association (Moerman and Sacks, 1971/1988), given with the anthropologist, Moerman, Sacks defined 'culture' as 'a system of common understandings'. The implication of Sacks' proposal is that the systematic study of conversation as he conceived it provides a powerful and comprehensive tool for the empirical study of the system of shared understandings which is culture. Through the systematic application of CA methods, context need not be invoked as a self-evident background to the processes of culture and social action; rather, it is empirically identifiable in its own right as an orderly product of social interaction, generating common understanding through a set of procedures which can be observed. The micro-processes of interaction embed the processes of social systems and cultures, and reveal that relevant context is created on a moment-to-moment basis by speakers and hearers through the production of what Sacks termed 'adequate descriptions'. The analysis of conversation is both *context free and context sensitive*: it seeks to reveal how speakers draw upon universal procedural rules to create locally relevant shared understanding. This view links 'macro' and 'micro' levels of analysis, previously considered to be inevitably separate, and it also has important implications for the study of culture.

By asking '*how*' at the level of interaction, we can build the answers to '*why*' questions in a disciplined and systematic way (Silverman, 1985). From the perspective of interaction, if we are truly to grasp the nature of context in its relevance to the people engaged in activities which we call 'culture' – whether they be 'macro' level activities, such as the law, medicine, education, the 'news', the 'market', on the one hand; or 'micro' level phenomena such as celebrations, feasts, trading, cooking, child-rearing and so on, on the other – then *how* it is demonstrably relevant becomes the analytic task. According to this view, the setting, the rules which govern correct behaviours in a given setting, the clothing, the roles, the age, race, class or gender of the individuals – all of these are treated analytically as resources, available to social actors in creating a potential space for action which is the relevant context. Context, in this analysis, exists in time. It is sustained in time, through the methodical activities of social actors, which can be rendered observable through the study of talk as interaction. In the following chapters, we will see how categorization analysis can shed light on the ways in which the orderly construction of context can be studied in a variety of interactional activities and settings, using talk, text and images as sources of data.

The question asked by Sacks, and developed through the detailed analytic work of those who followed him, addresses this question: how can the relevant context of any particular utterance demonstrably be shown in the talk? If we can show that, then we can show how it is that speakers and hearers ascertain what is being referred to at any given moment in the talk, and align themselves relevantly to each other, and, by tying their utterance relevantly to the task at hand, constitute a common understanding. *How* do they do this? In a very strong formulation of the task, Schegloff notes that 'If *context* is in the conduct itself, if it *is* in a sense the conduct itself, then . . . context is the omnipresent job of analysis' (1992: 215).

Procedures

Let's revisit Sacks' original proposal on method:

> A culture is an apparatus for generating *recognizable* actions; if the same procedures are used for generating as for detecting, that is perhaps as simple a solution to the problem of recognizability as is formulatable. (1992a: 226)

For Sacks, hearability, or meaning, is not a product of the linguistic features of the utterance, but an outcome of the application of procedures, embedded in the 'shared understandings' of culture, locally employed for the immediate purposes to hand. It follows that language, context and culture are not linked in a hierarchy of complexity, nor should any priority be given to one kind of analysis over another. If 'culture' is the orderly product of human action at the level of talk, then the study of the procedures by which contexted meaning is achieved in talk becomes a powerful natural observational tool for empirical study at different levels of complexity.

Here is a restatement of Sacks' original proposition, from the perspective of more recent research on the sequential telling of stories:

> Listening to talk thus involves constructing a continuously changing horizon of projected possibilities for what the unfolding talk might become. Moreover, making such projections is not simply an individual cognitive process, but a relevant component of the visible actions that the recipient is engaged in. If recipients were not engaged in such projection, co-ordinated action of the type found in these data might not be possible. In brief, within interactive activities, cognitive operations can be analysed as processes embedded within particular modes of social practice. (Goodwin and Goodwin, 1992: 163–4)

In his introduction to the Lectures, Schegloff suggests that much of Sacks' thinking points to a wide variety of potential applications, which Sacks himself never pursued. Many applications remain to be explored. Analysing the progress of situated talk involves two major accomplishments: the management of relevance – that is, how does each speaker contribute to the creation of a shared meaning through the selection of, and response to, the categories-in-use; and the management of turns, or 'sequencing'. As we have already seen, the mainstream of conversation analysis, following Sacks' concerns at the time that he died, has focused on sequential analysis of conversation. The analysis of Membership Category Devices, which occupied Sacks' attention for much of the time, has been very much sidelined, and even denigrated as not 'scientific'. Sacks' interest in a 'machinery' which underlay the orderly processes of turn-by-turn talk came to dominate what was seen as a legitimate continuation of his work. Schegloff, in his introduction to the Lectures, suggests that Sacks turned away from MCD analysis because of its potential for 'wild analysis' – analysis in which the 'interpretations' of the analyst can easily take precedence over the evidence in the talk itself. On the one hand, critics of CA, like Goffman, accuse it of 'empty formalism'; on the other, many practitioners of CA restrict their analysis to turn-taking procedures, fearing, with Schegloff, that categorization analysis is too prone to the dangers, as they see it, of hermeneutic, rather than empirical, analysis.

I do not believe Sacks would have taken this view – his interests and imagination were too wide for that. Yet, there are serious points to be taken into account on both sides of the argument about the applications of CA. There is some justification in Goffman's criticism of CA's 'empty formalism', and the exclusive pursuit of the analysis of turn-taking as the only legitimate project for CA is vulnerable to that criticism. There is also a real risk, in the loose application of categorization analysis, of a loss of the empirical and intellectual rigour which Sacks pursued.

A solution to this dilemma lies in an understanding of Sacks' approach to the study of talk in terms of systems constraints which need not be, and should not be, reductive, (nor was that Sacks' intention). The important innovation which Sacks made to the study of contexted interaction, was to find a route by which the choice between 'structures' and 'processes' can be bypassed altogether. Through his demonstration of the *procedures* by which speakers and hearers attend to 'the shifting and changing possibilities about what the talk might become', Sacks showed that *the phenomenon we are dealing with – 'context' – is neither structure nor process, but both.*

Procedures, in order to be recognizable, are inherently conservative – that is, they must be adhered to recognizably in practice or they cease to work. They may be formalized, in the form of documents – 'to do' lists, instructions, or recipes, for instance; or they may be tacit – greeting rituals would be an example of unwritten, but widely practised and recognizable procedures. Garfinkel (1967) demonstrated this property of procedures when he got his students to conduct an experiment. The experiment consisted of the students behaving as if they were boarders on returning to the family home at the end of the day. That is, they were instructed to behave in a formal, polite fashion. In four-fifths of the cases, 'family members were stupefied. They vigorously sought to make the strange actions intelligible and to restore the situation to normal appearances. Reports were filled with accounts of astonishment, bewilderment, shock, anxiety, embarrassment, and anger' (1967: 47).

If they are inherently conservative, at the same time, procedures are practices whose aim is fundamentally pragmatic. Unlike the rules of a game, for example, they are subject to alteration: as circumstances change, so will procedures. As system conditions change, so will the relations which constrain them. Normally, this process will be slow and incremental. However, it may also happen that circumstances will change dramatically. Greeting rituals may be dispensed with in an emergency, for example. In that case, familiar procedures may suddenly become irrelevant, and the interactional field they underpin may break down. Other procedures will be sought to organize immediate experience and provide for mutual understanding and shared action.

This fact – that procedures are simultaneously conservative and subject to change and alteration in the course of changing conditions – requires high levels of interactional competence and adaptability on the part of those participating individuals who depend on them to generate shared understanding. Operationalizing the concept of context in terms of procedures, which attends to both system change and system stability, provides a powerful conceptual tool for linking both individual practices (including, as Goodwin and Goodwin suggest, cognitive strategies) and systems constraints, in a model which allows for the empirical investigation of how 'context' and 'culture' are constituted and sustained by individuals engaged in situated talk and action.

These theoretical considerations place the micro-analysis of talk within the domain of the study of culture. But how, you may be asking by now, can we link these theoretical considerations to the practice of categorization analysis? Here, the contribution of Lena Jayyusi is significant. Consider for example this methodological injunction she proposes:

> The issue then is not a mechanical application of the consistency rule where one *decides* what device these two membership (or any co-selected) categories *are drawn from*, but rather to see what device-category they could, strictly or conventionally, imply *for the task or relevance at hand* that is displayed in the talk within which this category is embedded. . . . The device is then not so much *presupposed* as *implicated* by the selections. (1984: 62)

Jayussi, faithful to Sacks' principle that the procedures for generating meaningful utterances are the same as those for hearing them, reminds categorization analysts that, like the hearer, it is *the task or relevance at hand* which *implicates* the device within which the selected categories are to be heard, not presuppositions imposed on them by the analyst with an interest in 'culture', for example. Let's see how this applies to the headline with which this discussion of context began.

We have seen that the writer employs categories from two devices in such a way that a disjunction is created: on one hand are members of the device 'family', who, by applying the rules of duplicative organization, and the consistency rule, we read as the recipients of the activities of members of the device 'criminals'. The level of description is constrained by the task at hand – the creation of a newspaper headline, the purpose of which is to attract the reader by suggesting the nature of the story to follow. Such a task is of interest to categorization analysis because it involves appealing to the shared knowledge of the community of readers to provide for inferences about the story which follows in the fewest number of words possible. The nature of the task means that the use of categorization devices must be very finely tuned. Analysis of the newspaper headline focuses the question: what are the procedures by which the recipient of the communication (the reader) is enabled to hear an upcoming story, and to take the next action desired by the writer (to go on reading)? The relevant task at hand is 'newsworthiness', the success of which, as for any successful narrative (to be considered in detail in Part III) is to engage the interest of the reader. By analysing how this is achieved by the headline writer, through applications of the categorization procedures at the finest level of detail, we can also see how the relevant context is oriented to: the headline writer appeals to the shared knowledge of her community of readers to capture their interest, through the application of categorial procedures, which locate the story to follow – what is hearable – within the device 'the troubles'.

The consistency rule, as we have seen, enabled the reader to make some inferences about the story to follow: first, that this is a story about violence visited on innocent victims, rather than violence generated between warring parties. Second, that this is a story about more than just victims of crime ('drug pushers'); it is also a story about 'cross border terror' –

transgressors of national boundaries. Selection of the CBA 'terror' is specific to the setting of the story – Londonderry, in the mid-1990s. For a reader without this point of reference, the inclusion of 'terror' might carry other implications. For readers of the *Derry Journal*, it implicates a powerful statement of the dangers of borders, and the powerful taboos that empower them.

Here, we can start to see how the wider analysis of culture emerges from the local detail of local relevancies.

Douglas, in her study of the cultural phenomenon of pollution as shaper of culture and thought, noted:

> Four kinds of social pollution seem worth distinguishing. The first is danger pressing on external boundaries; the second, a danger from transgression of the internal lines of the system; the third, danger in the margins of the lines. The fourth is danger from internal contradiction, when some of the basic postulates are denied by other basic postulates, so that at certain points the system seems to be at war with itself. . . . I show how the symbolism of the body's boundaries is used in this kind of unfunny way to express danger to community boundaries. (1966: 122)

Douglas' analysis relies on the revelation, through the activities of the researcher of culture, of the categorial structures which underpin symbols and culture. For her, analysis began where members of that culture could not reveal to her *why* something was considered 'unclean'. In this brief analysis of a headline, without reference to pre-existing structures, we have been able to unravel the same kinds of attention to the reality of *external margins and internal contradictions in the form of categorial procedures which are members' resources.* In following the ethnomethodological injunction to treat topic as resource, asking *how* rather than *why*, categorization analysis yields a powerful means of showing how categorial procedures are attended to by speakers and hearers, and generate the recognizability which, for Sacks, provides for the possibility of culture.

Summary

> [I]t is in the use of categories that culture is constituted. . . . It is in their use that the collectable character of membership categories is constituted and membership categorization devices assembled in situ: membership categorization devices are assembled objects. (Hester and Eglin, 1996: 20)

In this chapter, I have used one particular example of a cultural phenomenon – the newspaper headline, now common to all literate cultures – to investigate the nature of context as an empirical matter, and to show how categorization analysis can be brought to bear on the study of culture and its products. The newspaper headline provides a particularly intensive site for analysis. The conditions of its production – 'the relevance at hand'

– set a task for writer and reader alike to deploy the categorial procedures to maximum effect. Some new concepts, developed by Jayyusi and others, were introduced to deepen the analysis of the way in which categories are assembled to generate a new headline.

It is on the basis of its analysis of procedures-in-use that categorization analysis can provide a robust empirical method which, applied across different interactional settings, can yield powerful insights into the fine-grained working of culture. In the chapter which follows, I will use another media form universally common to contemporary societies – the news broadcast – to show how categorization is generated in talk.

Recommended reading

Douglas, M. (1975) *Implicit meanings*. London: Routledge.
Structuralism has passed out of fashion, but its insights, and Douglas' use of the Durkheimian tradition of analysis still has much to offer.

Duranti, A. and Goodwin, C. (eds) (1992) *Rethinking context: language as an inter-active phenomenon*. Cambridge: Cambridge University Press.
The most comprehensive statement of current thinking across disciplines on the relationship between context and action.

Jayyusi, L. (1984) *Categorization and the moral order*. London: Routledge and Kegan Paul.
In this book, Jayyusi builds on the original concepts of Sacks' lectures to develop a full analysis of the procedures by which categorizations build a moral and social world. The book is dense, but a must for anyone intending to work intensively with the method of categorization analysis.

Schegloff, E.A. (1997) 'Whose text? Whose context?', *Discourse & Society*, 8(2): 165–87.
In this article, Schegloff makes the contemporary case for a conversation analytic approach to the study of context.

Note

1.   Thanks to Kay Fensom for these data and for the analysis.

5

Analysing Talk

CONTENTS

In this chapter, some samples of talk will be analysed. I will assume that the concepts already introduced in Part I are by now part of your basic understanding of the method. We will concentrate on discovering how everyday talk – using data easily collected for analysis – can be employed to analyse context and culture. One of the advantages of conversation and categorization analysis is that much data are readily available.

A radio news interview

Talk is offered in public settings and is easily recorded. The following extract comes from a BBC Radio News interview. The participants are the Presenter, Mr M (a Conservative member of Parliament), and Dr G, a demonstrator, who, because of a technical fault, misses his first turn to speak.

```
1   Presenter:   Mr M. First, do you approve of this injunction?
2   Mr M:        Yes. Good. Let's not forget it's not peaceful demonstrators
```

3		that are being injuncted. It's those that have caused trouble,
4		those that have made a situation very dangerous from time to
5		time, and I just hope that kind of demonstrator will now go
6		home.
7	Presenter:	So you're saying that every one of those fifty is a known
8		troublemaker?
9	Mr M:	Well, I, I'm saying that the court has looked at this matter, it's
10		taken its decision, and I back that thoroughly.
11	Presenter:	Are you a troublemaker, Dr G? Hello Dr G? Ah. We have a
12		problem there. He's just been called a troublemaker and he can't
13		defend himself. Let's see if [we can
14	Mr M:	[It was the court that called him a
15		troublemaker.
16	Presenter:	Indeed, indeed. But I dare say that if he were there he would . . .
17		But look, Mr M, surely people ought to be allowed to
18		demonstrate and (.) and it's a question of defining what a
19		troublemaker is, isn't it?

One of the basic principles of Sacks' method was that no part of a conversational exchange is incidental, and that no single utterance can be understood except within the overall structure of the conversation. Every part of an utterance is 'recipient designed' – that is, each element plays its part in the overall delivery of a communication which is designed to be hearable. In this segment, an interactional disturbance occurs when the presenter addresses the second interviewee – Dr G. – and discovers that he is not 'there'. This creates a 'problem' (the words of the interviewer). In the following exercise, use the principles of categorization analysis to analyse the presenter's 'problem', taking seriously Sacks' claim, that in the relationship between context, culture and language there are no absolute analytic or conceptual priorities. It may help to refer back to the 'how' questions on page 55.

EXERCISE 5.1

Describe the 'problem'. Remember, that it is not *your* common sense interpretation which is at issue here, but the common sense understanding displayed by the interactants which provides the evidence for the procedures which are operating in this interaction.

I was struck by this interview when I heard it because I was already studying the way the category 'troublemaker' is employed in institutions (Lepper, 1994, 1995). I was lucky to be able to get a recording of the interview from the BBC, because I do not usually audiotape the early morning news! The point of entry into the analysis was my analytic interest in the incidence of a specific phenomenon – in this case a categorization. The principle of selection of data depends upon several factors – the interest which drives the investigator, the availability of data, the usability of data. In this case, all converged nicely.

A troublemaker

When I did my first analysis of this sequence, I was interested in comparing the production of the category 'troublemaker' with another example from some textual data I was working on. I noticed how differently they were produced in the two sites. In the setting of the radio interview, it was evident that the absence of the 'accused' caused an interactional 'problem': 'He's just been called a troublemaker and he can't defend himself' (lines 10–11). In the text, which was a report, the absence of the 'troublemaker' was not an issue in the same way. Was this, I wondered, evidence for the way in which setting becomes a resource for interactants? But *how*?

You will probably have identified the presenter's 'problem' in the first instance as one of turn-taking. The interviewer's dilemma, having provided for a reply with a question, is that no answer is forthcoming (the participant isn't 'there'). The news interview, especially on the British radio and television, typically takes the form of a panel discussion, in which participants of opposing views are invited to debate their positions. The interview often takes the form of a disagreement, managed by the interviewer in the form of questions (as it were, on behalf of the listening audience), to be answered by the interviewees, who should be given equal time. The setting, therefore, constrains opportunities for speakers under the control of the interviewer (Greatbatch, 1992). In addition, news interviewers are under a constraint of neutrality, or apparent neutrality, which is primarily achieved through the management of 'footing' (Goffman, 1981). An analysis by Clayman (1992) of the televised news interview shows how Goffman's concepts of frame and footing can be rigorously demonstrated through the application of conversation analysis to situated interaction. Footing plays an important part in the way in which this presenter's management of the interview begins, and the 'problem' which is created for him when he discovers the second interviewee is not there.

Greatbatch, Heritage and Clayman have made ample demonstration of the crucial role that turn-taking plays in the interactional management of the news interview. What does categorization analysis have to add to it? This is a perfect example: you probably noticed that the categorization 'troublemaker' is introduced by the presenter himself, when, by posing the question in lines 7–8, he shifts the categorization offered by the first interviewee ('demonstrations'), which includes two versions of members – 'peaceful demonstrators' and 'those that have caused trouble' – to 'troublemakers'. By implication, the introduction of this categorization invokes the CBAs 'accuse' and 'defend', which then become relevant to the interaction. By 'accusing' someone, a 'defence' becomes not only relevant, but required ('He's just been called a troublemaker and he can't defend himself . . .'; lines 12–13). To be a 'demonstrator' is not to be accused. Once the footing is changed (the interviewer's shift of categorization from 'demonstrator' to 'troublemaker') a second range of constraints and opportunities within the interview dialogue is generated. The importance of turn-taking in this talk is thus shown to be not only one of the question and answer format as a feature of sequential order, but also one of right to reply on the part of an 'accused'. By examining the way in which the categorization device is deployed by the presenter, we begin to see *how* this sequence of turns generates a relevant category environment (or context), and how, through the application of the 'consistency rule' in the shift of footing from 'demonstrator' to 'troublemaker', the 'disagreement' format familiar to listeners of British news (the context) is generated by the presenter, and responded to by Mr M.

By looking further at this sequence, we can also see *how* the part played by categorization in the creation and maintenance of a moral order is deployed by the interactants. To the presenter's direct question (lines 7–8), Mr M responds with his own footing: 'Well, I, I'm saying the court has looked at this matter . . .' (lines 9–10). It is not *my* view, but the court's view. How does he do this? In this case, he makes use of another kind of resource: the pro-term 'you', embedded in the presenter's question 'So you're saying . . .'.

> **Pro-term**: A pro-term is an indexical term. Its referent, and hence its meaning, depends entirely on the function it plays within a sentence or utterance. Pro-terms include the personal pronouns, as well as indefinite locational adverbs ('there', 'here', 'before', 'after', for example) and indefinite prepositions. Verbs may also act as pro-terms where they are employed as actions, such as performatives (Austin, 1962) – for example, 'Look!'

In this case, Mr M uses a pro-term to shift the referent from the personal to a collective 'you' – it's 'the court' which has decided. When he then completes his turn – '. . . and I back that thoroughly' – Mr M succeeds in placing himself within the membership category of law-abiding citizens who back the court's decision, rather than within the membership category of 'accusers'. Pro-terms turn out to be an important resource for speakers in the management of footing. In the case of location categories, for example, they enable speakers and hearers to establish the relevant setting necessary for adequate descriptions to be constructed. As we have seen, the simple act of giving directions presumes that the giver of instructions is able to 'put himself in the shoes' of the hearer, and provide a description – the directions – which is relevant to the hearer's available knowledge. At a level of far greater complexity, pro-terms – particularly the pronoun forms – can play a crucial role in debates about accountability for actions and meanings (for a detailed study of pro-terms, see Watson, 1987).

As we shall see when we look at the production of the category 'trouble-maker' in the text which is discussed in the next chapter, speakers do not generally wish to appear in the role of accuser, and have a variety of inter-actional means by which they avoid that ascription. Further evidence for this occurs in lines 14–15: here Mr M 'defends' himself against the possi-bility of being perceived as an 'accuser'. His use of the pro-term in order to achieve a shift of footing is an important means to this end. Each speaker's perception of the moral implications of the topic, and the way in which they want to be perceived within it, is finely managed on a turn-by-turn basis. Mr M defends himself against the possible ascription 'accuser' by placing himself within the category 'law-abiding citizen'; just as the presenter demonstrates his 'fairness' to all sides by ensuring that listeners are aware of his intention to make sure everyone gets a hearing (lines 12–13). Once more, we see how close empirical attention to the details of the talk provides evidence for the ways in which context is generated and sustained on a turn-by-turn basis through the generation, recognition of, and response to a relevant category environment. In the next chapter, we'll look at another method by which speakers and hearers (report writers and readers, in this case) use the constraints of the 'genre' to manage issues of moral accountability.

Disorderability

Staying for the moment with the 'problem' before the presenter, another level of analysis can now be attempted. What additional significance could Mr M's introduction of the 'court' have? Having begun on the 'micro' level of analysis, we have seen, in the interaction between two speakers, the 'moral' problems they face in presenting themselves and their motives. The interviewer seeks to sustain his neutral, 'fair' role of giving right to reply; the interviewee seeks to avoid the ascription of 'accuser'. We have seen something of how the setting of the contempor-ary news interview constrains the ways in which the speakers take up their roles and form their responses to each other. We have seen the ways in which the category collection which is invoked by the membership categorization device 'this injunction' (line 1) has created a relevant category environment in which the authority of the 'court' provides a relevant and available resource to Mr M in his defence of his position. Looking more closely, again there is evidence of the ways in which the procedures employed by the presenter generate the disagreement, which is, in fact, a contest of versions between 'demonstrator' and 'trouble-maker'. In the first line, he sets up the categorization device which will provide the frame for the rest of the interview, with his question, 'Do you approve of this injunction?' In doing so, he invokes a 'macro' level of

discourse – the institutions of the law, of the courts, and of their procedures – the 'law of the land'. In response, Mr M invokes relevant
membership categories – those who are and are not 'being injuncted'
(line 3), who comprise two versions: 'peaceful demonstrators' and 'those
who make trouble'. In lines 7–8 ('So you're saying that every one of those
fifty is a known troublemaker?'), the presenter shifts the footing: now the
focus is on the persons, rather than the institutions, and on the adequate
description of the behaviours which persons engage in. What level, then
are we (the listeners) to hear this interview? Is it about demonstrators,
about troublemakers, or about the law of the land? How are they related?
Perhaps this interview is about adequate descriptions: about the 'question of defining what a troublemaker is' (lines 18–19). In fact, the rules
of evidence which provide for these participants' claims are similar in
kind to the rules of evidence upon which the 'courts' depend for the
practical business of interpreting the law. (Remember that Sacks' early
training was in the law.) Here is evidence for Sacks' claim that adequate
descriptions of the world and our experiences are everyday achieve-
ments, and are of as much concern to ordinary speakers and hearers as
they are to social (or psychological) analysts. Looking at this extract
more closely, can we see by what procedures, in the context of a news
interview, the debate – a contest of versions – draws on rules of evidence,
and the institution of the law, to achieve a 'definition' of a troublemaker?
In order to do this, another principle of the underlying structuring procedures of talk may help us.

One of the aspects of conversation which occupied a lot of Sacks' attention was the way in which the topic was managed over the course of an
extended exchange. He noticed that the movement from one topic to
another, or within a topic, is neither obviously smooth or self-evident. He
asked his usual question: *How* do speakers and hearers orient to a topic
across turns, and how do they change the subject while keeping the other
engaged? He sought to identify procedures by which this task is accomplished, and called those procedures 'tying rules'.

> **Tying rules:** The means by which one part of a conversation is tied to
> another on a local basis.

Tying rules are fundamental to the notion that 'context' is subject to local
control. This involves a principle which underpins the procedures which
provide for tying:

> **Disorderability:** describes a sequence which can be taken apart and re-
> ordered without loss of coherence. Its converse, **non-disorderability**,
> describes a sequence which loses meaning and coherence if its com-
> ponents are rearranged.

The ways in which the non-disorderability of sequence and topic can be demonstrated to be required for coherence is the basis for empirically identifying 'tying rules' – the procedures by which interactants structure their turns in ongoing interaction in order to achieve orderliness. Why, we might ask, does Sacks approach his analysis in this indirect manner? The answer lies in another aspect of Sacks' concerns about the nature of science. Sacks noted that mathematics, which formulates statements which are context-free, is the ideal case of 'disorderability'. If 'disorderability' describes the production of statements which are context-free, then non-disorderability becomes the focus of an empirical question: what principles of production would underlie the generation of a sequence for which its order makes a difference to its intelligibility?

> And if it's the case that we need some such rules and that if we had them they'd give us the non-disorderability, then, for one, we'd have some way of formulating some decent notions of 'context', seeing that context is something oriented to by Members, and not simply a matter of 'Of course it happened to happen at a certain time, so therefore you can't remove it from where it occurred.' (1992a: 371–2)

Here is another statement of Sacks' arguments about the nature of scientific method. It is interesting to note the similarity of Sacks' reasoning here to the logic of the 'null hypothesis' which underlies statistical analysis. In probability theory, the method of the 'null hypothesis' holds that disorderability (no significance) is presumed unless non-disorderability (significance) can be demonstrated by the presence of patterns of relations. Mathematics, Sacks argues, is not the only method of demonstrating patterns of relations in a systematic and empirical way. It is from this line of thinking that Sacks argued for the validity of the method of CA, which searches for procedural order on the basis that if you can't remove an utterance from where it occurred and still have the same meaning, then there must be some procedure for recognizing the ordering of a sequence, description, or narrative, which is used systematically and observably by speakers and hearers. This observation provides the basis for the empirical study of coherence.

> **Topical coherence:** 'Speakers specifically place most of their utterances. Where, by 'place', I mean they put them into such a position [that] what's just been happening provide[s] an obvious explanation for why this was said now (where, when they don't, a question could arise of why that now).' (Sacks, 1992a: 352)

The placement of utterances involves the co-management of both sequence and categories on the part of both speaker and hearer. Sacks had much to say about sequencing, and as much CA literature concentrates on that feature of talk, we won't focus much on that here, except to note that the question–answer sequence was of great interest to Sacks when he first started identifying tying rules (see, for example, 1992a: Part III, Lectures 14 and 15). He was also concerned to show how tying can be accomplished over intervening conversations, and in multi-party talk where speakers don't necessarily get the chance to speak in turn. These kinds of links are typically made through categorizations, and often the use of pro-terms plays an important part. Sacks suggested that topical coherence, achieved through the fine attunement of speakers to the management of tying, could be shown to account for socially acquired memory – on the basis of which, categorization analysis could prove an effective tool for the study of those aspects of cognitive development which depend on learning through 'mediated action' (Vygotsky, 1962).

The 'problem', we noticed in this interview, was the failure of a question and answer sequence. One of the methods by which the 'ordinary' can be made visible is by looking at what happens when something goes wrong. This is a practical means by which moments of non-disorderability can be detected by the researcher/analyst – the interactants themselves detect the breach in procedures, and move to correct the 'problem'. This failure in the sequencing relevant to the interview procedure causes a problem for the interviewer, which he has to resolve by improvisation. His repair involves the re-establishment of a question and answer sequence with Mr M, but it also involves some complex category work. This gives the analyst an opportunity to identify the procedures which the speakers are employing. What do the interactants do to repair the 'problem'? What resources do they draw upon? By looking at this interactional failure, it becomes possible to provide some evidence for tying rules which link sequence and categorization. Let's look at the sequence again. I am especially interested in lines 16–19, when the presenter is faced with the task of restarting the question and answer sequence, after the 'problem' has arisen. Note that he doesn't ask a new question. He reframes the existing question in a way which relates to the previous talk: '. . . surely people ought to be allowed to demonstrate and (.) it's a question of defining what a troublemaker is, isn't it?' Through use of the question, he ties his turn back to the previous talk, and reasserts his control over the interview by re-establishing the question and answer sequencing and his own membership categorization – 'troublemaker'. At the same time, he creates the opportunity for forward tying, by positioning two membership categorization devices – the 'injunction' and 'demonstrations' – in relation to each other. The questions he is asking are being asked of 'the court' (its injunction) on behalf of the listeners: What is the evidence for the definition of a 'troublemaker'? Does the injunction restrain demonstrators, or 'troublemakers'? This question goes to the heart of issues of concern to the study of the social and cultural order, both at the macro-level of analysis – issues of power and authority – and at the micro-level identified by Goffman and Garfinkel – issues of moral accountability and action. Here is evidence that they are issues of concern not only to social analysts, but to ordinary citizens, and that accounts at the level of individual action are ordinarily understood to be consequent to the determination of the just use of power and authority.

Accountability

When Dr G finally enters the talk, the presenter once more links his first question to him back to the previous talk without any attempt to put Dr G in the picture. Notice Dr G's first turn: despite the fact that he is a new entrant to the talk, his reply is relevant to the device, and produces another version – 'protest'. Dr G may or may not have heard the previous exchange. This provides additional evidence for the shared knowledge which underpins the interaction: it doesn't matter, because he knew what the topic of the interview was going to be – the injunction against him.

18	Presenter:	What have you been doing to cause trouble?
19	Dr G:	Wh. What I have been doing is protesting about what I regard
20		as a fundamentally wicked thing and . and that's consisted
21		with me of . of being involved in an entirely . in an entirely
22		peaceful protest. I have us I have uh. Effectively only
23		trespassed on land t . to protest against ah . . . this scheme.
24	Presenter:	You've not thrown stones at [people?
25	Dr G:	[I . . .]
26	Presenter:	or done anything like that]
27	Dr G:	[I've done no physical damage, I have never encouraged anyone to do physical damage, and I have never seen anyone doing it. I . . .
28	Presenter:	You've sat down in front of bulldozers and the like?
29	Dr G:	No I. . . . I uh have been in. In protest on . . . uh . . . on Twyford Down and the surrounding area.

Dr G now has his opportunity to 'defend himself'.

EXERCISE 5.2

Identify the procedures by which Dr G ties his reply to the question. Pay attention to sequence, and to categorization issues. What significance does his reply have for the setting? How does it contribute to the maintenance of the context by the three interactants? Derive your evidence from the text.

Note that the presenter does not ask Dr G if he has heard the first part of the interview, and that Dr G responds to the interviewer's opening question as appropriate. In another setting – say, at a local social event in the United Kingdom – the question might be heard, and replied to, in quite a different way – as an insult, perhaps; and one can imagine a very different reply (especially from a Doctor!) – for example, 'I beg your pardon?' In the context of the radio interview, the question is, on the evidence of Dr G's reply, taken as an opportunity to provide a defence. The defence, like the charge, is conducted in terms of 'versions'. Yet another version of the category 'demonstrator' is introduced – 'protester': not all demonstrators are 'protesters'. By shifting the footing to 'protest', he implicates a potentially more contentious activity, which he then asserts is entirely 'peaceful'. By introducing his version, Dr G mediates the account of the activities on Twyford Down, as one of 'peaceful protest'. In doing so, he provides for the case of just protest, and legitimate conflict: not all 'protesters' are 'troublemakers'. In response to the production of category bound activities which might be relevant to the 'definition of a troublemaker' (e.g. 'throw stones', sit down in front of bulldozers'), Dr G provides for an alternative version (line 29) which prepares for the later introduction of the term 'trespass' (probably derived from the injunction) as an activity potentially justified by circumstances: 'I have uh. Effectively only trespassed on land t. to protest . . .'. Did you note also the use of the category 'people' (line 24), here used as a 'pro-term'? By implication, in the context of a 'protest', 'people' would denote 'the police'. By using 'people', the presenter continues to pursue his objective of directing the talk away from 'the authorities' (the category which Mr M prefers) and towards the activity of 'defining what a troublemaker is.'

Whether or not he has heard the first part of the interview, Dr G orients quickly (though evidently not without some difficulty – notice the hesitations in the production of his turns) to the relevant category environment, and the sequential context, which includes the orderly answering of challenging questions. He takes his part in answering the question – 'it's a question of defining what a troublemaker is' – with minimum preparation. He responds to the question without demur, and he ties his reply to the interviewer-introduced topic through the use of versions, much as Mr M did in his turn. Part of the evidence for the operation of tying rules, then, consists in the ease with which this newcomer to the interview responds to the relevant context, as defined by both categorial and sequential procedures. One piece of evidence for non-disorderability in the talk lies in the observation that if Mr M had uttered the sentence, 'What have you been doing to cause trouble?', the course of the interview might have been very different indeed. Other examples of the production of the category 'troublemaker', in the following section, will provide further evidence for my proposal that Mr M is highly unlikely ever to have made such an accusation.

Tying and procedural consequentiality

Further purchase on the interview is to be had by noting that tying procedures link not only backwards to previous turns, but also can be identified in the forward movement of the topic. From the point of view of sequence, the question/answer format is a very restricted version of tying: the second part (the answer) of the Q/A pair must tie to the first, and the first part (the question) requires a certain kind of response – an answer. As we can see from Dr G's entry into the talk, the constraints of the question/answer sequence are unproblematically adhered to, and constitute a major tying procedure, to which all the speakers conform. From the point of view of categories-in-use, we can see how the categories link back to the previously introduced device at every turn, while the introduction of alternative categories within the device links forward to alternative versions/topics to be introduced at a later turn.

Here's another example, which occurs somewhat later in the interview, when Mr M is once more invited to defend his reasons for supporting the injunction:

30	Presenter:	Well, then. Mr M. Surely he should be allowed to carry on
31		doing that sort of thing – sounds fair, doesn't it?
32	Mr M:	Well, ah, I'm not going to get into the individual case of Dr G.
33		And what he has done. All I can say is that there have been
34		incidents over the course of the past few months where life has
35		been put at risk by the antics of some demonstrators, and this
36		is something that we're perfectly entitled to see the authorities
37		take action against and I'm rather glad they have . . . [and I don't
38	Presenter:	[Do you accept that
39	Mr M:	[Want to see that repeated this Sunday.
40	Presenter:	Do you accept that, Dr G?
41	Dr G:	Uh. . . . I hadn't been aware of uh incidents in which life has
42		been at risk . . . there was uh there was an accident . . . uh at least
43		I understand it was an accident uh . . . h . . . a few weeks ago uh
44		. . . near Twyford Down.

EXERCISE 5.3

Identify how forward and backward tying is employed to widen the range of versions in these six turns.

Can anything more be said about the way in which 'macro' (culture) and 'micro' (context) levels of social process can be treated by the analysis?

In this exchange, the speakers do further work on the question of the accountability of Dr G. Once more, Mr M, under pressure of a question from the presenter, conforms with an answer which evades the import of the question: is Dr G a troublemaker or a legitimate protestor? Using the question/answer sequence as the framework on which the procedure for the interview is built, the management of categories continues to do the work of procedural relevance.

> **Procedural relevance:** The orientation of the speakers and hearers to the relevancies at hand. These relevancies are not presupposed by the categorization analysis in terms of theoretical constructs, but demonstrated through analysis of the devices, with their relevant membership categories and category bound activities, implicated by the interactants in their talk.

In this case, the responsibility of the analyst to the text is not to use the theoretical construct of 'boundaries' in order to analyse the social and cultural order; rather, it is his/her responsibility to demonstrate how the speakers' orientation to the sequential and categorial procedural consequences of each turn implicate the movement between the categorization device 'troublemaking' (with its relevant membership categories, and category bound activities) and the device 'protest', with its alternative collection of categories. The procedural relevance of the interaction embeds and displays the shared cultural knowledge of everyday speakers, of how these boundaries, which are categorial, are to be negotiated and sustained in practice.

Summary

By now, you should be able to apply a wide range of analytical tools to demonstrate how, through the management of categories, and the procedural constraints of participation in the setting of the radio interview, the speakers orient to a shared understanding, implicated by the assembly of the categorization device 'troublemaking', which constitutes the relevant context at several levels of significance, and in doing so, enact the process called 'democracy'.

We are able to demonstrate how an institution which resides at the heart of culture – the 'court' – is employed on multiple levels, for various interactional purposes, as a member's resource. These speakers and hearers do not think of the court as a resource in their talk; but we as analysts of that talk can see that the ways in which they deploy the court as a resource in the negotiation of blame, in the management of accountability, in the orderly process of defining what a 'troublemaker' is, create the legitimacy upon which the Court depends for its authority through their focused talk and actions.

As we observed in the previous chapter, the phenomenon of

'transgression' is a rich site for the investigation of how categories are deployed in order to define and locate what will, and what will not, count as lawful, coherent and meaningful action. In the next section, we will look at an example of a transgression from a very different source of data, in which the task of 'defining a troublemaker' is accomplished through the medium of report writing.

Recommended reading

Clayman, S.E. (1992) 'Footing in the achievement of neutrality'. In P. Drew and J. Heritage (eds), *Talk at work: interaction in institutional settings*. Cambridge: Cambridge University Press.
Clayman subjects Goffman's concept of 'footing' to detailed CA analysis, using television interview data.

Drew, P. and Wootton, A.J. (eds) (1988) *Erving Goffman: exploring the interaction order*. Cambridge: Polity Press.
A collection of theoretical and analytic papers evaluating the contribution of Goffman to the study of interaction. A paper by Schegloff addresses the dispute between Sacks and Goffman with some contemporary thinking on the issues.

Hester, P. and Eglin, S. (1996) *Culture in action*. Washington DC: International Institute for Ethnomethology and Conversation Analysis: University Press of America.
The authors address practical analytic problems of interest to categorization analysts, incorporating Jayyusi's dense analysis in a user-friendly way.

Watson, D.R. (1987) 'Interdisciplinary considerations in the analysis of pro-terms'. In G. Button and J.R.E. Lee (eds), *Talk and social organization*. Clevedon: Multilingual Matters Publishers.
Watson's attention to fine analytic detail provides an example of best practice in the principle of the analytic saturation of a text.

Empirical studies

Baker, C.D. (1997) 'Membership categorization and interview accounts'. In D. Silverman (ed.), *Qualitative research: theory, method, practice*. London: Sage.
Analysis of accounts provided in a variety of interview settings.

Greatbatch, D. (1992) 'On the management of disagreement between news interviewees'. In P. Drew and J. Heritage (eds), *Talk at work: interaction in institutional settings*. Cambridge: Cambridge University Press.
Among many useful articles in Drew and Heritage's collection of CA analyses of institutional interaction is this study of radio interviews, which examines how sequencing is managed by interviewers and interviewees.

Have, P. ten (1996/1998) 'Essential tensions in (semi)-open research interviews'. In Ethno/CA News Website: http://www.pscw.uva.nl/emca/index.htm
A useful study of the interview process from the perspective of conversational sequencing which may add to categorization analysis.

For those whose core discipline is anthropology/ethnography, there is a growing body of studies employing CA techniques, which will provide a good foundation for applications of categorization analysis:

Duranti, A. and Goodwin, C. (eds) (1992) *Rethinking context: language as an interactive phenomenon*. Cambridge: Cambridge University Press.

For examples of empirical studies of interaction as ethnography, see chapters by Lindstrom, Cicourel and Philips in this volume.

Givon, T. (1997) *Conversation: cognitive, communicative and social perspectives.* Amsterdam: John Benjamins Publishing Company.

Moerman, M. (1988) *Talking culture: ethnography and conversation analysis.* Philadelphia, PA: University of Philadelphia Press.
Moerman developed the application of conversation analysis techniques in ethnographic study of culture. This book brings together the work of two decades. It provides a useful starting point for those wishing to apply categorization analysis to the ethnographic study of talk.

6

Analysing Text

CONTENTS

In this chapter, I examine how the analysis of a textual form – a report – can be undertaken, using the tools of categorization analysis. Reports provide a means of communication between persons who, in the complex tasks of organizational and institutional life, use them to 'talk' to each other, in ways which, no less than face-to-face talk, take into account other parties, and the management of accountability for actions in multi-party tasks. By holding constant the categorization device 'troublemaker' as a lens of enquiry, the ways in which different media are employed to accomplish the interactional work of culture are compared and contrasted.

Text and talk

The first question to be addressed in turning attention to text, rather than talk, is what relevance the principles of conversation analysis, which address the processes of talk-in-action, have to the apparently stable form of a written text, which, unlike conversation, can be read and reread in different situations, by different readers at different times. Sacks used textual data on many occasions – but primarily, when he was considering membership categorization analysis. It needs to be noted that this is the point at which the categorization analysis and conversation analysis diverge in an important way. Conversation analysis, with its emphasis on sequence, relies entirely on spoken interaction, in transcript form, for its data. Categorization analysis, with its analytic focus on the ways in which membership categorization devices are assembled to generate locally occasioned meaning and action, has the potential for a wider application. Modern industrial cultures which rely on written forms as a primary means of communication and organization, provide a rich source of data in the form of texts which act as an alternative to talk in 'conversations' which, no less than face-to-face talk, involve all the constraints of 'recipient design' which have been noted in the previous analysis of some talk. Examples of 'conversational' writing abound. Letters, reports and memos (both formal and informal) constitute a large part of the routine communications of modern employment. E-mail is rapidly growing as a day-to-day medium of communication of both personal and working life. In all these cases, writers and readers, no less than speakers and hearers, use categorial resources to debate, negotiate, conceal and impugn, and to act to gain the concurrence of other parties to the 'talk'. Through written, no less than through spoken, interaction, the work of shared understanding is routinely accomplished according to observable procedures which can be formulated and verified. Here is another rich source of naturally occurring data, through which the processes of culture can be systematically studied and formulated.

In his article on 'hotrodders', Sacks makes the following observation:

> The important problems of social change would involve laying out such things as the sets of categories, how things are used, what's known about any member, and beginning to play with shifts in the rules of application of a category and with shifts in the properties of any category. (1979: 14)

Working with some data from an inner city Further Education College, I came across a bound notebook, which contained daily handwritten entries by the 'Duty Principal', a role occupied in turn by senior members of staff, who assisted the Principal in the daily overall management of the college. The function of the 'duty-rota logbook', as the notebook was called, was to report any incidents which the next Duty Principal should know of, and to inform the Principal of what had occurred. The Principal initialled and occasionally commented on the reports. What became obvious, on reading the logbook, was the way in which reports about day-to-day events – mainly disciplinary matters – were entered and referred back to by subsequent reporters, who linked subsequent events and comments to earlier reports. The reports were, in fact, a kind of conversation, between the members of the group of Duty Principals, and the Principal herself. Studying some of the entries in this notebook, it occurred to me that this logbook might provide a site for the formulation of some 'rules of application of a category and shifts in the properties of any category' which interested Sacks in this article on 'hotrodders'. The category I was interested in was 'troublemaker'. Through formulation of rules of application of the category 'troublemaker', I anticipated being able to demonstrate some aspects of the social processes of authority and control which were practised in the college.

The 'Logbook'

Here is the text of an entry that describes some events which occurred during one Duty Principal's rota:

1   DW BTEC First Bus&Fin OSD came to see [Principal] to report harassment
    by security staff.
2   This arose because she has broken her pass and asked to come into the
3   building to go to the Library (6pm). She queried whether any rule stating
4   f/t student cannot enter college in the evenings. R and M [security
5   guards] reported that (a) she has been in and out of B . . . all of the term, (b) she is
6   rude and aggressive, (c) spends her time in the refectory and not the library
7   and (d) she was involved in some of the troubles last term. I will discuss the
8   matter with her tutor tomorrow and take any action within my powers as
9   HOD. I will refer the matter to R [Principal] only if necessary.
[in the margin there is initialling by RS [Principal] accompanied by an arrow pointing to the last sentence.]

This entry revealed a conversation-like exchange which, like the radio interview, is designed to address readers (hearers) who are not present, but whose importance is implicit in the communication. One piece of evidence is the arrow pointing to the report writer's statement 'will refer the matter to RS only if necessary', which accompanies the Principal's initialling. At least one reader wanted the writer to know that the message had been received. The report also refers to 'some of the troubles last term' which were also documented in the logbook. A cursory inspection reveals the way in which tying mechanisms, both forward and backward, are employed in this textual account in order to create a recipient-designed communication, which entails a reply.

But what was the message? In line 1, the writer reports a 'complaint' on the part of a student; then, in lines 5–7 s/he rather carefully documents what could be evidence in support of an accusation. I noticed that this evidence also implicated the category 'troublemaker'; however, in this report, the accusation, 'she is a troublemaker' is not explicitly made. It is, rather, assembled in the form of a list of 'facts', which relies on location categories, category bound activities and membership categories for its 'force'.

EXERCISE 6.1

Demonstrate how the category 'troublemaker' is generated by the report writer. What membership categorization device is employed to assemble the evidence? How are location categories used to provide 'evidence' for the ascription 'troublemaker'.

You probably noticed that, in contrast with the straightforward use of the category 'troublemaker' by the presenter in the radio news interview, in this case the simple ascription, 'she is a troublemaker' is not offered. Rather, the writer of the report goes to great lengths to establish an impression of neutrality by using the kind of report writing which is familiar as the style, for example, of a police report (Cicourel, 1968). The form of this kind of 'report' is typically headed by facts which state the time, the place, and an account of the person or persons who are the subject of the report. That is, report writers establish a relevant context in terms of membership and locational categories in order to create the adequate description of events which is to follow. Inferences can be made from these introductory facts about how that description of events is to be read/heard. This provides for the 'procedural relevance' of the report: it implicates certain categories of hearer, and certain categories of action on the part of hearers. Notice that the assembly of the 'facts' which provide the evidence are reported indirectly through the voice of the security guards: 'R & M reported that . . .'.

It can be seen from even a brief study of this report that a description of the subject of the report in terms of her status as a student is given an important place. The writer took care not only to identify her course, but the department and the fact that she is a full-time student. All of these facts are implicated in the list of statements which follows to constitute an 'adequate description', within the principle of the 'economy rule'. That is to say, each item in the list provided as evidence contributes non-redundantly either directly (the ascription 'she is rude and aggressive') or indirectly through the location categories ('queried whether any rule stating f/t student cannot enter college in the evenings') to the production of the category device 'troublemaker'.

It is important to note the nesting that occurs between the procedural relevance which is constituted by virtue of the use of the report form (similar examples abound throughout the 'logbook'), and within that form, the procedural relevance which is implicated through the relevant categories which are employed. Did you notice how the membership category 'full-time student', in combination with the location category 'evening', provides for inferences about the nature of the 'complaint'? Students who come in the evening are primarily 'part-time' students. In line 1 of the report we are invited to expect a report about 'harassment' of a student by those in authority; by the end of the report, we may infer that here is an account of a troublemaker defying legitimately exercised authority. How is this shift of versions accomplished, and what relevance does it have to understanding how hierarchy of relevance (the context) is constituted? One way of addressing this question as one of procedural relevance is to ask, and to show, how the writer of the report sought, and received, a reading of the report. I took the arrow to be an important piece of evidence for the recipient design of this report. It seemed that it might have been produced not only to report on an incident, but also to provide for negotiations about the relationships between the readers of the reports.

EXERCISE 6.2

Identify the standard relational pairs which have relevance for the 'reading' given to the report (i.e., the arrow). What hearers are being addressed, and what is the hearing being invited? It may help to consider the category bound activities implicated, and their relevance for the possible readings of the 'facts'.

By exploring who saw what, and what evidence there is for that seeing, several new levels of implication can be identified. Not only the motives of the actors who are subjects of the report (security guards and students), but also, the actions of the writer, and the readers of the report, are constituted as observable, accountable and relevant to how the report is to be read, and possibly used (as evidence in the event of a formal complaint, for example).

This raises another important claim which Sacks made about the functions of categories as constituting procedures for shared understanding of social reality. Here is an observation he made on 'exchanging glances' – and an empirical study which he set for his students. Here is how he formulated this principle:

So the classes and their categories permit you to see. That's a start. It's not enough to make a glance an action . . . it's not merely that some observer is seeing by reference to some category, but that one being observed sees what the observer is, and is seeing.

And if you can see what it is that is doing that looking, you could have a pretty good idea of what it is that would be at the end of it. So this complementarity is equally as crucial as the fact that one is able to see what somebody with whom you are a member of a class in common is seeing when they are looking at you, or another. The sense of there being 'a society' is that there are many whomsoevers, who are not members of this or that class, who are able to see what it is that one is looking at. (Sacks, 1992a: 87–8)

By looking at the ways in which the writer of the report positions his/her 'gaze', by what categories s/he constructs the report, and attributes possible readings, we can see another hierarchy of relevancies which is operating within this act of reporting. That hierarchy is the authority structure within the institution, which includes managerial staff, teaching staff, service staff and students. At the top of this hierarchy of relevance is the Principal herself. The report attends to, and implicates, the relational pairing security staff/student, a pairing which generates a lot of activity: in practice, security guards control entry to the college. Evidence of the report shows that both student and security staff attend to their accountability to managerial staff, through their presentation to the Duty Principal in charge. The student launches her 'report of harassment' by going to the Duty Principal, evidently aware of the hierarchy of relevance through which her report will be heard, and treated, as a potential 'complaint'. Through this act, she creates the conditions in which the college staff must account for their actions. The security guards, in their turn, offer a version of events, and an account of their reasons, through the same hierarchy. They are accountable to management. The duty officer in turn, attends to the events by fact-finding, and by invoking the next level of accountability – the tutor. S/he completes the report by stating (and remember, that s/he expects the Principal to read this report) that s/he intends to 'refer the matter to R only if necessary'. RS is both informed, and reminded that the matter can be dealt with by the duty Principal within [his/her] powers as HOD [Head of Department].

All of the actions displayed in this report demonstrate awareness of the observability of acts, the awareness of others' observation of acts, and the inferences which will be drawn about accountability. 'Power' is demonstrated as a categorial resource, dynamically constituted by each actor as s/he asserts his or her 'rights' to a hearing by attending to procedural relevance at the level of culture (reporting, publicly recognized hierarchies of authority); context (the situated actions through which authority is enforced – in this case, security guards and gates), and categorial procedures which draw relevantly on cultural and local practices to constitute the shared understanding which is 'the sense of there being a society'.

Notes on method

This chapter has focused narrowly on a few examples to demonstrate how the method of categorization analysis can be applied consistently to data coming from very different sources. Many other examples could have been shown of the analysis of text and talk which draws upon Sacks' theory of categorization. Many of those studies are referred to in the recommended reading at the end of each chapter, and I would urge the reader to explore that wider corpus of work in order to develop his or her own skill and practice in researching any of the major areas of potential for analysis. The purpose of this chapter has been to focus on method, and on how findings can be derived from analysis, rather than on the findings themselves.

In conclusion, therefore, I want to consider two further points of method arising from the data we have looked at in this chapter, in the light of Sacks's claims for the study of context and culture through the study of talk.

Comparative method

One of Sacks' major published papers was an analysis of the ways in which teenagers create identities through the use of membership categories. He uses the example of 'hotrodders' (Sacks, 1979) in a key analysis of this aspect of categorization. In the lectures, he concludes a similar discussion by noting the following:

> Now I just want to notice one thing, and it's extremely tough to give a decent formulation of. The term 'bad' can gain a lot of its power . . . by virtue of the fact that it can have two ways of being heard. One is 'bad', and one is "bad", in quotes. Where "bad" in quotes means 'bad' by reference to adult considerations, and 'bad' means by reference to our [teenagers'] considerations. Now that could be just in general, where a quotative use of such terms might refer to that use of it which would be made by some category that stands in alternation to ours. And the non-quotative use could stand by reference to our use. What we want to find are some activities which hold for anybody, not formulated by reference to say, 'kids' or 'hotrodders', in which that systematic situation for ' bad' holds for some action that they expectably all face. (1992a: 449)

This analysis provides just such an instance. The news presenter, in declaring 'it's a question of defining what a troublemaker is, isn't it?', refers precisely to the distinction Sacks makes between 'bad' and "bad". So, it would appear that we have located, through the application categorization analysis, an 'activit[y] which hold[s] for anybody, not formulated by reference to, say, "kids", or "hotrodders", in which that systematic situation for "bad" holds for some action that they can expectably all face.' The analysis of 'troublemaker' provides just such evidence of the generalizability of the systematic situation in which an ascription holds for two potential, and competing, versions. In the case of the news interview, we see how speakers negotiate this categorial procedure by contesting a 'definition' in the setting of the radio interview.

The example of the logbook report shows that even those of the 'hotrodder' generation may contest definitions through finely tuned category work which attends to the continuous dynamic of power-in-action. The 'systematic situation' Sacks observed is revealed as a members' issue.

This has important implications for method: by analysing the production of the device 'troublemaking' across two different interactional sites, it has been possible to show that procedures are flexible and can be employed flexibly for situated interactional purposes. In each of these cases, the shared knowledge of the procedures for a readily recognized form (and note that evidence for this recognizability was demonstrated in the data) – the 'radio news interview', and the 'official report' – provides speakers/writers with resources for generating an adequate description of a 'troublemaker', which met the expectation (again, evidence for this expectation can be demonstrated in the data) for a 'fair hearing'. This application of a formal, and recognizable, procedure provided for stability. At the same time, however, it has been possible to demonstrate that within the constraint of a formal procedure, the generation of an adequate description (one that attends to the difference between a troublemaker and a 'troublemaker', or a complaint and a 'complaint') has been achieved in a locally relevant way through the management of categorial resources. The moral accountability of 'accused' and 'accuser' are rendered observable in the situated act of the interviewing and reporting, leaving hearers/readers to take an active part in the 'definition of a troublemaker' as a process which attends to the 'right' to protest (complain). Procedures, by this means, also provide for dynamic, flexible interpretative action in the constitution of social process. The 'systematic situation for the use of bad', and its constraints, compares across the two sites. It is by such incremental steps, Sacks held, that the validity of the method is demonstrated.

'Emic' and 'etic' as members' resources

This analysis of some talk, and of some text, provides a demonstration of the way recognized forms – a news interview, a commonplace institutional report – are foregrounded or backgrounded by interactants themselves in the systematic acts of providing for shared understandings of the task to hand – in this case, defining what a troublemaker is. 'Emic' and 'etic' aspects of context are also demonstrated to be members' issues. In the case of the news interview, all three speakers attend to each other's utterances, to the setting of the interaction – the radio interview – with its implicit rules – and to the macro-level – the topic of the injunction introduced by the interviewer's first question – with talk which attends at all these levels, and to matters both of structure and of substance. The report attends to issues of public accountability for the actions of managers, and the observable 'rights' of students, while at the same time negotiating who shall have the right to 'take any action within my powers as HOD' at the level of the relationship between the Duty Principal and the Principal. This analysis shows that a 'definition of what a troublemaker is' involves actors' continuous attention and participation at several levels of relevance. In the social world, a definition is not a matter of dictionaries but a matter of shared understanding of what actions mean at the moment of the observing.

Summary

It has been the intention of this chapter, in conjunction with the other chapters in Part II, to demonstrate that both talk and text provide opportunities for close analytic attention to the observable procedures of interactional process, grounded in Sacks' consistent theoretical framework for the study of conversation, from the perspective of both sequential and categorization analysis. As a site for the study of context and culture, such an analysis can meet the demands of a theoretical synthesis of 'macro' and 'micro' levels of analysis. Silverman, following Bhaskar (1979/1989), has argued for the interdependence of macro-level (social structure) and micro-level (social process) phenomena, according to three principles:

1. Interpretative procedures are central to the reproduction of social structure.
2. Social structures are real, constraining and enabling forces.
3. Social structures are the condition of social action and are reproduced and changed by it (Silverman, 1985: 77–8).

Recommended reading

Baker, C.D. and Freebody, P. (1987) 'Constituting the child in beginning school reading books', *British Journal of the Sociology of Education*, 8(1): 55–76.
Demonstration of a textual analysis of children's school books shows how categorization is used to define and build the category child-at-school.

Cicourel, A. (1968) *The social organization of juvenile justice*. New York: John Wiley.
This early but still important interactional study of policing shows how routine reports are employed by authorities to 'do justice' in the inner city.

Have, P. ten (1998) *Doing conversation analysis: a practical guide*. London: Sage.
See ten Have's introduction to conversation analysis for a clear discussion of validity in the practice of C.A.

McHoul, A.W. (1982) *Telling how texts talk: essays on reading and ethnomethodology*. London: Routledge and Kegan Paul.
McHoul challenged the dominance of ethnomethodological concerns with talk as social interaction by showing how texts constitute social realities.

Watson, R. (1997) 'Ethnomethodology and textual analysis'. In D. Silverman (ed.), *Qualitative research: theory, method, practice*. London: Sage.
Watson argues the case for treating everyday texts as topic rather than resource.

7

Analysing Images

CONTENTS

This chapter ventures into a domain not yet explored by categorization analysis – the image. Study of the image has become an important feature of cultural studies, crossing traditional academic boundaries, and opening up new areas for research. An example demonstrates how the conceptual tools of categorization analysis can contribute to the study of the image as cultural object. This is followed by a discussion of the overlap between some of Sacks' concerns, and those of Foucault, and the potential for using categorization analysis as a tool for investigating 'orders of discourse'.

Seeing and believing

Just as we take everyday talk for granted, so we take what we see for granted. We do not need to analyse in order to see things – well, not consciously, anyway. However, as we have discovered, what we can observe through the application of categorization analysis is an embedded 'analysis' which is the remarkable, though unremarked, accomplishment of every ordinary speaker and hearer. Perhaps the same applies to images.

Sacks began to study everyday talk building on the ethnomethodo-logical idea that the resources employed to do systematic social science, could be treated as topics – an object of study in their own right. Sacks put forward a novel way of thinking about science. He proposed that it consists of two stages: first, the application of a set of procedures, whose outcomes are then reported in words. It follows, Sacks argued, that the reporting is as much a part of the procedures of discovery as the 'experiments', and as such, as of much interest as the 'findings'. There is a second point, which Sacks, at that time, didn't notice: that the reporting of scientific procedures and outcomes often takes the form of images – tables, graphs, photographs. However, it wasn't long before the same kind of questions that were being asked of words, started to be asked of images.

Like those social scientists who began to investigate the social world not as an objective phenomenon, but as something to do with human agency, those with an interest in images noticed that photographs, in their early days presumed to be the means of objective recording of the real world, were not so objective after all. When it was first developed, there was great excitement at the thought that through photography, the means of capturing objective images of the world had been achieved. Very soon, however, its images entered the domain of the symbolic, to become the provider of a kind of 'magic': the moving picture – a 'real' world conjured up out of images, to which people could go for the perceptual experiences (sight and sound) which could represent the reality of their imaginations – the wonders of the natural world, or the myths of their social existence. Where the word – often in the form of story-telling, or drama – provided the magic of experience beyond that of the individuals in the pre-literate and pre-modern eras of cultural evolution, the photographed image quickly took its place.

The image has had a paradoxical relationship to our understanding of the world since the early philosophers of classical Greece. Though the word 'idea' derives from the Greek 'to see', we do business in words, and in the academies, traditionally, have valued the language world of ideas over that of images. Yet it is the link between the observed and the real world – the assumption that what is seen represents what is really there – which has driven the agenda for both the natural and the social sciences, and has obscured a critical evaluation of the relation of observation to the nature of thought and language.

Recently, however, that unquestioning assumption of the uncompli-cated relationship between what is observed and what is real has come into serious question, in the natural sciences as well as the social sciences. In the physical sciences, the certainty which accompanied belief in obser-vation was undermined by the findings of quantum mechanics. In psy-chology, the nature of perception has been demonstrated to be an active, rather than a passive phenomenon: the eye, in its complex neural relation-ship to the brain, is not a passive receptor but an active agent in the order-ing of perception (Gregory, 1977). In philosophy, too, the nature of the relationship of the seen to the thought has undergone dramatic change. The early thinking of Wittgenstein went along with the Logical Positivists who sought to develop a model of a logically ordered and orderable universe. At first, Wittgenstein held that 'A picture is a fact' and that 'a logical picture of facts is a thought'. Later he changed his view of the relationship of the observed to thought thus:

> A rule stands there like a sign-post. – Does a sign-post leave no doubt open about the way I have to go? Does it shew which direction I am to take when I have passed it, whether along the road or the footpath or cross-country? But where is it said which way I am to follow it; whether in the direction of its finger, or (e.g.) in the opposite one? – And if there were, not a single sign-post, but a chain of adjacent ones or of chalk marks on the ground, – is there only *one* way of interpreting them? – So I can say, the sign-post after all does after all leave no room for doubt. Or rather, it sometimes leaves room for doubt and sometimes not. And now this is no longer a philosophical one, but an empirical one. (1953: para. 85)

A picture, like a sign-post, and like a word, points the way, but not to certainty.

A similar shift – from the search for invariant rules, to the search for understanding meaning as an achievement – has occurred in the social sciences. We have traced, in the first chapter of this discussion of the study of culture, the development in thinking about the concept of context. The earliest theorists of social science sought to establish that society as phenomenon existed at a logical level above that of individuals, and that its study would reveal formal and quantifiable properties. When the hope for a science of society which would deliver law-like rules similar to those in the natural sciences proved elusive, social scientists turned to these newer models of the relationship between the observed and the observer for an alternative mode of enquiry and description. For example, it was the philosophical school of 'pragmatism' which led to the idea that communications are rhetorical – that is, that communications are made in order to get a response from someone, to interest, to engage, to convince. The social psychology of Erving Goffman transformed this line of thinking into a question for social science enquiry. Sacks continued the tradition with this observation on 'exchanging glances'. In it he proposes a fundamental link between observation, language and action which provides, at the micro-level of individuals in relation to each other, for the procedures which underpin the possibility of meaningful communication, which, ultimately, emerge as context and culture. It is the formulation of the basis for an empirical, rather than philosophical, approach to the question of signs, which Wittgenstein proposed above. I will quote it again, because it is so vital for understanding what it was that Sacks was trying to accomplish:

> So the classes and their categories permit you to see. That's a start. It's not enough to make a glance an action . . . it's not merely that some observer is

Mental health poster campaign, 1993

seeing by reference to some category, but that one being observed sees what the observer is, and is seeing.

And if you can see what it is that is doing that looking, you could have a pretty good idea of what it is that would be at the end of it. So this complementarity is equally as crucial as the fact that one is able to see what somebody with whom you are a member of a class in common is seeing when they are looking at you, or another. The sense of there being 'a society' is that there are many whomsoevers, who are not members of this or that class, who are able to see what it is that one is looking at. (Sacks, 1992a: 87–8)

For Sacks, the sign points the way to which direction to take, through the orderly processes of interaction. It is the complementary relationship between members as Members of a class of categories which creates the possibility for speakers and hearers to find their way through a social world of sharable, meaningful category collections. It is the act of observation, organized through that complementarity, which provides for the very possibility of talk, relevance and, ultimately, culture. It is the analysis of that complementary process, constellated by speaker/writer and hearer/reader/observer – who is seeing what, and what is being seen whom – as topic, rather than resource, which underpins the empirical logic of categorization analysis. The following analysis explores that rhetorical relationship through the medium of a photo-image.

Leaving home

This poster was one of a series produced in the early 1990s for 'Young Minds', a voluntary organization which promotes knowledge about, and action on behalf of, mental health issues for young people in the United Kingdom.

EXERCISE 7.1

- What categorization device does this image implicate?
- What location categories are employed?
- What membership categories are created through the images?

This poster is a contemporary example of the magic and the paradox of the photographed image. Through contemporary electronic techniques of manipulation, it creates a virtual world out of representations of the real, which generates an image of social reality which its observer might well rather not see: the world of the homeless. Some children leave the family home protected, with belongings, packed in boxes, which will carry their personal history with them. Some children leave home for a boundariless space, unprotected, story-less and forgotten, with only a cardboard box to shelter them.

The distribution of space which is manipulated in the construction of the image uses the visual image to generate Sacks' glance – the beginning of the conversation between viewer and image. Location categories operate on three levels:

- [top/bottom]: The full box which occupies the upper part of the picture seems to sit on top of the underground inhabitant of the box below.

- [inside/outside]: A hall, with a door, provides the backdrop for upper image; beneath, an undefined space.
- [home/underground]: The hall door signals a home; the underground sign represents to its likely audience the location of the inhabitant of the box in a system of underground passageways connecting parts of a complex London junction, at the time home of the homeless.

It is the location categories which implicate the two versions of the membership category 'kids': the protected, and the abandoned. The text points towards the device, 'family', to the category 'kids', and the CBA 'leaving home'; but it is the image which signals the existence of versions, and 'whomsoevers, who are not members of this or that class, who are able to see what it is that one is looking at'. Image maker becomes lens for the gaze of the other. At this first level of analysis, a reading of the image could be available to viewers who share knowledge of many urban environments throughout the world: the category of 'homeless' persons is not a local phenomenon.

However, implicit in the categories which generate the image are other possible paths of shared understandings which can be followed. There are further levels of a 'hierarchy of relevance' which are implicated by the location categories, which assemble further readings of the image. The first is the device 'public/private'. At the centre of the image is the symbol of the London Underground, which functions as signpost, but also as symbol of the organized system of spaces and tunnels which make up the underground railway system. It marks points of entry into the system, but also, represents the authority which manages, controls and requires payment for use of its services. It is a social system in its own right, complete with barriers which require formal rights of entry in the form of tickets, and a police service of its own which enforces its authority. It is a public space, but one which polices and excludes those who do not, or cannot, pay.

Further reading of the sign points in yet another direction. If the presence of the underground symbol places the homeless young person literally underneath the world of the city, the wording on the sign, not actually the name of the underground station, yields yet further information about what paths might be taken by the viewer. The text 'Waterloo Bridge' points the way not to the underground system itself, but to the site of a series of underground walkways near Waterloo station which have become home to the homeless and 'down and out'. For those who inhabit the surface spaces of the city, it is a lawless and dangerous space. Though public, it is unpoliced by any effective authority; not private, it is home to those with no access to the personal spaces of domestic self-determination and identity.

What then is the observer to make of this pathway of interpretation? Are we to see that among those who drink, urinate, share needles and swear at passers-by in the underground world of 'Waterloo Bridge' are young persons who have been abandoned by their families and societies to a dangerous underground world, where no identity can be claimed? Are they 'troublemakers' or 'victims'?

The visual as social theory

The contemporary study of the visual takes two important forms: one, the study of the image as the product of sign-systems, or 'semiotics'; the other, the study of the image as a medium of discourse. The difference in emphasis mirrors the relationship, in the study of language, between form ('langue') and practice ('parole'). The two are not separate: the recognition that each creates the conditions for the other is a topic of study in itself. Barthes (1998), in an article entitled 'Rhetoric of the image' addresses this convergence in a discussion of the advertising image. The image of the photo-image discussed above shows how both sign-system and categorization elements can operate together: the use of the Underground symbol, with its electronically imported text, exploits aspects of both elements to construct its message.

In this section, and for the purposes of this discussion of the image, I am primarily interested, however, in the visual as a social phenomenon, emergent from the rhetorical character of discourse. With his suggestive proposal about the action of the glance, Sacks offers an analytic view of the complex interplay between seeing and talking which underpins human action. In order to construct a meaningful communication, the speaker must take into account what the hearer is, and what the hearer sees the speaker to be; the hearer in turn uses this same procedure to construct a next turn which ties to the previous turn, and carries the conversation forward. In order to construct a meaningful conversation, on a turn-by-turn basis, the speaker and hearer must also be observers of each other's actions and interpreters of each other's motives. The analysis of motivated action has occupied an important place in the ethnomethodological tradition (Jayyusi, 1984; McHugh, 1970). Sacks' contribution was to provide an empirical method for discovering the ways in which glances (motivated actions) *combined with the procedural rules of categorization* generate observations about social facts which provide the conditions for next actions, next sequences, and so on, throughout the order of social complexity, to culture.

We have seen, in all the previous analyses of everyday communications, how important the recognition of who was observing was to the next actions of the speaker/hearer pair. Each of the parties to the radio interview had an eye(ear) to the receiving audience, in a rhetorical contest to achieve a version of 'troublemaker/protester'. In the newspaper headline, the writer's main task is to construct a mini-story which will act as an enticement, and entry, for the reader into the story proper. The report writer of the logbook is constructing a story which sends messages to several different viewers/readers with implications about what has been observed and how it is to be interpreted.

It is but a short step to the realization that images too can be rhetorical – not just the representation of what is, but communications designed to interest, engage and convince the viewer to follow a path in a certain direction. The image-maker, no less than the speaker, seeks to present his/her communication in such a way that the observer is invited actively to participate in the process of putting together the way things are. The hypothesis is this: that the relationship between image and observer is a 'conversation' no less than one constructed with words, and makes use of the shared knowledge of observers in a similar way.

Linking the processes by which both images *and* words act as sign-posts to shared understanding leads us to the heart of the study of culture through **discourse**, a discipline of wide-ranging interest across disciplines in the contemporary academy. One of the major formative theories of discourse analysis is that of Foucault, whose historical, analytic method of 'archaeology' has revealed the changing relationship over time between gaze, text and the shared understanding about the nature of the human existence as social body, social subject which characterizes different epochs. Foucault, and the discipline of discourse analysis which emerged through his analytic techniques, drew attention to the spatialization and temporalization of word and image which creates what he termed 'discourse domains'.

For Foucault, in the study of culture the micro-analysis of language was as insufficient as the macro-analysis of structures:

> I believe one's point of reference should not be to the great model of language (*langue*) and signs, but to that of war and battle. The history which bears and determines us has the form of a war rather than that of a language: relations of power, not relations of meaning. History has no 'meaning', though this is not to say that it is absurd or incoherent. On the contrary, it is intelligible and should be susceptible of analysis down to the smallest detail – but in accordance with the intelligibility of struggles, of strategies and of tactics. (Quoted in Silverman, 1985: 71)

Describing the practice of such an enquiry, Foucault proposes in 'Politics and the study of discourse', as an object of analysis, a discursive field of 'limited practical domains which have their boundaries, their rules of formation, their conditions of existence' (1991: 61). He goes on to define his project in terms of the *limits of analysis*, by putting 'the analysis of discourse itself in its conditions of formation, in its serial modification, and in the play of its dependencies and correlations. . . . Discourses would then be seen in a describable relationship with a set of other practices.' He would 'advocate a procedure which maps the roles and operations exhausted by different "discoursing" subjects' (1991: 61). Foucault defined a new object of enquiry: *a discourse domain*, which is bounded not by constants, but by the practical field of activities deployed by speaking subjects. For Foucault, the discourse domain is defined by 'a set of rules which at a given period and for a given society define what is *sayable*' (1991: 59). Spatialization, temporalization and the conditions of the production of words and images, become important components in the analysis of 'the sayable'.

Like Sacks, Foucault was interested in the analysis of practices. Unlike Sacks, his focus was historical, his method textual, and his critique anti-empirical. However, I believe that the analysis of the above image demonstrates how his advocacy 'of a procedure which maps the roles and operations exhausted by different "discoursing" subjects' could be well served by the empirically inspired methods of categorization analysis. Analysis of the ways in which a categorization device is deployed – that is, the *procedures* by which the creator and the observer assemble an image – creates a complementary pathway for the interpretation of the spatialization, of the conditions of production, and the interdependence of word and image, which Foucault sought to place within the space of analytic attention. The image, which disturbs perception of the category 'homeless' and creates alternative versions, acts like a lens no less than the interview, the headline, or the report, for doing the work of visibility which, Foucault showed, defines the discursive domain of culture.

EXERCISE 7.2

Visual images, together with headlines, or copy, dominate our passage through the public spaces of towns and cities, in public transport, street, waiting areas.

Practice identifiying the procedures which underpin the assembly of categorization devices in visual and print media as you go about your daily travels. Take notes of interesting observations. (These may lead you to new ideas for analysis.)

Using filmed data

The potential for linking images with CA or categorization analysis has been little explored. However, there exists a small but growing body of research which has widened the remit of CA to include visual as well as vocal data, through the use of filmed interaction. Goodwin (1980, 1981), using video recording, made the first studies of the relationship between gaze, gesture and turn-taking. In a later study (1984) of the interaction at a social dinner party, he analysed the co-produced telling of a story in relation to the gaze, gesture and visual cueing of the tellers. Heath (1997), using video-recordings of medical interviews, explored sequencing in the medical consultation in terms of the non-vocal behaviours of doctor and patient. These studies suggest another potential site of enquiry for categorization analysis: What would such a study reveal, if the play of categorization devices were linked to the non-vocal aspects of the talk?

In all these cases, the video-recording was an instrument of the research, and the cultural site chosen for study was chosen with the aim of researching a particular cultural domain. These forms of naturally occurring interaction are not typically recorded, and the availablity of the resources, and permission to record them, are difficult and time-consuming to obtain. However, our culture is saturated with filmed representations of itself. These 'naturally occurring' representations have for some time been an important site of enquiry for the semiotic study of culture, now a well established discipline, with a large literature. The novice researcher does not need to invest in expensive technology in order to study the production of culture in naturally occurring settings. There is the entire advertising industry to exploit!

EXERCISE 7.3

Video-record some television advertisements. What categorization devices are used to construct a shared cultural reality? How are they assembled? How do both vocal and non-vocal elements work together to deliver the 'message'?

Compare your findings with some of those from 'semiotic' analyses.

Summary

In this chapter, I have introduced principles of application of categorization analysis across a wide range of sites of production of 'culture'. In order to grasp the nature of the phenomena which come under that broad term, it has been necessary to consider some of the approaches to context which have informed the ways in which the social sciences have attempted to investigate the institutions of culture, and the ways in which that study has given way, in recent decades, to the study of the practices which make up the ongoing evolving character of the 'object' under study. Harvey Sacks was an important figure in these developments in the understanding of social phenomena. The breadth of his interests and the depth of his conception of the relationship between talk and social structure provided a generation of researchers with both new tools and new insights to carry the practice of research into new conceptual frames, and across traditional boundaries.

In its subsequent development, conversation analysis has become a major discipline, and created its own culture. In keeping with Sacks' original spirit of wide-ranging enquiry, backed up by empirical disciplines, this chapter has been written to introduce the reader to a wide range of potential applications across the lively and unbounded domain of culture and discourse studies. I hope it communicates two messages.

First, the purpose of research is to build on the findings of others in the search for further understanding of the world we inhabit. It must tread a fine balance between, on the one hand, respect for the traditions, coherence, and findings of the disciplines from which it arises; and, on the other, the duty to cross boundaries into the unknown, at the risk of misunderstanding, such as Goffman's disagreement with Sacks; or of failure.

Second, research is a disciplined activity. The practice of categorization analysis, which, like conversation analysis, can cross into so many different domains of study, depends for its strength and coherence as a method on its roots in the formative thinking which underpinned Sacks' original work. Constant return to the *Lectures on conversation* during the course of developing an analysis repays the effort in rich dividends of Sacks' observations of countless interactional events which he did not have time to pursue. We do not know where he might have gone with this work, had he had the opportunity to follow those insights, but endless ideas for possible analysis are there.

Recommended reading

Burchell, G., Gordon, C. and Miller, P. (1991) *The Foucault effect: Studies in governmentality.* Hemel Hempstead: Harvester Wheatsheaf.
In addition to articles discussing Foucault's thinking on the rationalities of government, this volume also contains an article by Foucault which gives an insight into his method for the study of discourse.

Heath, C. (1997) 'The analysis of activities in face to face interaction using video'. In D. Silverman (ed.), *Qualitative research: theory, method and practice.* London: Sage.
Heath provides an introduction to the use of video to study 'the social organization of the actions and activities accomplished through the body and physical artefacts'.

Jenks, C. (1995) *Visual culture.* London: Routledge.
A collection of articles on the study of the image as social phenomenon.

Lindstrom, L. (1992) 'Context contests: debatable truth statements on Tanna (Vanuatu)'. In A. Duranti and C. Goodwin (eds), *Rethinking context: language as an interactive phenomenon.* Cambridge: Cambridge University Press.
Lindstrom analyses a dispute on the Pacific island of Vanuatu. He demonstrates the usefulness of CA in analysing 'orders of discourse' (Foucault).

Miller, G. (1997) 'Building bridges: The possibility of analytic dialogue between ethnography, conversation analysis and Foucault'. In D. Silverman (ed.), *Qualitative research: theory, method and practice.* London: Sage.
Miller outlines areas of complementarity between conversation analysis, ethnography and Foucauldian analysis, and argues the case for cross-fertilization.

Part III

ANALYSING NARRATIVE

8

What is a Narrative?

CONTENTS

We started to explore categorization analysis with one of Sacks' earliest demonstrations of his technique: the child's story 'The baby cried, the mommy picked it up'. Throughout his work, one phenomenon of everyday talk which Sacks returned to over and over for his examples was the telling of stories. Sacks noticed that story-telling was ubiquitous in naturally occurring interaction, and that it was orderly in the same ways that the interaction of the telephone conversations he studied were found to be – that is, that stories are told in orderly sequences, governed by embedded rules of production and turn-taking. In this chapter we will explore the phenomenon of naturally occurring story-telling, drawing as before on examples from Sacks' original work, and from later developments in the field. I will place Sacks' work in the wider context of contemporary empirical research into narrative and life stories, and show why categorization analysis offers a powerful tool to the researchers of narrative across the fields of sociology and anthropology, as well as social and developmental psychology.

Defining the phenomenon

Sacks was studying conversation at a time when there was rapidly growing interest in the study of narrative as a social and psychological phenomenon, rather than solely as a formal literary or historical genre.

Competing theories of narrative surfaced, and a complex language of terms emerged. Researchers sought to address some basic questions about what a narrative is:

1. What are the minimum conditions which define a narrative?
2. When does a narrative stop being a narrative and become something else?
3. What is the relationship between different versions of a story? (Mitchell, 1980: ix)

You will notice immediately in this list of questions, that the terms 'narrative' and 'story' are both used. First we must consider what these basic terms might mean for those embarked on the study of so complicated a phenomenon.

In the early part of the twentieth century, the growing interest in the study of language and text was shaped by the distinction first drawn by Saussure between 'langue' (the study of form and structure) and 'parole' (the study of the manifestations of language in text and talk). An example of the analysis of 'langue' would be the 'generative grammar' of Noam Chomsky, who worked at the same time as Sacks. The theory of generative grammar seeks formally to describe the elements of a universal grammar which underpins all languages, and has a neurophysiological substrate which is inherited. In contrast, Sacks' attention was directed to the study of 'parole' – he sought to describe formally the elements which underpin the achievement of everyday talk.

The study of 'parole' had previously been avoided by linguists, as too 'messy': actual talk rarely conforms to the principles of structure and form which they traditionally studied. Sacks sought to show that the manifestation of 'parole' was not as 'messy' as it appeared to be. It is important to note that the study of 'parole', as undertaken by Sacks, is not in competition with the study of 'langue', as exemplified here by Chomsky. A generative grammar may exist (there is now some research evidence which supports it), but it would not be sufficient to explain what Sacks sought to describe: the orderly processes of talk-in-interaction. Conversation analysis may make a contribution to understanding the process of development of language in children, as we shall see later in this discussion of narrative, but it is not a theory about mental processes.

In common with much of the work on language and text in the first half of the century, narrative has been studied as a formal entity – usually in relation to literary or historical text – and scholarly interest has been concentrated on issues of form and structure. However, in his seminal works, the most influential of which was *A grammar of motive* (1945), the theorist Kenneth Burke crossed the divide from the formal study of literary and historical text to the study of narrative as a manifestation of human action. Burke proposed a view of narrative as motivated and rhetorical. Narrators, whether writers or speakers, act with purpose and that purpose is to affect the reader/hearer. His work was an important influence on the developing sociology of everyday interaction, and particularly on both the 'interactionism' of Erving Goffman, and on ethnomethodology – and thus, ultimately, on Sacks. By the 1960s it was becoming interesting to ask, what effect does the context of a narrative – the relationship between the producer of the narrative and the receiver of a narrative – have on the nature of the phenomenon and how we study it?

In this chapter, I will preserve the distinction between 'langue' and 'parole' by using the term 'narrative' to consider the structural elements of conversational story-telling; and I will use the term 'story' to refer to the interactional aspects of telling. As we shall see, Sacks had some interesting points to make about the connectedness of the structure and the telling.

Labov: analysing the structure of stories

Among those who became interested in the study of story-telling was the sociolinguist William Labov, who was studying the everyday language of the streets in the cities of America (1972; Labov and Waletsky, 1967). Labov wanted to identify empirically the most basic elements which would define a narrative. How do we know that a narrative has been produced? He proposed a minimum structure which would provide for a unit of analysis: 'any sequence of clauses which contains at least one temporal juncture' (Labov and Waletsky, 1967: 28). The basic condition for identifying such a sequence as a narrative is that the reversal of the sequence changes the meaning. 'The mommy picked it up. The baby cried' would be a different story. The actions map onto a temporal order, Labov argued, which exists outside the narrative and on which its coherence depends. In addition to this core narrative unit – a 'first' and a 'then' – Labov also observed that we introduce a story, and end a story, in characteristically recognizable ways, such that a minimum narrative will typically have the form: Preface–First–Then–Coda.

Additionally, in the course of intensive fieldwork, Labov noticed that the stories he was studying seemed to be characterized by a need to be recognized as worthy of telling. He noticed that told stories include evaluations. Sometimes evaluation is simply a reflection on the story already told – a coda which says, for example, 'And then everything was fine', indicating an upbeat assessment of the tale just told. However, Labov noticed that sometimes the whole story is interjected with evaluative commentary, which may even start with an introductory preface, which prepares the hearer for the kind of story to follow. In his later work, Labov (1972) identified the following elements of the fully formed narrative, its 'ideal form':

Abstract
Orientation
Complicating action
Evaluation
Result or resolution
Coda

Labov provided the basis for the analysis of the structure of narrative in spoken discourse. Virtually all analysis of narrative in contemporary research has been influenced by his study. However, his initial analysis and subsequent work left out the context of the telling of the story – the relationship of the speaker and the hearer at the moment of the talk. Though Labov was aware of the need for a story to be recognized by the recipient as worthy of telling, his primary focus was on the relationship of the parts of the narrative to each other (the aspect of 'langue') rather than the relationship of the producer to the recipient of the story (the aspect of 'parole').

Sacks: analysing stories in conversations

Sacks was working at the same time as Labov, and it is clear in Labov's later work that he was aware of Sacks' work and influenced by it. Though he does not make any specific mention of Labov, it seems clear from some of his analyses of talk that Sacks must have been aware of Labov's approach to narrative structure. In view of his main concerns, however, it isn't surprising that what interested him most was the study of story-telling as interaction. One of the things he noticed and talked about in some of the earliest lectures – in Spring 1966 – was that children use stories of troubles to legitimately attract the attention of adults. (Troubles-telling was to become a major area of empirical study for conversation analysts.) For Sacks, the interest in the study of story-telling was to reveal the under-lying rules of production and hearing which he proposed underlies the recognizability of actions in the situated context of the telling. To the basic questions about narrative being asked by many others, Sacks added his own characteristic question:

> We want to see: is the fact that someone is telling a story something that matters to the teller and the hearer? How can it matter and why does it matter, and of course when does it matter? We're assigning the candidate name 'story' to some-thing for which that name is provably warranted, provably relevant to the thing coming off as a story. If it isn't provably relevant then it's of no particular inter-est that its a story or not. (1992b: 223)

Stories, Sacks argued, are descriptions of the world, which orient speakers and hearers to the continuity of ongoing talk, and to the continuous main-tenance of a sharable, and comprehensible, social reality. The telling of stories, the exchange of stories, and the recognizability of stories are subject to rules of production and to rules of turn-taking. In order to maintain the viability of turn-taking in conversation, permission must be sought to take the extended turn-telling a story requires.

Consider this example:

```
 1    Stan:      En hyou know a' jing go ups go down eh
 2    Gordon:                                         [
 3                                  (check 'm out,)
 4    Stan:      duh — de waduh
 5    Gordon:             [
 6                             Better check 'm out.
 7    Gordon:    (he) did: d too
 8               (2.0)
 9    Stan:      Hal you know things go up go – down water
10    Hal:                                      [Yeah
11               The roller coaster?
12    Stan:      Yeh one – rollie coaster broke loose eneh down it landed–BANG
13               uv went – ow – down the ocean
14    Hal:       ((softly)) Yeah.
15               (4.5)
```

(Data extract from: Ryave, 1978)

EXERCISE 8.1

This is a perfectly formed story. Can you identify the minimum story structure – Preface, First, Then, Coda (Evaluation)?

Although the language of the speakers seems somewhat limited, the participation in the exchange is orderly and all the normal rules of turn-taking are observed. The speakers are learning disabled, but their grasp of the embedded rules of turn-taking is fully competent, as is their grasp of the structural principles of a 'good' narrative. As with the speakers from the psychotherapy group, studied in Chapter 2, these speakers attend to the next turn and, in this case, co-produce a story which is perfectly formed. This empirical observation offers evidence that *the rules of production and hearing of a good story constitute a powerful object of study, and that the defining characteristic of a 'story' is the fact that it has been heard as such according to those rules.* (For a full discussion of this story see Ryave, 1978.)

Summary

In this section the basic principles, developed by Labov, for identifying the structural elements of a narrative have been introduced. Sacks observed that even very young children have a basic grasp of how to put a story together. These original investigations into the phenomenon of oral story-telling provide the basis for the systematic study of story-telling as a pervasive social phenomenon. Labov demonstrated in his research, that speakers of black vernacular English in fact can be demonstrated to have a high degree of narrative competence, and that, contrary to the then prevailing opinion, dialects are as complex as 'standard' speech. It was demonstrated, from the CA analysis of a story-telling sequence of learning disabled speakers, that a sophisticated grasp of how to put a story together in order to share news is not dependent on conventional notions of 'intelligence', but on social competence.

Recommended reading

Labov, W. (1972) *Language in the inner city*. Oxford: Basil Blackwell.
In this study of black English vernacular in the inner city of America, Labov demonstrated the highly developed narrative competence of street corner gang members. His methods, as well as his findings, are well worth revisiting.

Riessman, C.K. (1993) *Narrative analysis*. Newbury Park, CA: Sage.
This is a short but thorough general introduction to research in the field of narrative analysis.

Sacks, H. (1972a) 'On the analyzability of stories by children'. In R. Turner (ed.), *Ethnomethodology*. Harmondsworth, UK: Penguin.
Returning to Sacks' own analyses repays efforts with new insights and ideas.

Sacks, H. (1992a) *Lectures on conversation*, vol. I. Ed. G. Jefferson. Oxford: Basil Blackwell.

Sacks, H. (1992b) *Lectures on conversation*, vol. II. Ed. G. Jefferson. Oxford: Basil Blackwell.
The lectures contain countless examples of analysis of data: use the index to browse and locate those which pertain to the phenomenon of story-telling.

9

Applying Categorization Analysis to the Study of Naturally Occurring Stories

CONTENTS

In this chapter, we will look at some naturally occurring stories, and explore how the principles of categorization analysis can be employed to reveal the inter-actional resources used by story-tellers to engage their hearers. Using an extended telephone conversation, analysed by Sacks for its sequential organization, we will look at how categorization is employed as a resource by the story teller to produce a relevant story, which is then responded to by the production of a linked second story. An analysis of categorization in a co-produced story, analysed by Jefferson for its sequential features, shows how a group of speakers orient to categorizations to generate a story with features of 'poetics' – an aspect of conversation which Sacks turned to in the later lectures.

First analysis of a story

Here's an example of a story, told by friends in a phone conversation, which Sacks analysed extensively.

```
 1  A:  Say, did you see anything in the paper last night or hear anything, on the local
 2      radio. Ruth Henderson and I drove down to Ventura yesterday,
 3  B:  Mn Hm
 4  A:  And on the way home we saw the::: most gosh awful wreck.
 5  B:  Oh: : : :
 6  A:  - we have ev – I've ever seen. I've never seen a car smashed into sm – such a
 7      small space.
 8  B:  Oh: : : :
 9  A:  It was smashed from the front and the back both it must've been in ¬ caught in
10      between two cars.
11  B:  Mm hm Uh huh
12  A:  Must've run into a car and then another car smashed into it and there were
13      people laid out and covered over on the pavement.
14  B:  Mh
15  A:  We were s – parked there for quite awhile but I was going to listen to the local r -
16      news and haven't done it.
17  B:  No. I haven't had my radio on either.
18  A:  Well I had my television on, but I was listening to uh the blast off, you know
19  B:  M, hm.
20  A:  | The ah - / / astronauts.
21  B:  | Yeah
22  B:  Yeah
23  A:  An I didn't ever get any local news
24  B:  Uh huh
25  A:  and I wondered.
26  B:  Uh huh,
27  B:  no I haven't had it on, and I don't uh get the paper, and uhm.
28  A:  It wasn't in the paper last night, I looked.
29  B:  Uh huh
```

(Data extract from Sacks, 1992a: 764)

Sacks begins his analysis of this story by noticing its 'recipient status' – the method by which the teller designs the story for this particular hearer. This orientation to the intended hearer is demonstrated in the 'preface', which in story-telling is designed to engage the hearer in terms relevant to the hearer's experience or interest. As Sacks shows, the request sequence employed here gains the permission of the hearer to take an extended turn, sets the scene in a way which is relevant to the speaker's knowledge, and indicates what would count as completion of the story. Let's look at this sequence in some detail.

The request ('Say, did you see anything in the paper last night . . .') gives the hearer an indication as to how the story can be responded to as 'heard' on completion ('Yes, I did', or 'No, I didn't'). The request indicates that what follows is a possible news story. This has two implications for the production and hearing of the story: of all the possible tellings, it allows the hearer to identify it as a possible news story, and to reply with a negative or affirmative to the 'request' in relation to 'have you heard the news?'. The request format, as preface, is related to the body of the story in that what's told is constructed in the form of a 'news story'. Therefore, the story-teller focuses on the objective 'facts'. In another format, the story could have been offered as one of her subjective reaction to the event. In this way, recognizability is provided for by the teller, and constitutes part of the telling: the story-to-be-heard as news story (one that might be heard on the radio, the television, or read in the newspaper) can be identified by the hearer as such and responded to in this way. The preface therefore constrains the way the story to follow will be organized.

The story preface can also be seen as a pre-sequence element which announces the upcoming story sequence, with its promise of 'news' in exchange for an extended turn of talk. In conversation, all talk is sequentially organized. Story-telling is no exception.

EXERCISE 9.1

Using the tools of categorization analysis what evidence can you produce for the situated relevance of this preface? What inferences can you make about the relation of the teller to the hearer? For example, what shared knowledge is presumed? What does this imply for the way the story is offered?

By my reading, this is a preface which could only be employed by someone talking to a hearer who knows the local geography, and who is likely to have access to the local news. The request format, therefore, is oriented to the specific conditions of this speaker/hearer pair, through the employment of a location category. Were the hearer someone who lived elsewhere, the preface would have to be very different, and this in turn would have implications for how the story to follow was constructed.

Sacks records that he was working on the story for a year-and-a-half assuming that it was a witness story, until he noticed that it was in fact a story about an aftermath, not about an event. The construction of the story-as-reportable-event had to be produced to make a tellable story. Like Labov, Sacks was interested in the way tellers make stories both hearable and worthy of telling: 'I want to argue that the story that's being told is found, and that an appropriate story has been found to tell, of the possible stories that could be told' (1992b: 232). Having noticed that this was the story of an aftermath, rather than the story of an event, Sacks shows that the story being told here is in the form of a 'course of action' – the course of the teller's actions – which is one of the most common story forms. The story of the wrecked car – in fact, a description – is embedded into that course of action story, which is prefaced by the statement 'Ruth Henderson and I drove down to Ventura'.

EXERCISE 9.2

- Identify the main elements of the 'course of action' story in terms of Labov's minimum story structure as outlined above.
- Identify the main elements of the 'wreck' story in terms of the minimum story elements.

(Note that the two stories are embedded in each other. A minimal story, in fact, seldom appears in actual discourse.)

In order to tell a story about a course of events about which she was not a witness, the story-teller in this case had to construct a story-about-an-event from her observation of an 'aftermath'. In order to construct a hearable story, several parts had to be assembled:

- *a preface*, which engages the hearer relevantly to the story to come ('Did you hear the news?');
- *a course of action* (sequence of events in time): first 'drove to Ventura'; then 'saw the::: most gosh awful wreck';
- *a description* which has been constructed as a sequence of events in time (the 'story' of the wreck): first 'must've run into a car', then 'then another car smashed into it and there were people laid out and covered over on the pavement';
- *the coda*: 'I didn't ever get any local news . . . and I wondered', which links the ending of the story to the preface and provides the opportunity for the reply which acknowledges receipt of the story, and a hearing: 'No I haven't had it on, and I don't uh get the paper, and uhm'.

EXERCISE 9.3

Examine the story for elements of evaluation. You will find them in the choice of descriptors, and in the non-verbal sounds which have been transcribed. Can you see how they work to orient the story-telling to its hearing?

The first evaluation appears in the teller's second turn – 'the::: most gosh awful wreck'. On receipt of permission to carry on with a story (the hearer's 'Mn Hm' in turn 2), the teller provides an evaluation of the story to come. The evaluation is constructed through the categorization device ('wreck'), which provides for a disaster (and thus newsworthy) story, plus the descriptor 'gosh awful' – this is not just a small wreck, the effect of which is heightened by a vocal cue – the lengthened 'the::: '. The hearer acknowledges receipt of this evaluation with her response – 'Oh: : : :' – a lengthened vocalization which reflects the evaluative tone of the previous turn. This co-produced evaluation affirms the orientation of the hearer to the bad news to come, and serves to introduce the sub-story, or description, of the wreck, in its sequence of action form, assembled within the device 'wreck' in terms of relevant category bound activities ('smashed from the front and the back') and Members 'people laid out and covered over on the pavement'). This complex assembly of categorization device and evaluation satisfies the constraints of the preface: the story to follow must report on events most likely to be witnessed in the course of driving somewhere, and of newsworthy significance, which are reportable in the context of being received by a hearer who acknowledges readiness for the (terrible) story to come with her 'Oh: : : :'.

Evaluation plays an important part in story construction, and has been studied in far more detail recently. I will return to that topic later in this chapter. For the moment, let's stay with Sacks' analysis, to which he returned in the lectures over a period of several years, and see how an important aspect of categorization analysis – the 'economy rule' – operates in this extended narrative sequence.

Sacks was particularly interested in the fact that a course of action seems to be a favourite principle of organization for a story-teller. As we have seen, the course of action in the story – first 'drove down to Ventura', then 'saw the::: most gosh awful wreck' – provides the basic structure for another telling, the story of the wreck. He then observed that the description of the wreck was also organized into a sequence of actions, although that sequence occurred before the teller arrived, and was not in fact part of the witnessing. An aftermath in itself does not constitute an event, and must be made into one, in order to become storyable, or hearable as 'news'. So the embedded story of the 'wreck' has been made into a course-of-action story, although in fact it is a description of an aftermath rather than a course of events.

The production of the categorization 'wreck' links both these stories, and delivers the 'promised' news of the preface. We've also noticed how the elements of the preface – the location categories – provide both an invitation to the hearer to listen, and to have reason to go on listening, and to wait for a report worthy of the telling, which might be recognizable as 'news'. The 'drive' was not the purpose of the outing to Ventura, but for the purposes of the story, it is the organizing principle for its telling. The 'drive to Ventura' provides both for the relevance to the hearer (the location and the appeal to 'local news'), and for the course of action which embeds the story which the speaker wants to tell – the story of a 'wreck, which is most likely to be observed in the course of a drive. Sacks shows that the economy rule, which as we have seen is a primary organizing principle for orderly categorization, applies to narrative organization as well. Parts of the narrative embed each other, and may serve more than one purpose.

In the subsequent chapter, I want to take up more recent developments and issues in narrative analysis and examine ways in which Sacks' approach to narrative, and the application of categorization analysis, may offer some valuable analytic tools. But before going further, it may be helpful to return to the questions posed by Mitchell, at the beginning of Chapter 8, in order to see how they can be addressed from the perspective of Sacks' approach to the study of story-telling:

1. What are the minimum conditions for the identification of a narrative?

Sacks both simplified and widened the minimum conditions which define what a narrative is. He restricted his study by focusing analytic attention not on the formal characteristics of the structure or on the content, but on the procedures by which stories are produced and recognized by speakers and hearers. He widened the scope of the study by demonstrating that stories embed principles of production which constitute hearable descriptions of the experienced social (and natural) world. It is through stories that we organize the world into meaningful and sharable reality. More recently, it has been proposed that 'narrative is the natural product of language; it precedes and is the source of theoretical thinking' (Donald, 1991, quoted in Nelson, 1996: 184). Sacks was tentatively making a similar proposition, based on his observation of naturally occurring talk.

2. When does a narrative stop being a narrative and become something else?

Narrative analysis, like any kind of analysis, has several aspects, some of which we've looked at in this chapter. The question 'when does a narrative become something else?' is handled by Sacks' observation that stories act as potential descriptions of the world. They are stories, and not something else, when they are treated as stories by the interactants. By analysing the details of the production and reception of stories, we stand to gain an operational understanding of the construction of narrative as a phenomenon of naturally occurring communication. 'Stories', by this definition, precede the evolved narrative forms found in literary and historical texts. The link between occasioned stories, and formal textual narrative forms, is found in the formal traditions of oral story-telling, prevalent in pre-literate societies – *The Iliad*, and *The Odyssey*, the Arthurian legends are those most familiar to Anglo-American culture. What Labov and Sacks have shown, is that formal story-telling, which employs observable procedures of production and hearing, plays a critical part in our everyday communicative world as a vehicle of meaningful, shared social reality.

3. What is the relationship between different versions of a story?

Taking the interactional perspective that Sacks offers, this question yields up its answer readily: stories are 'worked up for the occasion. You might tell the same story differently for different persons, or on different occasions' (1992a: 790). By looking at the procedures for telling stories, rather than their content, the question of 'versions' becomes one of relevance, rather than 'verifiability' – how does the version of the story, told in this interactional context, provide for its hearability? The purpose of telling a story is to represent events in a recognizable way. The hearing of the story demonstrates acceptance or rejection of the situated representation of events. What is represented is a matter for negotiation and agreement.

Here's an example from Sacks' lectures. He is addressing a problem:

> Sometimes the hearer picks up one part of a story and not another, and will say 'That's good' (evaluation) when apparently the teller will have intended that they pick out another part of it. For example, a lady is renting her house. Now the story she's telling can be heard to be, not that she rented the house within a day of putting the ad in the paper, – i.e., so quickly – but that instead of turning it over to a rental agent she put an ad in the paper so as to have some fun and see what would happen. She finishes the story with the fact that the house has been rented, and the hearer says 'that's good'. She says 'Isn't that surprizing'. What she had wanted, apparently, was a comment on the experience, rather than on the efficacy of the transaction. (1992a: 766)

The teller means something to be heard; the speaker misaligns to the 'story'; the teller restates her evaluation, in order to correct the representation of the event – the story – on the part of the hearer.

> How it is that you should talk when you see the story is finished, is told to you at the outset; where your task is then to see from what was presented, (1) that the story is finished, and (2) that it makes the point it proposed to make. Such procedures are heavily present in story structures, and make things like 'That's nice' as compared to 'Uh uh' interesting. They also make the 'That's nice' and the pre-story information relevant to each other and make them interactional phenomena. (1992a: 767)

Sacks demonstrates that the relationship between possible stories is indeterminate. In the case of interaction, that indeterminacy both requires the parties to the talk to attend to the utterance, and to align their responses accordingly. Narratives – and this may apply to both text as well as to talk – rely on indeterminacy for their 'force' – it is what makes them interesting and worthy of the telling (i.e., commanding the attention of the reader for an extended time).

Relevant to this discussion is a distinction made by the literary critic, Jonathan Culler. He discusses the debates in the study of narrative, between the 'formalists' and the 'interactionists', and concludes that they all make a fundamental distinction between what he calls 'story' – a sequence of actions or events, conceived as independent of their manifestation in discourse – and what he calls 'discourse' – the discursive presentation or narration of events (1981: 169). (Note that though he uses different terms, the distinction he makes is that of 'langue' and 'parole'.) He goes on to comment:

Analysis of narrative depends ... on the distinction between story and discourse, and this distinction always involves a relation of dependency: either the discourse is seen as a representation of events which must be thought of as independent of that particular representation; or else the so called events are thought of as the postulates or products of a discourse. Since the distinction between story and discourse can function only if there is a determination of one by the other, the analysts must always choose which will be treated as given and which will be treated as product. (1981: 186)

For Sacks, as we have seen, a narrative is defined not simply by its structure. What does define it is the way it is used and recognized for human purposes by persons engaged in social activity. It could be said, therefore, that by concentrating on the interaction, he foregrounds the analysis of discourse in favour of structure. However, I would argue that by concentrating on the procedures by which a narrative is produced by tellers and hearers as a means of structuring the relationship between the 'what happened' and the telling in a recognizable way, he shows us a way to link the two aspects of analysis. The link resides in the recognizability of an utterance as a story, subject to shared (and observable) rules of verification and acceptance of the 'story' as a representation of events. It is the procedures for the representation of events, and the agreement about the orderability of events which speakers and hearers share, which provides for the possibility of an analysis of a narrative in which representation and discourse cannot be separated.

Second stories

In the previous discussion, we looked at how Sacks placed the study of narrative within the context of the study of naturally occurring conversation. One of the findings Sacks emphasized, was that the interactional requirement for turn-taking imposes constraints on how talk is organized, and that this has implications for story-telling: the story must be prefaced by the speaker, and recognized by the hearer, as such in order for the tale to be told. A phenomenon which interested Sacks was that of 'second stories'. He noticed that the telling of one story was frequently followed by the telling of another. In fact, the exchange of stories is a commonplace human communicative activity. How, he asked, does the telling of a second story relate to the telling of the first? Here's the rest of the telephone conversation about the 'wreck':

30	B:	No, I haven't had it on, and I don't uh get the paper, and uhm.
31	A:	It wasn't in the paper last night, I looked.
32	B:	Uh huh.
33	B:	Probably didn't make it.
34	A:	No, no you see this was about three o'clock in the afternoon.
35	B:	[Uh huh

36 A: [Paper was already off the press.
37 B: Uh huh
38 A: Boy it was a bad one though
39 B: Well that's too bad.
40 A: Kinda / / (freak -)
41 B: You know, I looked and looked in the paper – I think I told you f- for
42   that uh fall over at the Bowl that night. And I never saw a thing about it
43   and I / / looked in the next couple of evenings.
44 A: Mm hm.
45   (1.0)
46 B: Never saw a th – a mention of it
47 A: I din't see that either.
48 B: Uh huh.
49 A: Maybe they kept it out.
50 B: Mm hm, I expect.
51 A: Uh huh, deli / / berately.
52 B: Well, I'll see you at – at–
53 A: Tomorrow / / night
54 B: at six at – hehhehh

(Data extract from Sacks, 1992a: 764)

Sacks spent some considerable analytic attention on the telling of the second story in this exchange. What is the link between the two tellings? The thing that interested Sacks was his finding that second stories are not necessarily tied to the *topic* of the first, which is what he expected to find.

EXERCISE 9.4

Examine the 'second story' in this conversation.

- How is the transition made from the conclusion of the first narrative sequence to the second?
- Can you detect the main structural elements of the second story?
- Can you identify what device organizes the telling?

Notice the repetition of the word 'bad' – what work is it doing in the transition? In the first instance, it serves to keep the first story in view – it is another category-description of the 'wreck' – 'a bad one'. In the response, 'Well that's too bad', it is repeated, but here, it is not clearly aligned to the story of the 'wreck'. Rather, it seems to function as an evaluative coda, which is directed to the experience of the witnessed event, rather than the facts of the wreck. By examining the hearer's response in terms of the device within which she frames her evaluation, we (categorization analysts) can demonstrate how the story was interpreted. In the next turn, speaker A may be about to confirm this evaluation ('kinda / / (freak –)) when the hearer interrupts and commences her own story, with 'You know, I looked and looked in the paper . . .' (first) 'and I never saw a thing about it [then]'. This story, as the teller acknowledges, has already been told before ('I think I told you . . .'). So, Sacks asked, why is this story chosen for a second telling? His suggestion is this:

> What seems to happen is that the character that the teller was in the story they tell you, is the character that you turn out to be in the story you tell them. So that in the first story here, the teller of it was somebody who saw it, saw it as news, and looked to see if it occurred in the paper and found that it didn't. And in the second, she gives us a method of search: Search for such a story as involved you in playing an equivalent role to the storyteller in his story. (1992a: 769)

The building of the second story, Sacks argues, serves two functions: it treats the first story as worthy of hearing; and it demonstrates this by showing the hearer playing the same role as the teller – one in search of a relevant news report. So, the 'news' finally proves to be the linking 'device' through which the two story-tellers align themselves to the interaction, and agree the relevance and congruity of their experience. The use of another device, Sacks argues, would have constrained the choice of second story, and involved a different sort of remembering in order to achieve the successful exchange of stories (and experiences).

Such exchanges demonstrate that the link between stories is often that the search for a relevant second story involves an understanding of the role of the teller of the first story. Perhaps, Sacks suggests, this may be one way of describing how memory would be organized. According to this perspective, it isn't memory that organizes stories, but stories that organize memory. Story-tellers use orderly procedures in their search for congruent experiences through which to acknowledge their attentiveness and connectedness to the story-telling and the story-teller. This then provides the basis for a shared experience and shared social reality. Findings from subsequent research into the development of language in children supports this intuition – some discussion of this appears in Chapter 10 in the section on 'Applications' (page 125).

Co-produced stories

Taking Sacks' preliminary analysis of second stories yet another step further, Gail Jefferson (1978) showed that story-telling may occur in rounds, include multiple speakers, and that a single story may even be co-produced by several speakers. Here's an example from the therapy group introduced in Chapter 2:

1 Al: (to Roger) Probly poured the *glue* over it. 'F I know you:, (0.4)
2 Ken: 'hhhh No:, yih gotta be careful evry so *often* he takes that cup'n 'e

```
 3             takes a deep whiff he's gotta tube a' glue in it (0.7)
 4   Roger:    New Years we:: split up the dues up so we each hadda buck fifty to
 5             buy booze with fer the New Years party?
 6   Al:       Mm Hm
 7   Roger:    So w' wen' around the room they were takin orders. "hh So Lance
 8             k– So:, one guy brought a dollar fifty worth a' Ripple, 'hh the next
 9             guy b(hh)ought a dollar fifty worth a' glue:, uhh!
10   ( ):      'hhh=
11   Ken:      =heh huh h u h
12                      [      ]
13   Al:            he – eh hehh he hh
14   Roger:                      [hhh! Ufff ff
15   Al:                             [hihhhh!
16   Jim:      (Hheh =
17
18   Roger:    = 'Planning on getting gassed. Huh La (h) nce.'
19                                     [        ]
20   Al:                              v e r y
21   Roger:    hh uhh hyihh hhh h
22             = [[              ] [
23   Al:           (good Roger)        he::::: h
24             (1.0)
25   Roger:    They were progressively gittin worse, ez we went aroun'
26             the circ(h)le,
27   Ken:      m hhmhh (     )
28                  [
29   Al:               he:h hehh uh hh nh
30                             [
31   Ken:                      (that's a true    ),
32   Roger:                                 I ordered rum n'
33             thought it wz ba: d y(h)kno(h)w
```

(Data extract from Jefferson, 1978: 222–3)

Jefferson observes that the occasion for the story-telling is the previous talk about 'glue', which she terms the 'trigger' word. Her primary interest in it is the sequential aspects of story-telling, so she does not attend to the way the deployment of categorizations contributes to the coherence of the story.

EXERCISE 9.5

Drawing on the categorization procedures, identify how the device is deployed by the speakers to link their contributions to the story. Identify how the evaluative elements contribute to the success of the conjoint telling.

The exchange between Al and Ken provides the preface to the story (did you notice the mini-narrative embedded in that preface?), introduces the device 'glue sniffing', and provides the opportunity for a 'remembering' – a story about the New Year's party. The story proper is prefaced by a 'once upon a time' opening – 'Last New Year' – and delivers a series of (category bound) activities (ordering 'booze' of various kinds) which deliver the climax of the story – 'I ordered rum and thought it was bad, you know' (until someone ordered glue) – delivered by Roger, who delivers the main elements (first/then) of the story by taking advantage of the story fragment produced in the previous turn to hear a potential story preface ('he takes a deep whiff he's gotta tube of glue in it'), and preface a story of his own (once-upon-a-time) 'New Year's Eve'. Roger's story about New Year's Eve provides a location category – a specific time with relevant category bound activities like drinking – as its preface, and then proceeds into its telling, the first/then sequence of the taking of orders, which elicits the evaluative encouragement of his hearers. The subsequent telling of the story hinges on the assembly of the order of events, told in a sequence of category bound activities ('planning on getting gassed'; 'progressively gittin worse'), in order to generate its ironic climax and the hearers' complicity in that delayed story evaluation – 'and I thought I was bad'.

It is interesting to note that the remembering, as evidenced in the structure of the telling, recreates the 'round' which the story was about. The story of the ordering, and the passing 'around the circle', is re-enacted in the evaluative comments of the hearers, which go around the circle of the group of hearers present. Sacks comments in several places in the lectures on the 'poetics' of talk which appear in the choice and placing of words. This story-telling is an example of such 'poetics', and also a topic of potential interest in the analysis of the production of stories-as-rememberings (or adequate descriptions). Similar kinds of reflexive activities in the production of stories have been observed in the exchanges of stories between care-givers and children (Nelson, 1996).

Summary

The previous sections have outlined some of the issues which captured the interest of Sacks and Labov in these first studies of conversational story-telling. At the later stage of his work, Sacks' attention turned to the mechanisms of turn-taking, and Gail Jefferson developed this aspect of his work in studies on the sequential aspects of story- and troubles-telling (1978, 1988). As discussed in the introduction to this book, sequential analysis subsequently dominated the development of conversation analysis. This chapter seeks to redress the balance and to provide the tools for an enriched analysis which includes both sequencing and categorization. As will also have been clear, there are many issues more generally about

the form and practice of narrative analysis which have generated alternative models of analysis and controversy. It would seem that the term
'narrative' covers a wide range of phenomena, related in the form of a
'family resemblance' (Wittgenstein). How to choose data, and what technique to apply to their analysis, depends on the interest of the researcher,
and the aspect of narrative which is being foregrounded for attention. In
the following chapter, some contemporary applications of Sacks' original
work will be considered, and we will see the richness of analytic possibilities which the original work generates.

Recommended reading

If you want to get started analysing stories, the best way to begin is by looking at some
of the classic studies:

Jefferson, G. (1978) 'Sequential aspects of storytelling in conversation'. In J.N.
Schenkein (ed.), *Studies in the organization of conversational interaction.* New York:
Academic Press.
A classic paper in the development of the analysis of stories, and an example of
best practice in sequential analysis.

Ryave, A. (1978) 'On the achievement of a series of stories'. In J.N. Schenkein (ed.),
Studies in the organization of conversation interaction. New York: Academic Press.
An early empirical study which employs CA to investigate how a series of stories
are linked.

Sacks, H. (1992b) Lectures on 'poetics' (Winter, Spring 1971). In *Lectures in conversation,* vol. II. Ed. G. Jefferson. Oxford: Basil Blackwell.
In these lectures, Sacks explores lexical choice as a function of sound, and the tex-
tured character of speech, employed by speakers and hearers to link utterances in
ongoing talk. They are rich in ideas for exploring how stories are constructed and
exchanged.

10

Contemporary Application of Sacks' Work on Narrative

CONTENTS

In the previous chapter, we've looked at some methods for analysing narrative sequences in naturally occurring talk, based on examples drawn from data of various kinds. Sacks made the case for working from singular instances, in order to build a model of the 'machinery of talk' which would be empirically grounded in the data. It remains to consider a practical research problem which turns out to have some complex implications for validity: how to search for, and identify, genuine narrative sequences in recorded data of ongoing, natural conversation. In the following chapter, we will look at two contemporary approaches to the identification and analysis of narratives.

Identifying stories in ongoing interaction

As discussed above, the early researchers in the social and psychological aspects of story-telling were concerned to identify the minimum conditions for a complete narrative. Labov, and most researchers of narrative, have relied on 'interview' data – elicited narratives which were part of the research process itself – in order to develop a model of narrative form. In practice, however, a simple expression of these minimum conditions is hardly ever met, or present, in naturally occurring talk. Recent research (Luebs, 1992, quoted in Ervin-Tripp and Kuntay, 1997) has shown that elicited narratives are more likely to demonstrate the elements of the prototypical form identified by Labov. Very considerable variations are observed in naturally occurring talk, which typically reveals only partially formed stories, and a variety of possible temporal connectives which do not necessarily link actions in the past. Natural talk is most likely to produce non-typical narrative-like sequences which include 'future plans and other kinds of sequences (particularly characteristic of children's talk), such as generic descriptions of scripted events describing what happens on a regular basis, or what happens if you don't do something, what results' (Ervin-Tripp and Kuntay, 1997: 140). Further, Ervin-Tripp and Kuntay find that stories are occasioned in everyday talk in a variety of different forms which are subject to cultural variation. These findings are consistent with Sacks' core proposal that the procedures for the production and hearing of everyday talk are the means by which social structuring and action are rendered meaningful and coherent. However, it follows that any part of the talk depends on the overall structure of the communicative event (whether it is spoken conversation or textual communication) for its sense (Sacks, Schegloff and Jefferson, 1974).

In the previous chapter, we saw how Sacks thought about the phenomenon of second stories. The example we looked at was typical of Sacks' method which involved collecting data, and searching for interesting examples of familiar phenomena to analyse in depth, in order to build his model of conversational interaction. Sacks noticed, however, that second stories do not necessarily feature in all kinds of story-telling. Stories appear in many guises, and under a variety of conditions. In studying story-telling as a naturally occurring phenomenon it is necessary to identify the many discursive forms in which story-telling may appear. For example, stories may be co-produced, rounds of stories may be told, stories may be elicited not for their own sake, but for other purposes – in teaching for example. Several problems of method result:

1. How to identify narrative sequences in an extended dataset;
2. How to explain the presence or absence of prototypical elements in the production of naturally occurring story-telling;
3. How to link the identified narrative to the context in which it was told.

Ervin-Tripp and her colleagues collected samples from a large dataset which included both elicited and spontaneous narratives, seeking to address some of these issues. Addressing the first question, they attempted to search their dataset for 'temporal markers' which would identify a 'first/then' sequence. They discovered that while this search identified many embedded narratives, the search for temporal conjunctions did not necessarily identify every narrative sequence. Trained judges also needed to search for story fragments which appeared in multi-party talk. Though these fragments do not match the prototypical narrative, they formed an important part of the data. Nevertheless, the method of searching for temporal markers yielded useful data from both child and adult talk in a wide variety of settings. This method seems a promising approach, in that it points towards a practical method of extracting relevant sequences for study from large amounts of data, and may be computerized (see Part V).

Addressing the second problem of method – how to explain the presence or absence of prototypical elements in stories told in a wide variety of settings, Ervin-Tripp and Kuntay have identified a wide range of occasioned story-tellings:

- *Elicited or prefaced narratives*: These are typically elicited by a question which invites the telling. It is important to note that in these interactions, prompting may alter the sequence of the story-telling.
- *Rounds of stories*: The use of rounds of stories as an interactional device was studied by Goffman (1974) in terms of framing. Ervin-Tripp and Kuntay's findings were that rounds of stories are ubiquitous in many settings of both adult and child multi-party talk and constitute an important communicative competence. The sequencing and linking of such stories, as revealed in Exercise 9.4, provides a rich site for categorization analysis.
- *Environmentally-cued stories*: Even more common than story rounds, environmentally-cued stories also appear in both adult and child talk. Because the story is prompted by immediate events, and embeds commonly shared knowledge, these stories show less consistency in structure – prefaces may be absent altogether.
- *Problem telling*: Stories about 'troubles' have formed an important part of the conversation analysis corpus – probably because Sacks used the data from helplines as the core of his early work. Later studies – Jefferson and Lee (1981), Watson (1987), Cuff (1993) – demonstrate some conversation and categorization analytic applications.
- *Narratives as performances*: Of particular interest to Goffman, narratives as performances form one distinct subgroup of story-tellings. All stories must get their point across, and be evaluable, but some story-tellings are characterized by a high degree of orientation to the 'audience', and by aspects of structure which support a high degree of evaluation and response. This kind of analysis reveals yet another set of formal constraints and possibilities for the study of stories. For example, what constraints of the context of the telling influence the structure of the story? Stories (testimony) told in court, in doctors' consulting rooms, in news interviews – all of these come to mind as examples, already given attention in CA literature (Drew and Heritage, 1992), of sites rich in possibility for the empirical study of the

relationship between narrative structures and the performance criteria implicit in the context of the telling.

- *Tactical narratives*: Many stories are produced to provide 'evidence' for a claim, a position in an argument, or statements about other's behaviour ('gossip'). An extended tactical narrative, put forward in the context of an organization, will be analysed in detail in Part IV.

In concluding their findings, Ervin-Tripp and Kuntay (1997) observe that an important aspect of the analysis of story-telling is the production conditions under which they are told. They argue that the degree of deviation from the prototypical story structure depends on the context of the telling, including the culture. Sacks' notion that a story has to be found, and crafted from what's available – the tellability of a story – has much to say about competence in the social world. It involves a natural sense of 'working to make the story. That is, a story is not just what someone makes, but what someone finds in competent engagement in a communicative world where stories constitute adequate descriptions' (Sacks, 1992b: 234).

The implication of Sacks' claim is that an important object of enquiry in the study of 'narrative' is the relationship between the production conditions (the context of the telling) and the systematic procedures employed by the teller in constructing the story. An 'adequate description' is measured by the degree to which it is heard as such, and treated as such, by speakers and hearers. In the service of this analytic logic, categorization analysis has the potential to provide a powerful tool for the study of the situated means by which 'culture' is sustained and generated in the varieties of story-telling which make up much of its everyday communicative activity.

Analysis of story evaluations

One of the things agreed on and studied by both Sacks and Labov was the centrality of the evaluation (Sacks), or coda (Labov), in the delivery of a successful story. Ervin-Tripp's findings confirm this aspect across a wide range of story-telling data. Goodwin and Goodwin (1992) studied what they call the 'assessment' segments of stories. They use the term 'assessment' to indicate what Sacks termed the evaluation element of the story, but they include in addition a wider range of evaluative phenomena: signals and sounds, as well as gesture and gaze which can only be captured on video-recording equipment. They demonstrate that assessment actions:

- may occur at any point in an utterance, not only at the end;
- involve the speaker in taking up a position towards what has been said, including his or her affective involvement in the telling;
- display the speakers' experience of what is being told.

Like Sacks, the Goodwins are interested in 'public structures such as this which display the experience of one participant and provide resources for the interactive organization of co-experience, a process that can be accomplished and negotiated in fine detail within assessment ' (1992: 154). The 'glue sniffing' story we looked at in Chapter 9 is a fine example of the organization of 'co-experience' through 'assessment', which makes use of a variety of methods for demonstrating the shared affective experience of the members of the group. Sacks, working with tape-recorded data, first drew attention to the fine-tuned orchestration of co-produced story. Later, Goodwin (1984), in a study of another short, jointly produced story, makes use of video-recording technology to expand on Sacks' original insights, by showing how both verbal and non-verbal aspects of the interaction contribute to the joint telling.

A more recent study (Torode, 1998) has developed a method for taking the analysis of this aspect of story-telling even further. Using computer-aided techniques, Torode shows how the structure of the conversation in a telephone encounter between a worried caller and an emergency service provider can be analysed as narrative, and that the evaluative elements provide a means of demonstrating how the encounter is successfully managed, in the terms Sacks identified in his caller/helper data: that is, that the 'helper' is category-bound to attempt to offer the client an acceptable solution. This, Sacks showed in his helpline studies, offers the client the possibility of employing that situated constraint as a strategy of his or her own motivated action.

Torode systematizes his analysis of the evaluative aspects of the narrative by applying a simple coding system to the overall structure of the telling. He too shows that the story shows elements of evaluation throughout its parts. In order to 'code', he simplified the story elements to the version Sacks identified as basic elements: Preface, First/Then and Response (evaluative coda). He then analyses the story elements in a sample of talk. Then, to each element of the identified story, he applied a simple code, representing the evaluative tone. The code he used involved a range of five possible values: +2, +1, 0, −1, −2, where the '+' values indicate positive tone, 0 represents neutral tone, and the '−' values represent negative tone. The process of analysis involves applying the code values to each part of the narrative. It simply describes the evaluative movement from one story part to the next. Following is an example of the application of the code to a simple story, taken from some interview data, in which the interviewer is eliciting stories about the death of a spouse. You'll notice that the story is very close to the prototypical narrative form:

and er a doctor came in and she said to me 'We've given your wife a thorough examination and we can't find anything wrong with her' (0.1) which seemed a bit odd to me (0.1) you know, they didn't X-ray her or anything like that. Now why I've pointed this out is because my daughter read a case in America. An American man collapsed with a stabbing pain in his back (like my wife). They took him to hospital, X-rayed him, found he'd got lung cancer.[1]

I have analysed the story like this (gaining agreement from several co-workers):

1	and er a doctor came in and she said to me	(preface)	0
2	We've given your wife a thorough examination	(first)	0
3	and we can't find anything wrong with her (0.1)	(then)	+1
4	which seemed a bit odd to me (0.1)	(response)	0
5	you know they didn't X-ray her or anything like	(response)	−1
6	that (0.2)		
7	Now why I've pointed this out is because [request sequence- 'keep on listening, here's the rest of the story]		
8	My daughter read a case in America	Preface	0
9	an American man collapsed with a		
10	stabbing pain in his back (like my wife)	First	−1
11	They took him to hospital, X-rayed him	Then	−1
12	found he'd got lung cancer		−2

My reasoning is this: the preface (line 1) signals a story which could go in either a positive or a negative direction – the doctor could deliver good or bad news. I coded it 0. This preface is followed by the core story elements – *first*, 'we've given your wife a thorough examination' – still neutral (could go either way); *then* shows an upward movement, evidently delivering good news – 'can't find anything wrong'. I coded it +1. The evaluative response suggests that the story maybe isn't quite so upbeat, however: 'it seemed a bit odd'. In fact, the response seems to incorporate two parts, and could be heard as falling in evaluative tone between the two parts. Maybe the hearer should be expecting a negative story. I coded it in two parts to show this: 0, followed by −1.

The story-teller then proceeds to provide a second story, which he prefaces with the sequence – 'Now why I've pointed this out is because' (line 7). With this clause, the story-teller indicates to the hearer 1) that there is more to come (request sequence); and 2) that the point of the story is up-coming.

By my reading, the second part of the story mirrors the first part and in its construction, but continues the falling evaluation which has been pre-figured in the last line of the first part of the story. First there is a neutral preface 'read a case' (line 8), followed by a simple two part first/then sequence: *first*, 'a stabbing pain in his back'; *then* 'took him to hospital' (coded −1, because it is falling in tone) and 'found . . . lung cancer' (coded −2 because the tone continues to fall).

There is no evaluation to this second part of the story. In fact, the second story in the sequence acts as an evaluation of the first part. In the case of this story, a story-within-a-story contributes to the overall narrative structure. Torode shows how embedded stories and evaluations produce a recursive structure in the complex exchange between his two callers, and how parts of the story become parts of other stories. All this complexity is easily handled by the speakers, who are intent on what they are trying to get the other one to do/hear, rather than on the way they are doing it! What Torode reveals with his coding method is the complex recursive structure which characterizes the evaluative movement of the story.

The analysis of the evaluation reveals a dramatically falling story-line. What relationship does it have to the deployment of the categorizations?

EXERCISE 10.1

Examine this narrative for its deployment of categorizations. What is the main organizing device? Using the concepts of membership categorization, category bound activities, the economy rule, hierarchies of relevance – show how the evaluative tone is achieved and managed in the story. How does the management of evaluative tone constitute a hearable message, and what is that message?

You should by now be able to show empirically, using categorization analytic methods, how the deployment of categories within a relevant device generates an evaluative movement, which cues the hearer about what kind of story to expect, and how to react to it. This strategy adds great power to the potential for an empirically based and precise narrative analysis.

This method, however, holds some potential dangers which you should be aware of. The driving force behind Sacks' work was the critique of contemporary social science that sought to impose its logic on data, in order to show what was 'really there'. For Sacks, the natural observational social science which he sought to create relied for its validity on the demonstration of how social actors create mutually shared and sharable understandings through their categorizations, not upon researchers' categorizations. He criticized the experimental work of Bales, who sought to code interaction 'variables' for analysis. Any coding procedure lends itself quickly to the illusion that it is revealing what is there, rather than opening up for observation what the talk is *doing*. The advantages and pitfalls of computer-aided analysis are discussed in Part V.

Applications

Narrative analysis is a rapidly developing field of study across a wide range of disciplines. In the following section, I want briefly to indicate several potential applications of categorization analysis to the study of narrative in adjacent fields of study.

Developmental psychology

Sacks' work has great potential for the empirical study of the micro-processes of the development of language and cognitive structures in the context of adult–infant interaction. Though the work of the great Russian developmental psychologist, Vygotsky (1962), had not yet been widely read at the time Sacks was working, the two methods converge in many interesting ways, and constitute an important potential direction for future empirical research.

As we have seen, Sacks used many examples from children's stories to demonstrate that categorization devices are used by even quite young children to represent their understanding of their social world. In this chapter, we have examined how stories are used in adult interaction to accomplish interactional ends. Vygotsky was interested in studying the relationship between the cognitive development of individuals and the culturally embedded interactions between care-givers (and teachers) and developing children – a process which he termed 'mediated action'. He viewed development as an interactional process rather than as the relatively autonomous unfolding process proposed by the Piagetian model of genetic epistemology. The ascendance of behaviourism during the 1920s and 1930s obscured the early work of psychologists interested in interaction, and established a culture of deductive method modelled on the natural sciences, which is generally inimical to the study of talk and social action. However, as we have seen, interactional models took root and flourished in sociology, and generated a variety of methods for the study of social action.

More recently, interest in interaction has reappeared in psychology, and the early work of Vygotsky is now highly valued. Important new research in the development of an interactional model of language and cognitive development was undertaken in a series of studies which examine the use of stories in exchanges between care-givers and young children (Nelson, 1996). Nelson demonstrates how stories are used to describe events and actions in the child's world, and how events are tied together through the medium of stories to provide increasingly complex accounts of the social world in which the developing child is learning to take his or her place. Nelson argues that the structuring aspects of narrative in the socialization of the child may be seen as acting indirectly as a means of providing the basis for a continuous sense of self. She argues that the primary function of stories in the interaction between the developing child and his or her care-takers is to map the social world in a way which is congruent with the cultural and social context of the family. The development of self, as a psychological phenomenon, is a product of that process. The coherence of the child's sense of his or her relationship to the people in his or her world, and the relationships between them, develops through and is constrained by those stories. These accomplishments underpin the development of other cognitive skills.

I would propose that categorization analysis, grounded as it is in the procedures by which adequate descriptions are produced and heard, has the potential to add sharp focus and precision at the level of turn-by-turn interaction, to these new initiatives in the development of empirical methods for the study of the development of cognitive competence through the agency of interaction.

Life stories

A life story is an oral unit that is told over many occasions. Conventionally it includes certain kinds of landmark events, such as choice of profession, marriage, divorce, and religious or ideological conversion, if any. Both in its content (the items that it includes and excludes) and in its form (the structures that are used to make it coherent) it is the product of a member of a particular culture. Other cultures may include different items and use different forms. Indeed, the notion of a 'life story' itself is not universal, but is the product of a particular culture. (Linde, 1993: 11)

The empirical study of life stories has been demonstrated by numerous researchers to be a powerful tool in sociological and anthropological inquiry (Riessman, 1993). Life story research is based on the assumption that the coherence of the self is an achievement which is grounded in the context of social interaction. Through the study of the life story – stories, elicited or naturally occurring, which are told by people to others about their life and experiences – researchers may gain access to both psychological and social/anthropological understanding of the relation of the individual to the social world. Research methods range from an unstructured, ethnographic approach, in which language is treated as transparent, and the content is foregrounded, to analytic approaches, using Labov's structural model to specify narrative features and analyse the story in terms of them.

'Life story' methodology was employed to investigate the use of explanatory systems in peoples' accounts of themselves and their histories (Linde, 1987), following Labov's structural model of narrative. In this study, Linde shows how systems of belief are employed to construct an account of life choices and life chances. Linde employs the concept of 'coherence', which she defines, in line with cognitive thinking, in terms of 'causality' and 'continuity'. The 'Adult Attachment Interview', a life story instrument designed by the psychologist Mary Main (1991), seeks to analyse the coherence of life stories as markers of cognitive styles (see discussion below). In both these cases, though they examine discourse, the notion of 'coherence' relies on structural aspects of narrative, as we have used the term in this chapter, rather than on the analysis of the telling of the story.

Though Sacks' work is mentioned by some of these researchers, it is not directly employed as an analytic strategy. I would propose that the methods Sacks developed for the study of categorization have the potential to add analytic rigour with an empirical study of the micro-processes which underpin 'coherent accounts'. As we have seen, Sacks was able to show that coherence is an interactional achievement, grounded in the capacity to generate adequate descriptions. Sacks' observation that stories are not found, but made for the occasion of the telling, and that rememberings are designed for the occasion of the telling, implies that the detailed analysis of the production of life stories as stories told to someone, and of the interaction which produces them, may have much to tell us about the nature and use of explanatory systems.

Psychotherapy

In her study of life stories as explanatory systems, Linde (1987) refers to the uses of psychoanalysis as an explanatory system, and she refers to the work of Harry Stack Sullivan, a psychiatrist and psychoanalyst who was interested in social aspects of human growth and development. She uses his model of the psychiatric interview – the elicitation of a life history – as one which demonstrates the cultural embededness of life stories, and how a well constructed one may be understood. Most contemporary psychotherapies which rely on interpretative interaction between therapist and client – the so-called 'talking therapies' – take the life history as the basis of their interpretative work, and derive directly or indirectly from the work of Freud, and the influence of psychoanalysis. As an occasioning of story-telling in twentieth-century culture, the influence of psychoanalysis and the practices of psychotherapy cannot be ignored. Critical studies of psychoanalysis as discourse, based on the relationship between discursive practices and culture, have been undertaken by numerous authors (see Parker (1999), for a recent example).

Recently, however, interest in the nature of the therapeutic narrative, and its function in the psychotherapeutic process, has grown within psychoanalysis itself. Psychoanalysts Roy Schafer (1992) and Donald Spence (1982) first drew attention to the discourse of the analytic session, and to the creation and recreation of the life story, as the core of the psychotherapeutic process. The empirical findings of the psychologist and psychoanalyst John Bowlby (1969/1982), also shifted the attention of some psychoanalytic enquiry from the intrapsychic to the interactional and social bases of human psychology. For Bowlby, who was strongly influenced by concurrent developments in ethology, the primary factor in the development of the human infant was to be found in the instinctual drive to attach to others. This major stream of thought has generated a wide empirical research programme which investigates the developmental aspects of human relating, both functional and dysfunctional, as well as direct research into the psychotherapeutic process itself. Based on the work of Bowlby, Mary Main and her colleagues developed the Adult Attachment Interview (1985), a research tool which elicits a life story from subjects. The resulting life story is then analysed for its narrative properties – coherence – in order to demonstrate links between the stories and characteristic patterns of attachment and relating which subjects favour.

Both cognitive science (and its associated therapies) and psychoanalysis, though very different in many ways, derive from a common assumption about the nature of 'mind', in which language is treated as a system which 'represents' things in the 'mind'. This assumption causes methodological and theoretical problems for both practitioners and researchers, who face the familiar problem of 'structures' and 'processes' which we have explored in relation to theories of narrative. Cognitive scientists, developmental psychologists and psychotherapy share a vocabulary of concepts such as 'inner working models' (Bowlby), 'proto-narrative envelops' (Stern), and 'relational scripts' (Trevarthen). If 'representations' are structure-like 'mental models', how can we account for the plasticity of human thought and action?

Sacks offers a nice way out of this dilemma. With his method for the empirical analysis of conversation – based on the study of language-as-action (parole) – he accounts for both the stability of talk and its dynamic properties by focusing our attention not on what is in their 'minds', but on how, in practice, hearers and speakers demonstrate that they make inferences about what the other has 'in mind', on a turn-by-turn basis, in order for conversation, and relating, to occur at all. Sacks' observation accords very well with recent studies in cognitive science, which show that a 'theory of mind' is a developmental achievement which is the precursor to competent speech (Baron-Cohen, 1992).

Sacks demonstrated through his detailed analysis of naturally occurring stories, that remembering is not something fixed 'in the mind', but something designed for the immediate puposes of relating to present hearers. That this is the case is well understood in psychoanalysis, and is described in practitioner accounts (Stern et al., 1998), but no method of analysis has ever offered a way to evaluate this phenomenon empirically. By focusing on the procedures by which interactants produce adequate (hearable) descriptions of their remembering and their experience, categorization analysis has much to offer to this project.

Summary

In this chapter, contemporary developments in the analysis of narrative have been discussed in relation to Sacks' early focus on the telling of stories. Interest in everyday story-telling as a phenomenon of general interest to social scientists of many kinds is developing rapidly. Sacks' insight into the relationship between story-telling and adequate descriptions, and the centrality of adequate descriptions to human social life and the possibility of culture, continues to provide an important empirical foundation to the study of narrative in contemporary research. The sequential properties of story-telling have been absorbed into research in several domains of social science. Attention to categorization has yet to be fully exploited, and constitutes a rich new site for the CA researcher to explore.

Recommended reading

Bamberg, M. (ed.) (1997) 'Oral versions of personal experience: three generations of narrative analysis', *Journal of Narrative and Life History* (special edn), 7 (1–4).
Contributions by a wide range of researchers in the field of narrative study. The original paper by Labov and Waletsky (1967) is reprinted, and the volume finishes with Labov's current thinking on his theory.

Edwards, D. (1997) *Discourse and cognition.* London: Sage.
For those with an interest in following up applications of categorization analysis to developmental psychology, Edwards provides a good introductory discussion of the ways in which Sacks' work is being applied to the contemporary analysis of discourse as a way of approaching the study of cognition and cognitive development. Among others, there is an excellent chapter on narrative analysis.

Givon, T. (1997) *Conversation: cognitive, communicative and social perspectives.* Amsterdam: John Benjamins Publishing Company.
This excellent collection of papers 'were originally presented at the Symposium on Conversation held at the University of New Mexico in July 1995. The symposium itself brought together scholars who work on face-to-face communication from a variety of perspectives – social, cultural, cognitive and communicative.' The book contains the published studies of a wide variety of empirical studies, including the study by Ervin-Tripp and Kuntay (1997) discussed in this chapter.

Goodwin, C. (1984) 'Notes on story structure and the organization of participation'. In J.M. Atkinson and J. Heritage (eds), *Structures of social action: studies of conversation analysis.* Cambridge: Cambridge University Press.
In this study, Goodwin builds on Sacks' analysis of the audio-taped 'glue sniffing' story, using video-recording technology to show how both gestures, posture and gaze contribute to the co-production of a story by several speakers.

Goodwin, C. and Goodwin, M.H. (1992) 'Assessments and the construction of context'. In A. Duranti and C. Goodwin (eds), *Rethinking context: language as an interactive phenomenon.* Cambridge: Cambridge University Press.

Linde, C. (1993) *Life stories: the creation of coherence.* Oxford: Oxford University Press.
Defines and demonstrates methods for the study of life stories – good on both theory and practice.

McLeod, J. (1997) *Narrative and psychotherapy.* London: Sage.
An introduction to the social constructionist study of narrative processes in psychotherapy.

Note

1   Thanks to Moira Kelly for the data.

Part IV

ANALYSING ORGANIZATIONS

11

Background to the Study of Organizations

CONTENTS

In this chapter, I will briefly review how the identification of organizational phenomena, and methods for studying them, have developed in the social sciences. Then, in Chapter 12, I will show how the tools of categorization analysis can be employed as an empirical resource in the analysis of organizational phenomena. Finally, in Chapter 13, an extended case study will demonstrate how an in-depth application of categorization analysis to the study of a single document can contribute to the understanding of how organizations work.

Institutional talk

```
1           (26.3)
2   JFK:    How many copies of this have you made, Dave?
3   Bell:   Well they're - they're all here . . . in the room, sir except uh (0.6) for
4           about three more that are in our (0.8) in Bob Turner's office.
5                   (2.9)
6           This is handled (.) the way
7   JFK:                    [Yes]
8                    [  Ea]ch of these things has been handled
9           over the last number of years. . . .
```

(Data extracts from *The Kennedy White House Tapes*, quoted in Boden, 1994)

This extract is from a discussion in the White House, between President Kennedy and his economic advisers. They go on to discuss the management of the forthcoming Federal budget proposals. As with much data used by conversation analysts, the exchange seems mundane, and insignificant in relation to the 'important' matters – the 'Economy' – which they are about to discuss. What analytically relevant relationship could there be between a discussion about photocopies and the processes of policy making in the White House? In this chapter, we will explore how and why the analysis of such exchanges may be valuable in the study of social process and structure, and what contribution categorization analysis in particular can make to that undertaking.

As in the previous chapters, in order to identify the phenomenon to be studied, it is important to be precise about what is meant by the use of the abstract terms such as 'organization', which describe a field of enquiry. Many conceptualizations of what an organization is have been generated, and ways of studying them accordingly developed. The concept of organization as a domain of enquiry, both theoretical (sociology, psychology, anthropology) and applied (management studies, accountancy, industrial psychology), now occupies an important place in many university teaching programmes.

In some ways, the extract above could be treated as an example of 'institutional talk' – an example of 'government' for example. The concept of organized collective processes which structure human social life begins with the notion of 'institutions'. The term derives from the Latin 'instituere' – to establish, arrange, teach. Medicine, education, the law, the media: all are examples of institutions through which the collective affairs of society are conducted in the context of recognized practices, systematically inculcated through learning and adhered to through established convention. Culture is instantiated in and worked on through institutions. Social institutions have been traditional objects of sociological enquiry since its inception as a theoretical discipline.

As we have seen, Sacks' primary analytic interest in the lectures was to develop an alternative to conventional sociological analysis through the development of an empirical method by which to study the 'machinery' of everyday talk which, he proposed, underlies all social interaction. In a later article, co-authored with Schegloff and Jefferson (1974), the authors explored the idea that the universal 'speech exchange system' which was being revealed through the study of talk in many different settings, might be adapted in specific institutional settings, and that the ways in which it is adapted constitute a potential application of the CA method to the study of social institutions. The authors identified a 'linear array' of turn-taking systems:

- those in which the turn-taking sequence is highly constrained and organized (such as courtroom procedures);
- those in which a mixture of pre-allocated rules, and locally organized

exchanges (the news interview example in Chapter 5 is an example); and
- those in which locally organized sequences predominate – the therapy group which Sacks studied in the lectures would be an example of such institutional talk.

The important methodological potential created by Sacks, Schegloff and Jefferson in this seminal statement of the CA project was to open up the possibility of 'a comparative investigation of speech exchange systems' across this 'linear array', as a rigorous empirical method for the study of institutions.

As conversation analysis has developed in the years since this early paper, a substantial literature in the study of institutional talk within areas of traditional sociological concern has emerged. Education, law and governmental/political process, media studies, and medical, social work and counselling consultations: all have proved rich sites for analysis (a brief guide to this literature can be found at the end of this chapter). Such studies as these take social institutions as their site of enquiry, and demonstrate, as we have seen in Chapter 5, *how* institutional relevance is sustained and worked upon on a turn-by-turn basis through the recognizability of the procedurally consequential actions of individual speakers who organize their turns within a framework of locally relevant rules of exchange. In Chapter 5, it was possible to specify and demonstrate the ways in which the speech exchange system relevant to the 'news interview' was employed and co-produced by the interactants, in order to achieve situated interactional objectives. We also looked in some detail at how 'institutions' such as the 'court' are methodically employed as a shared resource in order to achieve a publicly agreed means of deciding what shall count as defining a 'demonstrator', and what as a 'troublemaker'; and how the institution of the 'media' is employed to achieve yet further cultural 'work' on these definitions. It was also possible to show how the 'court', as institution, was employed as a categorial resource for the interactants in the context of versions which the setting of the news interview invites/requires. As social objects, worthy of systematic study, institutions can be shown by CA to have relevance at multiple levels of complexity.

What is an organization?

The title of this part, however, is 'Analysing Organizations', rather than 'Analysing Institutions'. What is the distinction, and why make it? A relatively recent phenomenon, 'organizations' have come to play a dominating role in modern society, as well as in social theory. That there is a distinction to be made between organizations and institutions can be seen in sociological terminology. The notion of 'Macdonaldization' is a contemporary example of an organization which has come to be treated as an institution; the Ford Motor Company, and 'Fordism', an earlier one. If organizations may become institutions, it is also the case that organizations are created to do the business of institutions. The 'White House' constitutes an institution of American government, as the established locus of executive authority which houses successive generations of elected incumbents. It also houses an organization, formed around its incumbent, whose specific task is to serve the functions of the Executive. We speak of the 'Kennedy White House', or the 'Nixon White House' as of different organizations. The fact that their proceedings are tape-recorded has both institutional and organizational significance. It also provides CA researchers with a vast corpus of data. In this chapter, I will be looking at some extracts from those tapes to explore how they can be used to demonstrate some features of organization of the day-to-day business of the Kennedy Administration.

In Western societies we spend so much of our lives in organizations, and take so many aspects of them for granted, that the phenomenon of 'the organization' may seem as old and enduring as the traditional institutions which shaped the social fabric of pre-modern societies. It is, however, very much a concept of modernity. The early work on organizations was taken up in earnest with the rapid growth of large industrial corporations following the war. In most classical studies, organizations are conceived of as social entities, capable of 'acting' (for or against the workers, or governments, for example); of 'making decisions', and 'learning' (how to operate in the 'global economy', for example). Inherent in these models of organization is an assumption that the organization is structure-like, a boundaried 'body' which contains, and moulds, the lives of individuals working within it. Later models, built on Weber's (1964) account of human sociality, introduced the notion of social action into organization theory, as into all fields of social science enquiry, and the attempt to integrate 'formal' and 'substantive' models of organizational rationality began. As wide a continuum of concepts and theories now populates the field of organization theory as can be found in any of the social science disciplines. This raises the question: what is the nature of the object to be studied, and how are we to be sure what we are actually looking at?

Given the amount of time we all spend in organizations, these competing models of the relationship between the individual and the collective have powerful implications. In pre-modern societies, the relationship between the individual and the institutions which provided the framework for the conduct of individual lives was not subject to the kind of continuous critique which characterizes modern societies – particularly, modern democratic societies. With the arrival of the Enlightenment, and the notion that human beings are capable of understanding, and, through that understanding, controlling events in the physical world, the possibility of studying, and controlling, economic and social life began to be explored. The development of the 'organization' as an object of study is a relatively late development in that process. As we shall see, the evolution of the notion of 'organization' also has reflexive implications: how the 'organization' is conceptualized and studied has implications for how we understand the nature of the individual in relation to the social order. The organization conceptualized as an entity with structural properties generates very different methods of enquiry than the organization studied as the arranging and co-ordinating of the parts of a whole.

The emergence of organization theory

Organization theory has developed a vast and varied literature since its inception in the late 1930s. This section does not seek to discuss that development in detail (but see suggested recommended reading at the end of this chapter for indications about how to find out more about the different strands of organization theory). For the purposes of this introduction to categorization analysis and its applications, a particular strand of development of organizational theory is relevant to understanding the ways in which CA can provide a powerful tool in the analysis of *how* the structures and processes of organizations can be made observable through the study of 'structure in action' (Boden, 1994).

The conceptual conflict between social 'structures' and 'processes', which we have already considered in previous chapters, likewise characterizes the debates about method and meaning in the study of organizations. Much organizational theory and literature seeks to apply models of social systems theory to the phenomenon of the organization. It asks questions about the formal properties of organizations as social objects, in order to find answers in the form of general principles. During the early decades of organization studies, the attempt was made to study the organizational bureaucracy as a rational social system, capable of objectification. Organizations were conceptualized as self-sustaining social systems, capable of rational action such as 'making decisions', 'acting' and 'influencing' in their own right. The people in them, if they were seen at all, were the parts which are connected and co-ordinated by rational structures and management. Very much in the same way that Saussure viewed the phenomenon of 'parole' as too messy to study systematically, the micro-system of human actions was considered too idiosyncratic to be relevant to those seeking to establish a 'science' of organization theory. Throughout this period, organizational theorists sought to establish that the phenomenon of 'organization' which they were trying to describe and understand was different from traditional studies of social organization (including social institutions) by virtue of the fact that organizations are constituted for a purpose. An important distinction arose which was to have significant implications for the development of organization studies to come:

Formal organization: In contrast to the social organization that emerges whenever men are living together, there are organizations that have been deliberately established for a certain purpose. Since the distinctive characteristic of these organizations is that they have been formally established for the explicit purpose of achieving certain goals, the term "formal organizations" is used to designate them (Blau and Scott, 1963: 5).

Blau and Scott, in common with most early theoreticians of organization theory, conceived of the organization as a site of rational, goal directed action, characterized by unity of purpose, available to the systematic comparative analysis of structural variables. 'Formal organization' was distinguished from 'social organization' as the feature which defined a separate discipline of organizational theory. Very soon, however, problems emerged. It proved difficult to identify unity of purpose; observation of actual behaviour of workers at all levels of the organization showed that the theory of rational action was not confirmed by what actually happened at the level of the office or shopfloor. Closer investigation of organizational practices revealed that the formal hierarchy of relationships between 'workers' and 'managers' did not guarantee an orderly and agreed exercise of power and authority. The study of 'informal organization' – for example, the ways in which workers bend rules in the course of their work – was also needed to investigate how the actions of individuals in the organization operated within, and were affected by, the structures of formal organization (Blau and Scott, 1963). Even the early 'Hawthorne' studies, conducted in the 1920s, in the context of the 'engineering' model of business management, had shown that the 'parts' of the organization – its workers – did not behave like the parts of machines, and that the objective methods of study suitable for an engineering system were not adequate for the study of the behaviour of social actors. They discovered that when studied, the workers behaved differently, and this inevitably changed the methods and outcomes of research.

Out of this early phase of organizational study, three important theoretical models emerged:

1. *Structural functionalism*: Within this tradition, theoreticians such as Selznick (1949/1966), Parsons (1949) and Blau and Scott (1963) attempted to formulate lawful properties of organizations, reasoning from the perspective of macro-structures to the actions of individuals.
2. *Organizational psychology*: Theories within this school concentrate on the nature of 'social man', and on the needs and motives of individuals, and the ways in which they conflict with the demands of organizational structures and rationalities. For these organizational psychologists such as Schein (1987), Bennis (1966) and the solution to organizational conflict lies in optimizing organizational structure such that it meets those needs.
3. *Socio-technical systems theory*, like organizational psychology, focuses

on the 'human relations' model of human social needs, but derives ideas, as does structural functionalism, from systems theory. Starting from a perspective derived in consultancy, its early theorists (Trist, 1963; Miller and Rice, 1967) built a model based on the relationship of personal to organizational boundaries as they affect the 'primary task' of the organization and disturb rational decision making.

By the 1970s, in organization theory, as in other social sciences, new thinking began to emerge. These developments generated a new model of organization:

4. *The action model of organization*: Two early developments in particular were significant in changing the range of study available to those seeking to research organizations: the 'interactionist' approach, which yielded the notion of the 'negotiated order' (Strauss, 1978); and the ethnomethodological approach being developed by Garfinkel (1967) and his students, including, of course, Sacks. The concept of the 'action model of organization' (Silverman, 1970) emerged out of these new approaches to the study of social phenomena, and prepared the ground for contemporary approaches to organization study based on discourse analytic methods (MacKinlay and Starkey, 1997) and narrative analysis (Czarniawska, 1998), in addition to applications of conversation analysis – the so-called 'linguistic turn'.

These later approaches provide the basis for an alternative perspective on the nature of the organization through the study of the actions of the individuals within them. New solutions to old problems become possible and new problems are generated. Fresh debates about the nature of the phenomena under study emerge, which resonate with some classical conceptual and analytic problems in social theory:

- the relationship between macro and micro levels of phenomena and analysis;
- the nature of rationality;
- the nature of power and hierarchy in human social systems.

The relationship between 'micro' and 'macro' levels of phenomena and analysis

The concept of 'organization' denotes the 'connection and co-ordination of parts for vital functions or processes' as well as the 'arranging and co-ordinating of parts into a systematic whole' (*OED*, 1993). Implicit in this definition is the 'macro' (structures) versus 'micro' (interactional) divide which came to dominate theoretical debates in social science

(Knorr-Cetina and Cicourel, 1981; Silverman, 1985). Early organization theorists, like other social and language theorists, focused their attention on the study of the whole, rather than the parts – that is, on the study of the 'macro system' rather than the 'micro systems', on 'formal organization', rather than the actions of the individuals who make up organizations. The interactionists, under the influence of Strauss, turned this proposition on its head, collapsing the distinction between formal and social organization, and focusing entirely on the study of the interactions of the individuals who make up the organization. The order of the organization, according to interactionists, is rather conceived of as an achievement of negotiation, based on locally managed, temporally limited solutions which operate within the framework of whatever rules happen to be available and relevant at a given moment:

> The realm of rules could then be usefully pictured as a tiny island of structured stability around which swirled and beat a vast ocean of negotiation. But we would push the metaphor further and assert what is already implicit in our discussion: that there is *only* vast ocean. (Strauss et al., 1964: 313)

Rules, in this interactionist perspective, are merely epiphenomena of micro-processes of human action.

Ethnomethodologists who, in contrast, were concerned to account for the observable rule-guided orderliness of everyday action, sought a different approach. Following Garfinkel's central tenet, they proposed treating the 'formal organization' as resource rather than topic:

> a generalized formula to which all sorts of problems can be brought for solution ... [acquiring] through this reference a distinctive meaning that they would not otherwise have. Thus the formal organizational designs are schemes of interpretation that competent and entitled users can invoke in yet unknown ways whenever it suits their purposes. (Bittner, 1965: 249–50)

For Bittner, as for ethnomethodologists generally, the development of organization *theory* entailed first the development of a robust method of *enquiry*. The study of the situated interaction of members provides that site of empirical enquiry. However, it too, evades the question of how structures relate to individual action by reducing them to members' resources. Though each argued from the opposite end of the spectrum, a *method of enquiry* which would link structures to actions eluded ethnomethodologists just as it had those, like Parsons, who worked with a social systems models of organization.

Sacks, though he did not address organization theory in any direct way, developed that method: the systematic, empirical study of situated talk-in-action. In Sacks' conception of the study of talk-in-interaction, the systems to be studied are the procedures for the production of recognizable actions. Actions, he showed, are only recognizable to the extent that speakers employ available social resources (and learning) to generate shared understandings and coherent action (and to repair things when they go wrong). A commonly shared *field of relations*, which is based upon 'rules, techniques, procedures, methods, maxims (a collection of terms that interrelate and that I use somewhat interchangeably)' (Sacks, 1984b: 413) is a precondition for communicative action; and action is only recognizable to the extent that it draws upon that common field.

Once again, let's return to Sacks' core notion of the act of observing, and how it constitutes the precondition for communicative action, put in typically descriptive form:

> So the classes and their categories permit you to see. That's a start. It's not enough to make a glance an action. It's not merely that some observer is seeing by reference to some category, but that one being observed sees what the observer is, and is seeing.
>
> And if you can see what it is that is doing that looking, you could have a pretty good idea of what it is that would be at the end of it. So this complementarity is equally as crucial as the fact that one is able to see what somebody with whom you are a member of a class in common is seeing when they are looking at you, or another. The sense of there being 'a society' is that there are many whomsoevers, who are not members of this or that class, who are able to see what it is that one is looking at. (Sacks 1992a: 87–8)

Social structure, in Sacks' conception, is methodically describable in terms of the field of relations which is generated by talk-in-action, including the collection of membership categories, such that membership of a category (and all the shared knowledge that entails) provides the basis for shared recognition of what is going to happen next. The focus is on neither subjectivity nor objectivity, on neither structure nor process, but rather on 'the study of the cultural realities [which] are to be found in the technical practices through which sense and meaningfulness are constructed in speaking together' (Drew, 1999: 319).

Summary

In this chapter, the growth of organization theory has been outlined, not to provide a complete history, but to show how the 'action' model of organization, in which the CA methods are placed, evolved out of early thought about the nature and development of organizations. Although Sacks did not address the study of organizations in his own work, his analytic focus on the act of observing and categorization, as a members' accomplishment, provides a rich analytic site for the study of the practical reasoning and communicative action which underpin the ongoing process which is organizational life. The recommended reading which follows will provide the basis for a fuller understanding of the issues, and is essential reading if you are thinking of researching organizational processes using categorization analysis.

Recommended reading

Bittner, E. (1965) 'The concept of organization', *Social Research,* 32: 239–55.
This classic paper provides a basis for the debates from the perspective of ethnomethodology, about what constitutes an object of study in organization theory.

Clegg, S. and Hardy, C. (eds) (1999) *Studying organization: theory and method.* London: Sage.
A contemporary introduction to organizational theory and research method. A good place to begin.

Dingwall, R. and Strong, P. (1985) 'The interactional study of organizations: a critique and reformulation', *Urban Life,* 14(2): 205–31.
Addresses the key issues of method in the study of organizational processes.

Silverman, D. (1970) *The theory of organizations: a sociological framework.* London: Heinemann Educational Books.
An account of the development of organization theory which provides the background to the growth of the 'action model' of organization; still useful.

Suchman, L. (1987) *Plans and situated actions: the problem of human–machine interaction.* Cambridge: Cambridge University Press.
A model study of the application of the 'action' model of organization.

12

The Contribution of CA

CONTENTS

How does categorization analysis work to reveal structure-in-action? In this chapter, three examples of its application to the Kennedy White House Tapes are used to demonstrate how some of the 'macro' questions of traditional social and organization theory can be teased out through detailed analysis of the use of categorization devices, membership categorizations, and category bound activities. There are three exercises to help you apply the method. If you are not already familiar with these concepts, and how to work with them, turn back to Chapter 1.

Organization as structure-in-action

Little direct use has been made in the study of organizations through the medium of conversation analysis, despite the considerable attention paid to institutional talk by a variety of analysts. In recent years, however, that has begun to change. In *The business of talk*, Boden (1994) develops the proposition initially put forward by Sacks, Schegloff and Jefferson (1974) that the comparative study of speech exchange systems may be employed to study social phenomena. Moving beyond the analysis of talk in institutional settings, where such comparative analysis has generated many interesting results, Boden shows how analysis of the speech exchange system in the context of organization-specific activities – in meetings, both formal and informal, and in telephone conferences for example – can be employed to provide empirical evidence for the ways in which 'the reflexive properties of talk *necessarily* instantiate and creatively extend organizations' (1994: 215).

In the following sections, I will discuss the particular contribution CA has to make to contemporary organization theory, and how it addresses the traditional sociological concerns about structure versus interaction, about rationality, and about power and hierarchy. Examples from the tape-recorded meeting between President Kennedy and his economic advisers will provide a prism through which to investigate how CA tackles these familiar problems within the study of organizations.

Let's look at the extract which introduced Chapter 11.

```
1           (26.3)
2    JFK:   How many copies of this have you made, Dave?
3    Bell:  Well they're - they're all here . . . in the room, sir except uh (0.6) for
4           about three more that are in our (0.8) in Bob Turner's office.
5                           (2.9)
6           This is handled (.) the way
7    JFK:                            [Yes]
8                            [  Ea]ch of these things has been handled
9           over the last number of years. . . .
```

(Data extract from *The Kennedy White House Tapes*, quoted in Boden, 1994)

This exchange occurs at the very beginning of the meeting. The 26 second pause is time during which papers are being read.

First, let's consider it from the point of view of sequential analysis. It is a question and answer sequence, of the type which occupied a lot of Sacks' analytic interest, and has become the main focus of analytic attention in the subsequent development of CA. Boden (1994) uses this example to demonstrate the ways in which the analysis of a universal sequential feature of talk can provide the opportunity for a comparative study of organizational phenomena. She notes first that the President is 'not simply curious about Bell's photocopying habits', but that, in common with meetings in many different settings, there is a 'parallel agenda', which embeds the relevant context of the organizational setting – its rules, procedures and hierarchies.

EXERCISE 12.1

Using categorization analytic tools, can you identify elements of a parallel agenda in this exchange? What categorial resources are employed in the response, and what do they imply about the hearer's understanding of the question? Be clear about the evidence for your analysis.

In this exchange, it is clear that neither speaker is talking about the 'number' of photocopies. Evidence for this is provided in the answer to the question: it is the *hearer's* interpretation that the question is in fact a query about another agenda, and the relevant response to 'How many' is in fact expressed not in terms of quantities, but in location categories – *where* the copies are is the point of the query. Furthermore, the response is extended to make reference to the 'way each of these things has been handled over the years'. The response provides not only a fact – where the photocopies are – but an account. Additionally, the account may be read as a 'moral' account in that it embeds an explanation of the speaker's actions, based on the principle that correct procedures have been followed.

In this little example, it is clear that the query is uttered, and heard, as about macro-systems, rather than micro-systems. Not photocopying, but the uses to which photocopies may be put is the relevant topic; and the account offered by Bell employs as a resource the way 'things ha[ve] been handled' – the systems employed by that organization – to provide a relevant response to that query, which in itself orients to systems in order to address yet another level of relevance, implicit in the response – that of the distribution, and hence the availability, of information. The 'formal', or 'macro' level of the organization provides not only a framework for action, but a framework for accounts of actions. In this way, it is possible to demonstrate empirically that speakers, in the ordinary pursuit of their daily tasks, orient to many levels of task at one and the same time, from the micro-processes of interaction (including the interpretation of the speaker's intention and moral accountability) to the macro-processes of information management. This suggests that in empirically grounded study, it is not necessary to separate structures and actions. Careful analysis of categorization demonstrates that the two are consequent on each other in the following ways:

- that topic treated as resource – the insight offered by Garfinkel – is an ordinary, unremarkable speakers' accomplishment;
- that the category-environment relevant for the two speakers was (demonstrably) not photocopying, but information; and
- that structure is renewed by speaker's actions through the shared understanding and agreement implicit in the exchange.

The nature of organizational rationality

Turning to the second of the classical problems of social science, what can we discover about the nature of rationality in this little fragment of talk? On the one hand, the task is likely to be a high level one: this is part of a working discussion between a President and his economic advisers. Surely, one might suppose or even hope, rational, goal-directed activity would be the hallmark of their discourse. What we see, however, is what might appear on the surface, to be 'noise' – the kind of mundane stuff which was traditionally excluded from the serious study of organizations as rational social units. Is there anything in this exchange which could contribute to the understanding of organizational rationality?

Rationality has typically been conceptualized in terms of the cognitive capacity of individuals to make decisions and pursue rational action based upon them. Traditional organization theory conceptualized the system of decision making (or non-decision making) in organizations as an epiphenomenon of the capacity of individuals in pursuing goals: 'the concept ... of independent and responsible individuals acting freely and reasonably is deeply held and central to social order' (Boden, 1994: 184). However, there is a paradox here. When researchers begin to look at decision making in practice, what becomes evident is that it is not a clear step-by-step movement, but rather, a complex, discontinuous process which involves not only the assembly of facts, but also the practical and sometimes moral accountability of the decision makers (the actors) themselves. Furthermore, in forming those practical and moral accounts of their own and others' actions, decision makers assume that they are one of a group 'of independent and responsible individuals acting freely and reasonably'. It was Sacks' insight to see that this basic assumption – that others' actions and intentions are orderly, observable and consequential – forms the basis for the possibility of both talk and social order.

In the first extract, the application of categorization analysis demonstrated how the talk about 'photocopies' generated, within the framework of a question and answer sequence, an account. Let's look at the next part of the meeting between the President and his aides:

```
 1                        (31.2)
                          ((much squeaking of chairs and some paper shuffling))
 2   JFK:    It's a big difference, the CEA projection for the (0.5) second quarter of
 3           [19]sixty three? Five-hundred and fifty-nine billion?
 4   Bell:   Right
 5   JFK:    While the Treasury projections for the same is five-hundred and eighty -
 6           one?
 7   Bell:   Yessir
 8                        (0.6)
 9   JFK:    'S a major -
                          (0.5)
10   Heller: Yeah it's a-
11   Bell:   Actually the uh (0.4) the difference of view as to what's gonna happen to
12           the economy (.) after the first of the year [ (     )]
13   Heller:                                            [ The detail of] that is indicated
14           on page two in (.) the economic outlook under 'Housing', 'Plant and
15           Equipment', 'Inventories',
16                        (1.4)
17   JFK:    (Hmmm)
18                        (0.3)
```

(Data extract from *The Kennedy White House Tapes*, quoted in Boden, 1994)

Here is another question and answer sequence. Notice, however, that first utterance (line 2) which starts off as a declarative sentence, but ends as a question, and is treated as such by Bell, whose reply 'right' (line 4) seems to confirm the fact of the amount. The second reply, however, constitutes an evaluation – the confirmation is upgraded from a simple 'right'. Now notice what happens next: for a second time, an account is produced, jointly, in this case, by two hearers / other persons at the meeting (lines 10–15).

EXERCISE 12.2

Examine how the answer is tied to the question. The account is formed in two stages, co-produced by the two hearers. How does the second part of the account tie to the first? What implications do these ties have for the procedural consequentiality of the exchange?

In developing an analytic answer to these questions, some issues regarding the nature of rationality can be addressed in a different sort of way. First, the hearing of the question – again – as requiring an account, suggests that, in the context of this meeting, the question is not straightforwardly directed towards a specific answer. That is, it is not heard as a search for facts, but as a search for reasons. Bell ties his response to the question through the category 'difference'. As in the first extract, he does not hear this as a question about quantities (how much is the difference), but as a request for an account. He offers his account by shifting the version of 'difference' from the categorization device 'quantity' to the device 'points of view' – the '*diff*erence of view'. Unlike quantities, reasons are contingent – they depend on local, rather than invariant, conditions. Speakers and hearers know this as well as philosophers, and respond accordingly with accounts.

Sacks' aim was to establish that there is a 'machinery of talk' which is invariant ('context-free'), but which also accounts for the capacity of speakers to respond to the local conditions of the production of talk (context-sensitive). In this little exchange, we can see how the question and answer sequence provides a context-free machinery which organizes the rest of the exchange (the co-produced account which both hearers observably orient to). For Sacks, rationality is to be found not in the content of the utterance, or in a measurable outcome, but in the procedures by which subsequent actions – in this case, reasons – are accountably produced by speakers and hearers. This approach to the analysis of rationality offers to the researcher of organizations a way of empirically demonstrating that rationality is achieved through the application of procedures which generate locally produced and relevant accounts (reasons) which underpin the process of decision making. Taking this analysis one step further, using categorization analysis, then provides an empirical method for testing the proposition that for the purposes of effective collaborative action, such as decision making, rational action may be defined as the consequential communication of shared knowledge within a field of relations. In order for the decision making action to come off, speakers must presume that other rational agents share the same knowledge of that consequentiality, so that agreement, and repair in the event of error, can take place. The 'negotiated order' approach of the interactionists, no less than the structuralist or functionalist accounts of organizational rationality, assume this process; the approach of categorization analysis problematizes it in order to reveal it (Silverman, 1975). The empirical study in Chapter 13 will demonstrate this line of reasoning in detail.

The nature of power and hierarchy in organizations

A third area of concern to social science which has been a matter of enquiry and debate in the evolution of organization theory is how power is exercised and distributed through the hierarchy of the organization. In recent years, applied organization theory has undergone a dramatic change in the way that hierarchy and power are conceived and described in terms of 'formal organization'. The postmodern, 'flat' organization, as opposed to the hierarchical (bureaucratic) organization of modernity and early organization theory has become the contemporary model for understanding practical action and organizational change. Such a philosophy, however, depends heavily on the traditional models of rationality which we looked at above: it assumes that individuals are rational actors, engaged in goal-directed action shaped by the supra-ordinate organizational structures. If that structure is 'non-hierarchical', it is assumed, then the individuals will accordingly behave differently. Is this new conception of organization any more viable than the former?

An alternative approach to this question lies in the comparative method, hinted at by Sacks, Schegloff and Jefferson (1974), which takes the speech exchange system as its basis for rule-guided action, and then examines empirically *how* the speech exchange system is employed to achieve local rationalities in the form of reasoned and agreed plans of action. The question then becomes: *how* are hierarchies employed as strategies in the achievement of rational plans of action?

Let's start considering this by examining another exchange from the same White House tape:

1 Fowler: We haven't considered this at any length, Mr President, over at the
2   Treasury. I *have* discussed it informally with Secretary *Dillon* an-
3   (1.1)
4   And I have the feeling that *some* consideration *ought* to be given to - *if*
5   you *are* going to move forward on that, of having (0.3) *some* kind of
6   (0.7) outside (0.3) uh (0.2) eco*nom*ist – (0.9) *organizational analysis*
7   before you (0.5) *jump*

8 Bell: You mean as – as *win*dow dressing? Or (.) for a *real* purpose,
9 Fowler: Well . . . a little of *both*.

(From *The Kennedy White House Tapes*, quoted in Boden, 1994)

Here is yet another question and answer sequence. In this case, it is Bell who interrupts his colleague with a question (line 8), and in this case the hearer (Fowler) replies to the question with a statement rather than an account: 'Well . . . a little of both' (line 9). Comparing this question and answer sequence within the same interactional context as the previous examples gives us a useful opportunity to ask some more questions of the data.

Perhaps the first analytic question to be addressed is what is to be compared? Two differences between this and the previous question and answer sequences above seem worthy of attention:

* the question is not asked by the President;
* the reply is not an account.

This question and answer sequence in fact forms part of a larger unit of talk, the first part of which is Fowler's statement about 'some consideration which ought to be given to-' (line 4) (the topic of the utterance). So, rather than initiating a topic, as in the previous sequences, in this position, the question and answer sequence serves to develop the topic.

EXERCISE 12.3

Observe the turbulence of the delivery in Fowler's first utterance (lines 1–7). Who is the addressee? What membership/location categorizations or category bound activities are implicated? Do they account for the hesitations in delivery? Can you identify how the interjected question (line 8) ties to the previous utterance?

What part does this question and answer sequence play in the overall context of the utterance? (If you have read Part III on narrative analysis, you might want to consider it as an element in a narrative structure.)

Heritage and Sefi (1992), in an empirical study of advice giving by health visitors to mothers, define 'advice', for the purposes of CA, within Sacks' conceptual framework of procedures, as:

sequences within which the [professional] describes, recommends, or otherwise forwards a preferred course of future action. Our concern was with sequences in which the [professionals] were engaged in activities having an essentially normative dimension which, we propose, is central to advice giving as an activity. (1992: 368)

Building on Heritage and Sefi's empirical findings, Silverman (1997a), in his study of advice giving in HIV counselling, found that 'delicate' matters raised in HIV advice giving, are subject to 'expressive caution', which involves both the management of sequence and the management of categories. 'Delicate matters', Silverman found, are not intrinsically normative; rather they are constituted in the interactional context in which they arise, observably to other speakers and hearers, by the form of the delivery: the presence of hesitancy, repair and orientation to versions of membership categories stand as *markers of delicate topics*.

Turning to our extract, the presence of marked hesitations, and the management of versions (especially in the production of the membership category 'outside (0.3) uh (0.2) eco*nomist* – (0.9)' and the shift to the category 'organizational analysis') suggest that what is being raised is a delicate matter. Clearly, this utterance is a delivery of a piece of advice (it is a 'sequence in which a professional describes, recommends, or forwards a preferred course of future action'); it is also marked by the presence of delicacy. The question arises, what occasions the delicacy which is signalled here by the speaker, and how can we understand the function of the question and answer sequence which follows?

Looking at the utterance through the lens of categorization analysis provides an additional analytic vector. Notice how, in the second part of the statement (lines 4–8) Fowler uses a location category to create an inside/outside distinction: he suggests 'having (0.3) *some* kind of (0.7) outside uh (0.2) eco*nomist* – (0.9) *organizational analysis*'. Notice also the category shift from 'economist' (this is a meeting of economic advisers) to 'organizational analysis'. From the evidence of Bell's question – 'you mean as . . . window dressing? Or (.) for a real purpose?' – what has been heard is a shift from one membership categorization device – 'economist' – to another – 'organizational analysis'. Bell's hearing places the potential of this shift within a wider shift of categorization devices – '*win*dow dressing' or '*real* purpose'. Furthermore, it reflects another possible delicate matter: the 'hierarchy' of decision making. First is the hierarchy of decision making in the context of an interaction between (professional) advisers who are subordinate to the person being advised; and, second, in the context of a democratic government, the dependence of all those involved on the public's receipt of its decisions and actions for future electoral success or failure. The delicacy lies in the way in which the nominated hearer ('Mr President') is invited to take up the idea through the introduction of a change of categories. Bell accomplishes this (a co-produced rationality) by taking the next turn, at line 8, in place of the addressee, with his own hearing of Fowler's 'consideration', thus elaborating the production of the advice in a way which the President is still in a position to accept or reject (as advisers should). In fact, the proposed plan of action, through this complex co-production, becomes a joint venture, rather than the product of a single decision maker or adviser.

This is an example of the management of delicacy in a very different location from those studied by Silverman. It poses a new set of questions concerning power and authority as matters of the practical and everyday management of interactional delicacy and rationality – for example, how will the President receive the advice? Economic advisers, no less than HIV counsellors, are faced with the problem of presenting their 'preferred course of future action' in such a way that it is taken up. There is also a delicate matter here about the uses (and abuses) of power – how do politicians 'manage' the impression of a change of economic policy?

The comparative method

The comparative method first proposed by Sacks, Schegloff and Jefferson in 1974 can be seen, even in this limited analysis, to have great power in the exploration of social realities of interest to organizational theory – such as rational decision making, and the management of authority and power – at the level of their production in situated interaction. Two methodological strategies important to CA have come into this analysis: 'across type' comparisons; and 'within type' comparisons (ten Have, 1998).

First, by comparing the sequential and categorization features of these data extracts, 'across types' with findings from very different settings, we have been able to demonstrate how the production of 'delicacy' and the management of 'advice formats' operate as context-free mechanisms which enable the construction of complex interactional strategies, which have very different procedural consequences in different settings.

Second, through the use of 'within type' comparison, we have begun to establish a hypothesis about the ways in which 'delicacy' and 'advice formats' may have procedural consequentiality at several levels of shared organizational reality – in the production of rational decision making, in the maintenance of the hierarchy of power and authority, and in the management of 'inside' and 'outside' matters. Further analysis of the larger dataset of White House tape-recordings would be necessary to establish whether these phenomena explored here are singular cases, or whether they are recurring features of executive decision making and political management. Such an extended analysis would involve several further steps:

1. The 'saturation' of the full data corpus. This could be achieved using the 'constant comparative method', developed by Glaser and Strauss (1967), to identify all relevant cases of 'delicacy', for example, in such meetings.
2. Further analysis of each case, demonstrating common features through analysis of each identified exchange.

3. Analysis of any 'deviant cases' would then complete the analysis. It would establish whether a genuinely recurring feature has been discovered; whether a further refinement of the hypothesis is necessary; or whether a new hypothesis is required to explain all the cases analysed. (For a full discussion of 'deviant case analysis' see Chapter 14).

By such a process of rigorous data search, comparative analysis of single cases, and elaboration of accumulating findings, using sequential analysis, where analytically relevant, categorization analysis, where analytically relevant, and combining the techniques where needed, a powerful and comprehensive ethnographic tool for the study of social reality in the setting of organizations becomes available to the researcher.

Summary

In this chapter, we have seen how detailed attention to the deployment of categories within categorization devices can repay the researcher with a rich perspective on some of the core questions of organization theory. Three principles of analysis were observed:

1. Saturation of the data.
2. Comparison of sequential and categorial features – the question and answer sequence, for example – across the dataset.
3. Comparison of sequential and categorial features with interactions in other settings – the production of 'delicate matters'.

In the chapter which follows, an extended analysis of a single case will show another approach to the analytic problems introduced in this chapter. Here we have used situated talk of a kind common to organizations – the 'meeting'. In the next chapter, we will study another kind of common organizational object – a 'report'. In the extracts just examined, the 'speakers' and 'hearers' were manifest in the persons of JFK, Bell and Fowler. In the case of a 'report', as we shall find, the 'hearers' occupy a different, but no less powerful place in the production of the 'utterance'. We will also compare the ways in which the production of location categories 'inside' and 'outside' are brought to bear in the production of organizational rationality.

  CA does not study 'organizations' as formal entities; in that sense, it falls into the class of studies which take a view on 'social organization'. However, because of the nature of its theoretical basis – the procedural rationality of individual actors in the conduct of their talk – it does not simply subsume the organization under the rubric of 'informal organization'. It offers an alternative route to the study of organization, as a negotiated order which is subject to rules of rationality which are not the actions of individuals.

Recommended reading

Boden, D. (1994) *The business of talk: organizations in action*. Cambridge: Polity Press.
This provides a comprehensive introduction and discussion of the application of conversation analysis to the study of organizations. Its focus is on sequential analysis, but the basic principles for any CA study are there.

Drew, P. and Heritage, J. (eds) (1992) *Talk at work: interaction in institutional settings*. Cambridge: Cambridge University Press.
A useful collection of a variety of studies of interaction in the workplace.

Have, P. ten (1998) *Doing conversation analysis: a practical guide*. London: Sage.
The study of 'talk at work' will raise issues relevant to both categorization and sequential analysis. Use this introduction to conversation analysis to widen and develop your analysis.

13

A Case Study

CONTENTS

Organizational actors are, I suspect, of two minds: on the one hand they subscribe to the Weberian rational/technical distinction for their actions, and yet simultaneously they know that those actions only 'work' if they are fine-tuned and adjusted in a local manner. (Boden, 1994: 192)

In this chapter I propose to examine this statement of Boden's 'suspicions', using categorization analysis, to see whether they are well grounded in naturally occurring organizational data. The three primary areas of concern addressed in the previous chapter will be investigated:

- *The relationship between macro and micro levels of phenomena and analysis;*
- *The nature of rationality;*
- *The nature of organizational hierarchy and the exercise of power.*

Getting started

One of the conceptual phenomena of organizational life which has been of particular interest to its theorists is that of 'organizational boundaries'.

This interest derives from the systemic origins of the early theories of organization, in which the organization was conceptualized as an entity, with an internal structure, characterized by relations *within* the organization, as well as by relations between the organization and the 'outside' world. Unlike institutions, which may be represented in a multitude of places or contexts, the organization was conceived as having a core identity, in the form of its 'formal organization', or its 'primary task'; its problem was to align the interests of its 'workers' with the interests of the organization such that coherent 'management' might ensure productivity. Some theories sought to tackle that problem from the perspective of the overall structure of the organization; others sought to address it through attention to the needs and motives of 'workers'.

The following case study is part of a larger piece of research in which the phenomenon of 'organizational boundaries' was investigated empirically, using categorization analysis as the primary analytic method. Part of that study has already been presented in Part II as the analysis of the report on DW. The 'troubles last term' with which DW was associated are the subject of this report on 'an incident leading to injury', written by a staff member of the College.

As an analytical psychologist with a background in the 'group relations' school of organizational theory, I had become dissatisfied with the way in which the concept of 'boundary' was employed at the level of practice informed by group relations theory. How is one to observe boundary phenomena? Once introduced to categorization analysis, I was struck with its potential as a method for deriving empirically grounded observations on the nature of boundaries, and of boundary transgressions, in organizations. On the basis of a trial analysis of some documents, I started the research with the very general question:

> How are membership categorization devices used to generate and maintain 'boundaries' in multi-person settings. How relatively enduring are they? Does the management of membership categorization devices show evidence of 'narrative-in-the-work' (Silverman, 1985): a tendency to create orderly, relatively enduring 'stories' about perceived events, over time?

In order to address these questions, I used documents from an inner city Further Education College, in London, to which I had been given access by its Principal, who was new to the post. The next problem was to decide how to choose from the very large corpus of data which I had, what documents to study. To begin, I employed a version of the constant comparative method, developed by Glaser and Strauss (1967), in an initial analysis of one set of documents, by means of simple manual counting of the categories-in-use. This took quite a bit of time, but since the documents were not scanable, using a computer was not an option. (For discussion of the use of computer-aided methods see Part V.) This first analysis generated what I would call a 'categorial map' of the college. This map was generated by discovering the language which was actually in use, and it provided the basis for the analysis of membership categorization which followed: not *my* reading of the categories I found, but the shared field of categories-in-use as displayed by the community of speakers in the college provided the basis for understanding how situated actions were understood and managed by the interactants.

Some basic elements of this shared field of categories-in-use emerged, and these became the focus for the second phase of the analysis, which drew on the comparative method proposed by Sacks, Schegloff and Jefferson (1974): the comparison of turn-taking systems at different sites of interaction. In this case, the comparison was to analyse in different reports, the ways in which a membership categorization device – 'The Family Tree' (the term used by the college staff) – was employed by the members of this college to do the business of managing boundaries.

From this analysis, three features relevant to the discussion of boundaries emerged:

1. The use of 'standard relational pairs' to identify the structure of the 'Family Tree'. Among the important ones identified in the first analysis were: Management/staff; teaching staff/support staff; Staff/Student.
2. The systematic use of category bound activities to describe the relevance of activities within the MCD 'Family Tree'. An important set of activities turned out to be 'care' – the delivery of student benefits such as teaching and pastoral support; and 'control' – the management of student behaviour.
3. The mapping of location (and time) categories which were employed to define legitimate activities and loci of responsibility (within 'Family Tree'); and illegitimate, or deviant, activities and loci of responsibility. (Some of these have already been discussed in the example in Part II.)

The exterior doors, halls and cafeteria proved to be important sites of 'control' activities and these were reported in the 'Logbook' – a bound notebook in which the 'Duty Principal' recorded events during a day or evening shift. The 'Logbook' was instituted by the new Principal on her arrival in the College, along with a new role – that of 'Duty Principal', a rotating role taken up by senior staff members in turn. It was the function of the Duty Principal to cover for the Principal in any out-of-routine incidents which might arise in the course of a day (or evening). Each rota-shift was recorded in the 'Logbook', along with a report of any incidents which might have occurred, to be noted by the Principal herself, and other rota'd Duty Principals. Most reports concern 'out-of-order' events which occurred in the corridors and entrances, involving activities of 'care' and 'control' on the part of staff. The Logbook was intended to function as a means of communication between Duty-rota staff and the Principal. The notes were handwritten, and I soon found that they were linked by a kind of 'talk': handwritten notes in the margins constituted a commentary on several ongoing stories. They were mainly of a disciplinary nature. The reports were 'domestic' – that is, they were designed for internal consumption. They did not look to the world outside the College, or to an outside observer (like me). As such they provided a perfect sample of 'naturally occurring data'. They seemed an excellent site in which to investigate how boundaries might be generated and maintained in everyday organizational practice.

In the data analysis that follows, I will explore in detail how, in 'A report on an incident leading to injury', a laboratory technician in an inner city College of Further Education employs the categorization device 'I'. The writer is not a Duty Principal, and indeed, is one of the support staff. His report was loosely inserted into the 'Logbook', and was analysed as a *'deviant case'*. In comparison to the reports which were written into the bound notebook by the Duty Principals, the question which was being asked of the data, was: Why was this report found in the Logbook? As you will discover, the analysis is detailed. It is a principle of CA that the validity of its theory of the rule-governed recognizability of languaged action rests on the observability of those rules in action not only as an everyday matter, but as a scientific matter as well. Saturation of the data for every possible action which might be observable, and therefore relevant, is the core analytic task.

The analysis: 'A report of incident leading to injury'

Report of incident leading to injury.
To JC Technician grade 5.
Welding Shop. To RS Senior technician.

On Tuesday 26th Nov I was taking lunch at 2.5 p.m. this was due to a backlog of metal cutting. Therefore I worked until [sic] 2.00 p.m. before breaking for lunch. (Cutbacks in staff.)
    At approximately 2.5 p.m. I observed an argument taking place at the entrance to the refectory.

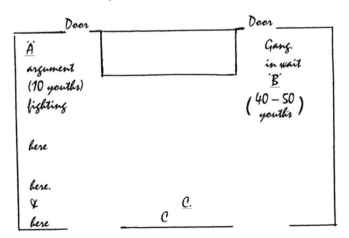

The argument developed into a fight with a girl being slapped on the face. Then a gang of youths who in my opinnion [sic] had been waiting for just such an incident attacked about 10 youths at position 'A'. I was in position 'C' and observed everything from start to finish.

I went to M [Refectory Supervisor] Told her to call security as there was a full scale riot developing I then ran to three of our Students (Welding Shop) and took them away from the scene of the fighting as I considered them to be in danger.

The fighting then erupted all down the stairway to the main entrance (B Bdg). I followed the combatants downstairs with the intention of giving first aid to anyone injured as I am a qualified first aider.

When I reached the main entrance, R [Security] said he was going to lock the front door and call the police. I agreed. He and I watched the fighting which then spread to B Rd. I then went to the admin office to observe the fighting, still with a view of pinpointing any injuries requiring first aid.

To my horror, the Principal appeared in the middle of the crowd. I considered her to be in grave danger of assault. I immediately attempted to go to her assistance. I left the building by the main entrance. I pushed my way toward the Principal. As I did so there was a large youth, defending himself against a virtual pack of youths by Karate Kicking. As I passed him, an attacker threw himself sideways and I received the full force of a kick to the Chest. I recovered and carried on towards the Principal. Shortly after, the Police arrived. We returned to the building.

Only then, did I notice a sharp pain in my chest some time later. (15 minutes) I was examined by Peter Morris. He addvised [sic] me to go to hospital. I did, and after examination, was told I had two or more broken ribs. There is no treatment for this. I was given very strong painkillers. and told to stay off work. for a couple of weeks. with no exertion. Report from Hospital and my G.P. following on written request.

First let us consider the heading of the report:

1. Above the author's heading, there is a marginalized note: 'FOR INFO'. I make the assumption that this note was added by the person who put the report in the 'Logbook': a *performative act* (Austin, 1961, 1962) which says to the community of readers (and categorizers) of 'Logbook': 'Look'.
2. Embedded within the title, the categorization of the 'incident' as 'leading to injury' invites the reader to expect a story, possibly about 'care' issues.
3. The setting out of the next three lines leads to an ambiguity about who is addressed which it takes a moment to decipher. This would not, perhaps, have confused the actual addressee, RS to whom the names

were already known; but it does suggest that the author is an inexperienced report writer. This makes it notable that he chooses this form of communicating, and that he shows his familiarity with the conventions of report writing. These conventions provide a cultural context for his actions.

4. Also included within this naming of report-author and addressee are their role-names – their formal designations within 'Family Tree': 'Technician grade 5. Welding Shop' and 'Senior technician'. Given that this appears to be a report from a subordinate, known to his manager, what is the function of these designations? Are there other potential readers of this reporting?

This observation suggests an analytic frame for an interpretative explanation: that his report is directed at someone else who will 'see' him, in the sense that Sacks raises the issue: 'it's not merely that the observer is seeing by reference to some category, but that one being observed sees what the observer is, and is seeing' (1992a: 87–8). Looking closely at the text which follows, is it possible to see how inferences about 'one being observed see[ing] what the observer is, and is seeing' are being provided for in these preparatory sentences?

The beginning of the report

Some features of reporting already familiar from the analysis of other 'Logbook' reports are immediately apparent; but there are some notable differences.

First, time and location categories locate the author at what we may assume will be the beginning of the story: (It is '2.5 p.m.'). (This report convention is frequently used in previously analysed reports.) That the location is 'the Refectory' may alter expectations about the report to come, since 'the Refectory' has been identified, by analysis of other reports in the Logbook, as a frequent locus of 'control' matters. This report begins with a location-categorization which has 'evidential' implications. Analysis of previous reports has already indicated that it is the production of such 'evidence' which will provide for subsequent inferences to be made from an introductory locating preface. In *Philosophical Investigations*, Wittgenstein remarks: 'In a court of law, the mere assurance "I know . . ." on the part of a witness would convince no one. It must be shown that he was in a position to know' (1953 / 1968: para. 57).

As a report, this document has qualities of providing for charges (as in police reporting – see Cicourel, 1968) which might be made. But what kinds of charges are being anticipated? And to whom would they be directed?

Second, in contrast with other reports in the 'Logbook', this author provides an account of his presence. He attends to his right to be there (time and place location categories) with reasons ('due to backlog of metal cutting. Therefore I worked untill [sic] 2.00 p.m. before breaking for lunch'). Here is a version of Sacks' 'one being observed' providing for inferences on the basis of 'what the observer is, and is seeing'. To do so, given his non-usual role as 'report writer', he accounts for himself with a category-description which places his activities in their positioned relation to the hierarchy of 'Family Tree', and allows for inferences both for his 'reasonableness' and his moral accountability. Finally there is the parenthesized interjection: ('Cutbacks in staff'). Now we may have to add to the possible readings of the story to come: is the incident being reported one of 'care', of 'control' or, possibly, of 'complaint'?

Third, completing this locating introduction is a map drawn by the reporter, which demonstrates what this observer sees. Now, the category description of the trouble is augmented see diagram p. 157: 'argument' qualified by ('10 youth's [sic] fighting'); and 'gang in wait' (40–50 youth's) tell us of a much more serious trouble, worthy of the title, and providing for an extended story to come. Placing himself in the picture as observer, he authorizes himself as the valid recorder of the incident: as we learn in the paragraph to come, 'I was in position 'C' and observed everything from start to finish.' Then, 'The argument developed into a fight with a girl being slapped on the face.' The nature of the trouble is now upgraded from 'argument' to 'fight', on the basis of the evidence 'A girl being slapped in the face' (something only one who 'observed everything from start to finish' could report). The picture is completed with the characterization of 'a gang of youth's [sic]'.

JC has been at great pains in this report to establish himself, to any observer (reader), as the sort of observer who can be trusted, through his introductory self-categorization. He has located himself appropriately within 'Family Tree' and demonstrated his reasonableness as a reporter. With this mapping, he places himself at the centre of the story as observer. He has in his view, his audience (the reader); the observed (the subjects of the report); and himself, as the observed, in relation to the higher-placed readers of the report, for whom it may be intended. It is still not clear who they might be; but the character of his introduction provides for the inference that 'for each [participant] there is an order of relevance which provides for the other as being an observable, and . . . the order of relevance of each was available to the other' (Sacks, 1992a: 88). The introduction to the report provides for JC being a possible, and credible, observer in terms of his positioning within 'Family Tree' and also locates his, and the readers', gaze in a marked way. Readers may now make the inference that he is a reliable witness.

The story continues: first

The body of the report employs category collections already discovered in 'official' Logbook entries which are primarily concerned with 'public areas'. First there are the location categories which define the relevant (previously analysed) description of the 'College', (e.g., 'entrance to the refectory', 'all down the stairway', 'to the main entrance', 'then spread to B Rd'). The membership categories, 'Management' (refectory Supervisor) – 'Staff ('called security') – 'Student' ('I then ran to three of our students (Welding Shop)') are invoked along with related activities which describe 'Family Tree'.

At the same time, the description of the trouble escalates from 'an argument' to 'fighting' to 'a full scale riot'. The subsequent paragraph confirms this characterization ('fighting then erupted all down the stairway'). Having assembled the categorization device 'Violence' the report writer discharges the 'control' functions associated with violence to 'Security', and further secures, and upgrades, his involvement within the rules of application of 'care' with the self-categorization 'qualified first aider'. This characterization, carefully assembled through an accumulating representation of 'facts', now provides for a highly relevant story. Relevance – and by implication, visibility – are bid for by this management of the categories. Let us see how this is accomplished.

Here is the whole sentence: 'I followed the combatants downstairs with the intention of giving first aid to anyone injured as I am a qualified first aider'. With this, the reporter justifies his presence as a 'caring' observer.

By thus relocating his gaze, the writer implicates the reader in the activity of 'care', permitting us to see – what? What is observed is a 'control' matter, but the report writer manages the gaze in such a way that the reader sees him in relation to the troubles as 'carer'. A possible charge of 'voyeurism' (he is just looking at a scene of violence, out of curiosity or excitement) is anticipated and rebutted. Through this realignment of his position of legitimate observer, he provides an accountable reason for being there. There appears to be a connection between how the rules of application of the device 'Family Tree', and those of 'reporting' provide for a reflexive system of inferences – that is, a system in which the inferences being made by the writer are displayed with 'intention', in order to present a constraining set of possible inferences before the reader – an 'I' addressing a 'you'. The problematic presented in this reporting appears to be to decide which author (that is, which version of 'I') and which reader (the nominated reader of the report, or some other reader) is in play at any given moment in the text.

> When I reached the main entrance, R [Security] said he was going to lock the front door and call the police. I agreed. He and I watched the fighting which then spread to B Rd. I then went to the admin office to observe the fighting, still with a view of pinpointing any injuries requiring first aid.

Familiar location categorizations describe the locus of the action. The correctness of JC's actions – as a 'qualified first aider' – is reaffirmed, and along with it, the inference that this is not the report of a 'voyeur'. Now the author continues his reporting with 'I agreed', and it again becomes (analytically) relevant to raise the question: Which 'I' is this? Is it the 'I' of 'Technician Grade 5'? Or the voice of JC? Within the frame of the activity 'reporting', it now becomes problematic whether his 'I agreed' is relevant or necessary; for within the context of 'Family Tree', he has already discharged his duties, having reported the matter, referring it out to the boundaries of 'College', to 'Security'. His continuing presence as reporter is in need of further explication in order to account for its reasonableness as an official, or serious (Silverman, 1975) and moral account (an account not motivated by voyeuristic curiosity, such that it might count as gossip, for example). It is, therefore, important for the reader to know that he is 'qualified'.

He continues: 'He and I watched the fighting which then spread to B Rd. I then went to the admin office to observe the fighting.' Again, the readers' gaze is interrupted by the repositioning of the reporter within his second self-ascribed participation-role: 'still with a view to pinpointing any injuries requiring first aid'. He is there, again, the 'I' as 'qualified first aider', engaged in a relevant activity for first aiders, 'looking for injured persons'.

So he is looking to those (bona fide) members of 'Family Tree', as 'one being observed', and who 'sees what the observer sees, and is seeing'. He not only sees as 'one being observed', but within the constraints of the activity, 'reporting', he employs strategies to be seen within certain categories. By this means he earns (moral) entitlement to go on, as reporter, being seen as having 'reasons', being recognized as having the right to continue his story, which we readers know is not yet complete, as it concerns an 'Injury to JC' which has not yet appeared in the story. Now it begins to be apparent what kind of problem it is to determine what kind of activity one is in at any moment in the course of ongoing interaction.

The story continues: then

> To my horror, the Principal appeared in the middle of the crowd. I considered her to be in grave danger of assault. I immediately attempted to go to her assistance. I left the building by the main entrance.

Now located within the gaze of a 'qualified first aider', the first phrase of the ensuing paragraph alerts us to attend to the next phase of the story: 'To my horror' implies a scene which might include activities relevant to the category 'first aider' – and to the readers' now thoroughly aroused interest is added the beginning of a story-within-a-story.

> I immediately attempted to go to her assistance.

Observably, this is the 'first aider'-I 'who left the building by the main entrance'.

I pushed my way toward the Principal. As I did so there was a large youth, defending himself against a virtual pack of youths by Karate Kicking. As I passed him, an attacker threw himself sideways and I received the full force of a kick to the Chest.

Finally, we reach the climax of the story, prefigured in the title – the 'injury'. There are several points to note about this description.

In the phrase, 'a kick to the Chest', the preposition 'to' is chosen, where 'in' might have been a more expectable choice. Echoes of the police report, with its evidential requirements, appear once more. In addition, the 'to' emphasizes the intention, rather than the effect of the act, thereby establishing its accountability in the context in which it occurred. The choice of the preposition therefore deepens the categorization work of locating the reported activity within the device violence, and implicates three relevant membership categories:

1. the membership category 'police' (who may be possible readers of the report?);
2. the membership category 'injured person' who can now be seen to be one who is injured in combat, and in the line of duty;
3. the 'I' of the reporter-observer, who has now been transformed into a participant in the trouble, in fact, the 'injury' of the title.

The point of view of the description has moved from that of a legitimate observer, whose 'I' voiced itself through a participant-role, into the voice of an 'I' who is an experiential participant, and who is the *subject* of the category 'injured person'. How does this 'I' locate the eye of the observer-reader, who now sees the observed as one of the parties to the trouble. Taken as a collection, the 'I' could be taken to include several possible incumbents: the 'Technician grade 5' to whom we are first introduced; 'qualified first aider', who earns his rights to carry on with the story; and the 'injured person' of the final segment of the story.

This reporter seems to want to anticipate every potential objection through a display of the completeness, and the seriousness, of his motives. There could be a possible interpretation of his motives – say, for example, that this is one of those injuries people might think up after an accident in order to get away with something. Such a set of inferences – about possible charges to be weighed by the evidence – would have implications for the relation between the author and the intended recipients, both nominated and indirect, of the report.

Here we find the production of a 'moral career' (Goffman, 1974), produced through the management of facts, embedded within the categorial practices of 'Family Tree', within the domain of 'College'. It is the moral career of an injured person, who is the author himself. Presuming that the 'report from Hospital and my G.P.' would provide sufficient evidence of injury to justify time off work, several questions arise: What is the overall function of this report, with its embedded production of a moral career? Who requested it (if anyone)? To whom is it directed?

Complaining

Sacks, Schegloff and Jefferson (1974) showed that the inferences that can be made from, or about, activities within a given speech event derive from the overall structure of the event. Take this document, 'A report on an incident leading to injury' as such an event; and take it as an activity generally familiar to ordinary members of society as the activity of reporting. The document shows that features of the organization of the activity of reporting were available even to a perhaps not-very-experienced report writer.

If the overall structuring activity of this document is reporting, one of the things discovered, through the analysis of 'Logbook', is a characteristic of reporting: as events are reported, activities are constructed – troubles, for example – in a way which makes them recognizable, and allows inferences to be made from them. It appears that the placing of any other activity within the overall activity of reporting is embedded in the practices employed by report writers, who are positioned, that is, constrained, and who employ practices relative to that positioning. Levinson describes these as strategies: 'optimal or self-maximizing patterns of behaviour available to participants in particular roles, under the constraints of the relevant activity' (1992: 100).

Taking just one category – the category 'I' – how does its play in the context of the overall structure of this reporting help to locate, analytically, what activities are in play at any given point in the text? In the course of the 'Report on an incident leading to injury', there was progressive development of the versions of 'I' in the course of the text.

1. An 'I' who, strategically placed (his map), was in a position to see 'everything from start to finish'. This 'I' would seem to be linked to the activity 'observing'. However, as noted by Wittgenstein, it is not enough for the witness to 'know'; it must also be the case that he was in a position to know, and that this should be observable. So, the positioning of this observing 'I', with its reflexive property, observable-by-others, embedded within this account, provides for the activity of 'witnessing'.

2. An observing 'I' who, having located himself as an incumbent of a recognized participant-role – that of 'Technician grade 5' – within 'Family Tree', can therefore provide, within the activity 'reporting', for the possibility of the participant-role, credible witness. Such an 'I' would be believed, for example, in his 'opinion [that the gang of youths] had been waiting for just such an incident'.

3. An 'I' who, as self-nominated incumbent of the participant-role 'first aider', has displayed, by the use of 'qualified', his right to make such

an observation outside the 'official' incumbency of 'Family Tree'. This shift of rules of application of the category 'I' provided for the observer's continuing presence, within a revised version of his participation role, within the activity of 'care', as opposed to 'control' – an activity category bound to the participation-role 'Security guards'. It also may provide for his implicit defence in anticipation of possible interpretation of his motives as 'curiosity', and the downgrading of his activity of 'reporting' to 'gossip'.

4. An 'I' who, as a consequence of his participation as 'injured person', has earned both rights to reasons and rights to 'care'. This 'I' was produced at the point where the rules of application of the category 'I' shifted from those relevant to a 'first aider' to those of an 'injured person'; who, having left by the main entrance, was no longer defined by, and constrained by, the rules of the membership category 'carer', but by the rules of 'injured person' (one who has rights to be cared for).

By what means might it now be possible to discover how these shifts in the rules of applications of the membership category collection 'I' might operate as 'strategies' in relation to their relevant activities? Sacks proposes that 'it's not enough to make a glance an action . . . it's not merely that the observer is seeing by reference to some category, but that one being observed sees what the observer is seeing' (1992a: 87–8). This gives some analytic purchase on how the activities implicated in this reporting could be understood. They can be seen as both constraining and enabling the possible relations between the categories which form the collection of the reporter-'I', and the recipients of his activity of reporting. The problem of identifying the relevant activities within which acts can be interpreted, is, I would argue, like any problem of context, finally one of the production of any context (or activity) by an 'I' to nominate and thereby get the attention, the participation, and even the concurrence of an observer. So it may be that through an analysis of what activities observing 'I's implicate, it is possible to get closer to discovering which observer is being addressed, and for what purpose.

Findings

Returning to some of the basic questions of organizational theory, discussed in the previous chapters, what contribution has this analysis to offer to the development of thinking on the questions of the 'macro/micro' debate; the nature of rationality; and the nature of power and hierarchy? Discovering, through fine grained analysis of the ordering of interpretative procedures observable in this report, the complex and multidimensional field of relations in which JC wrote his report, and the uses he has made of his (shared) knowledge of this field, there are some more general observations which can now be made.

1. *'Organizational actors are, I suspect, of two minds: on the one hand they subscribe to the Weberian rational/technical distinction for their actions, and yet simultaneously they know that those actions only 'work' if they are fine-tuned and adjusted in a local manner' (Boden, 1994: 192).*

In the light of this analysis, the problematic of 'formal' and 'social' organization can be reframed on the basis of empirical evidence to include both the systems (macro) perspective and interactional (micro) foundation of analysis. It shows:

- That organizations are *systems of relations*, within which the speaking subject provides the necessary but not sufficient condition for the possibility of rational action. It is evident that JC (successfully) relies both on his local knowledge of 'Family Tree', expressed in terms of location categories, membership categories, category bound activities, (the level of 'social organization') *and* on his knowledge of the 'rational/technical' level of 'formal organization' (how to write a report, for example) in order to construct and present his complaint in a form that it will be taken seriously.
- That the boundary of the organization as an 'entity' – what belongs inside, and what outside – is not fixed; but it's reality is nevertheless routinely invoked as self-evident by the members of the organization. Boundaries may be thought of as a system of practices which are co-sustained by speaking subjects.
- It therefore can be demonstrated through this analysis that the 'micro' and 'macro' levels posited by organizational theory are constructs which can only be separated in theory. In practice, they are members' resources, and are mutually co-sustaining.

2. The nature of rationality

Sacks' methodological innovation was to start with an observed social interaction, as 'social fact', and to try to find what kind of conditions might be required to produce that observed interaction. Commenting on Sacks' insistence on inductive analysis, Schegloff comments:

> how shall we as analysts describe the terms in which participants analyse and understand, from moment to moment, the contexted character of their lives, their current and prospective circumstances, the present moment, – how to do this when the very terms of that understanding can be transformed by a next bit of conduct by one of the participants. (Sacks, 1992a: xxviii)

Here Schegloff problematizes one of the key concepts of Sacks' work – its insistence on inductive logic both as a 'members' accomplishment, and an analytic method – its focus on single case, micro analysis as the key to understanding the ordering of interpretative procedures which underpin coherent social action and form. What contribution could this have to make to the generalized theory of rationality sought by organization theory?

On the basis of this analysis, it is possible to demonstrate that if organizational rationality does not proceed in the form of the step-by-step logic sought by early organization theory, it is, none the less, orderly. Through close analysis of his accomplished application of interpretative procedures, JC's report reveals a field of relations which underpins both the local, and the formal rationalities available to the members of the organization. His mastery of this field of relations relies on what Coulter (1979) calls '*presuppositional information*':

> We rely on presuppositional information for the adequate understanding of much ordinary talk. On occasion, it is not only what is said but where, when and by whom it is said which provides members with the basic data for presupposition-analysis as hearers in mundane situations. (Coulter, 1979: 51)

Presupposition-analysis was employed by JC to position himself in such a way as to be a believable witness; to write his 'report' in a fashion which would attract the interest of hearer's unknown, but recognizable in terms of 'Family Tree'; and to launch his 'complaint' on an uncertain, but ultimately successful trajectory into the hearing of senior management. It is his mastery of presuppositional information, which leads to the inclusion of his report in Logbook, which is an:

> '**upshot**': – the consequence of an action in which the agent's intentions played an important, but not determining, role.

The author of the report intended to communicate his complaint; he did not intend that this document end up in the 'Logbook' (about whose existence he was probably not even aware). Most of our actions are directed towards an uncertain goal, their outcomes unpredictable and their effects unknown. To have any chance of success they must be fine-tuned to the potential recipient, whether direct (as in a conversation) or indirect, such as in writing or broadcasting. We have seen how, across several sites of interaction, basic principles of the application of categorization devices are employed to deliver messages in which speakers and hearers take into account the indeterminacy of the outcome.

The term 'upshot' is commonly employed in ethnomethodological literature. It describes an alternative understanding of the kinds of 'facts' which can be described as 'outcomes' of social processes. Through the application of CA, the empirical study of this observable field of shared understanding reveals *how* a common stock of presuppositional knowledge makes rational action possible. Such rational action is not the product of 'intersubjective states of mind' claimed by interactionists. Neither, however, is it the objective process sought by early organization theorists – that is, independent of the actions and intentions of subjects. It is shown to be orderly, guided by rules, but indeterminate. JC could only launch his report into the field of relations 'Family Tree', not knowing what its outcome would be.

CA cannot predict outcomes; but it can uncover the fundamental rule-guided orderliness which underpins rational action.

3. *The nature of organizational hierarchy and power:*

> The important thing is not to attempt some kind of deduction of power starting from its centre and aimed at the degree to which it reproduces itself down to and including the most molecular elements of society. One must rather conduct an *ascending* analysis of power, starting, that is, from its infinitesimal mechanisms. (Lukes, 1986: 284)

The analysis of JC's report shows the robustness which is possible when following Lukes' methodological proposal. By analysing the ways in which JC attends to matters of hierarchy, from the perspective of its 'infinitesimal mechanisms', it is possible to demonstrate empirically the ways in which power manifests itself through that hierarchy. By taking the upshot of this report writing – the inclusion of its complaint at such a high level of visibility to senior management – as a social fact, and by analysing the conditions of its production, it is possible to show, in fine-grained detail, *how* the distribution of power, through the local practices of 'Family Tree', is attended to, and successfully managed, by those at the 'bottom' of the hierarchy.

From the perspective of power and hierarchy, the analysis of JC's report is an example of 'deviant case analysis'. All the other reports contained in the Logbook were handwritten notes, written by 'ratified participants' (Levinson, 1988): the nominated Duty Principals entitled to use the Logbook as a means of communication. The 'Report on an injury' constitutes a deviant example within this corpus of data. Through the close analysis of JC's report, we have been able to see how his appeal both to local practices of 'College' shares common ground with other members of 'College'; and how the rational/technical distinction – observable in JC's use of the formal conventions of report writing – is employed by JC to launch his message. We are able to observe, in fine detail, how he employs this knowledge to create his own opportunity to influence opinion and to exercise power. Its upshot is the inclusion of his report in the Logbook. Categorization analysis can be seen to offer a practical and robust method by which the infinitesimal mechanisms of power can be explored empirically.

Summary

In this chapter, CA was applied to a longer segment of data, which itself formed part of a much larger analysis (Lepper, 1994). Some of the benefits of working with a larger corpus of data, and some of the problems of method which arise, have been addressed. It shows the ways in which deviant case analysis can be used to validate findings, and to deepen analysis.

The basic rules of **analytic induction** have been applied, and the findings examined. This analysis was possible, however, only in the context of a larger piece of work (Lepper, 1994). It observed the principle of **saturation** (Foucault, 1991) – the crossing and re-crossing of the data in the conditions of its production. Its analytic force rests on the extent to which it forms part of a continuous process of comparative analysis which addresses the questions raised in greater and greater detail, and clarity.

Recommended reading

Boden, D. and Zimmerman, D.H. (eds) (1991) *Talk and social structure: studies in ethnomethodology and conversation analysis.* Cambridge: Polity Press.
Another collection of empirical studies of institutional interaction which will help the novice researcher explore how methods are applied and may generate ideas for new projects.

Czarniawska, B. (1998) *A narrative approach to organization studies.* London: Sage.
An introduction to the analysis of organizational narratives. Categorization analysis is a particularly useful tool in the analysis of narratives (see also, Part III of this volume).

Drew, P. and Wootton, A.J. (eds) (1988) *Erving Goffman: exploring the interaction order.* Cambridge: Polity Press.
This collection of articles contains a variety of important and useful contributions on theory and method which address issues of the 'interaction order', which may give a useful steer to any researcher seeking to apply categorization analytic techniques to organization studies.

Lepper, G. (1995) 'The uses of "formal organization" as an institutional resource', *Studies in Organizations, Cultures and Societies,* 1: 189–207.
An empirical study of the way in which the concept of the 'formal organization' is used as a members' resource.

Part V

THE PRACTICE OF RESEARCH

14

Reliability and Validity

CONTENTS

Throughout this introduction to the practice of categorization analysis, I have considered issues of method. In this chapter, I want to focus specifically on issues of reliability and validity as they relate to good practice. First, Sacks' original thinking on the scientific process, and his placing of his own work within the scope of scientific method, will be reviewed, in order to introduce his argument for the proof procedures he proposed for conversation analysis. Then, the specific issues arising from rigorous attention to validity will be discussed, ending with an example of the way in which attention to validity must be built into each stage of the process.

CA and science

An important feature of any scientific procedure involves the two important concepts of *reliability* and *validity*. Both refer to the objective nature of the scientific process. To meet the criteria of reliability, the findings must be shown to be independent of the circumstances of the research (Kirk and Miller, 1986: 20). That is, the researcher must show that the research process would yield the same result if it were repeated. In order to claim validity, the researcher must show that what is being described is accurately 'named' – that is, that the research process has accurately represented a phenomenon which is recognizable to the scientific community being addressed. Two kinds of error may occur (Kirk and Miller, 1986: 29–30):

- Type I error: believing a statement to be true when it is not (in statistical terms, this means incorrectly rejecting the 'null' hypothesis);
- Type II error: rejecting a statement which is in fact true (incorrectly supporting the 'null' hypothesis).

The quantitative sciences rely on statistical tests to validate research findings and claim 'objectivity'. In some traditions of qualitative social science research, however, issues of validity and reliability have been treated as irrelevant to the task of interpreting social data, which is seen as essentially 'subjective' in nature.

Although Sacks held that rigid adherence to the quantification of social facts distorted the object under study, nevertheless it should have become clear by now that he was very concerned with the objectivity of the new science he wished to create. He started out with an argument for the possibility of a 'natural observational science' of sociology by separating the scientific process into two aspects: the account of the findings; and the account of the scientists' methods in arriving at the findings (the principle of replicability). The underlying principle of scientific method, Sacks argued, involved this two-part strategy, by which findings are not simply asserted, but are reported in such a way that anyone with the requisite technical knowledge can reproduce them, and generate the same findings.

> So, Sacks concluded, from the fact of the existence of natural science there is evidence that it is possible to have (1) accounts of human courses of actions (2) which are not neurophysiological, biological, etc., (3) which are reproducible and hence scientifically adequate, (4) the latter two features amounting to the finding that they may be stable and (5) a way to have such stable accounts of human behaviour is by producing accounts of the methods and procedures for producing it. The grounding for the possibility of a stable social-scientific account of human behaviour of a non-reductionist sort was at least as deep as the grounding of the natural sciences. (Schegloff, 1992: xxxii)

In contrast to ethnomethodology, with its 'anti-scientific' tenor, Sacks' attitude towards 'common sense', which in ethnomethodology was conceptually opposed to empirical science, was that 'common sense' provides an object of study for empirical analysis. His critique of many forms of data analysis in social science was that it is often the common sense of the researcher which is used to interpret data. For Sacks, it is not the task of the researcher to open a piece of talk or text for interpretative exploration (the social constructionist position), but rather to demonstrate through the data an account of the systematic procedures (called 'common sense') employed by the interactants. How those procedures are reproducibly recognizable becomes the research question.

Sacks' main concern was to place sociology within the scientific tradition of enquiry, by showing that its object of study – human social life – could be subjected to detailed empirical enquiry, which could yield formal descriptions of as much rigor as the formal descriptions of the natural world. Sacks linked his project to Darwin's naturalistic method, the result of which was the theory of evolution, which rested on decades of detailed observations of the patterns of biological forms and structures (Sacks, 1992a: 28). If Sacks' project was to develop the possibility of a natural observational social science, then issues of reliability and validity must be considered as of paramount importance.

The principle of 'next turn' validity

> It is a systematic consequence of the turn taking organization of conversation that it obliges its participants to display to each other, in a turn's talk, their understanding of the other turn's talk. More generally, a turn's talk will be heard as directed to a prior turn's talk, unless special techniques are used to locate some other talk to which it is directed ... but while understandings of other turns' talk are displayed to the co-participants, they are available as well to professional analysts, who are thereby provided a proof criterion (and a search procedure) for the analysis of what a turn's talk is occupied with. Since it is the parties' understandings of prior turns' talk that is relevant to the construction of next turns, it is their understandings that are wanted for analysis. The display of those understandings in the talk in subsequent turns affords a resource for the analysis of prior turns, and a proof procedure for professional analysis of prior turns, resources intrinsic to the data themselves. (Sacks et al., 1974: 729)

Validity in conversation analysis must therefore rely on its accountability to a body of data. Three important principles must be observed:

- *Transparency*: The data must be available for inspection, and the report must show each stage of the analytic process.
- *Validation by next turn*: It is not the analyst's interpretation of the utterance but the understanding displayed by the hearer which provides for valid analytic inference about the procedures employed.
- *Deviant case analysis*: In common with the principles of 'analytic induction', it is through analysis of all features of the data, including deviant cases, that validity for analytic inference can be claimed. If a deviant case cannot be explained within the emerging pattern being studied, then the working hypothesis about the pattern must be revised.

Later research within the CA tradition describes two further standards of accountability:

- *Distributional* and *sequential accountability*: When an analysis provides a comprehensive understanding of coherence in a text, we may say that it has sequential accountability. When an analysis provides an explanation of why an element appears in one discourse environment but not in another, we may say that it has distributional accountability (Shiffrin, 1987: 19).

Sacks' work, without spelling out this distinction, was concerned with both kinds of accountability. What do they mean?

The principle of *sequential accountability*: in Part II we considered the analysis of topic, and how topic is sustained and generated. We examined the situated use of tying rules across a sequence of utterances. That analysis entailed sequential analysis. Questions to be asked might be: how do the interactants link each turn to the preceding turn, and provide the hearer with the opportunity to continue the conversation? Or, if there is a break in the linking of one turn to the preceding turn, by what other means did the turn-taker provide for a link to some other preceding talk? If there was a failure in the tying such that the conversation was in danger of faltering, then what did the turn-taker do to repair the failure? The source for the analyst's claims is the data, and the data must be available for inspection by others in order to secure the validity of the researcher's claim. By this means, the procedural relevance of the analysis, as well as of the data analysed, is reproducible. As Sacks noted, a report on a scientific experiment is no more than the making transparent of a set of procedures by which the results were achieved, rendering them reproducible.

The principle of *distributional accountability* – the building up of evidence, both across different sites, and within the same site – has been built into the text of this book. It was intended to demonstrate how the second form of accountability – the generation of distributional accountability – can deepen analytic penetration of a social/interactional phenomenon. Here is a summary of the process by which such evidence was built up, over several analytic stages:

1. By using *the constant comparative method* (Glaser and Strauss, 1967) – building up a 'dictionary' of the categories-in-use in a set of documents which involved all members of staff in describing the college– I established, through a simple counting exercise, what categories members used to describe their world at work in the college. I was also able to build evidence for the importance of some categories, which might, in the context of a single sequence, have gone unnoticed as having special significance. An example was the distribution of location categories, and the significance halls, stairways and doorways had for both students and staff as sites for potential 'boundary disputes'.

2. Next, I selected documents to analyse on the basis that they would represent a common site of textual interaction – reports which derived from a single source, and which were intended to 'inform RS [the

Principal]' (in the words of one report writer) of disciplinary incidents which happened in her absence. This analysis provided the opportunity to study *the distribution of categories across different textual accounts* of 'troublemaking'. It also provided for an examination of how the procedures of report writing are employed to do the interactional work of defining a 'troublemaker'.

3. This led to a *deviant case analysis* – the analysis of a report which did not 'belong' to the document 'Logbook', in that it was loosely inserted into a bound notebook, and was not written by one of the legitimated report writers. Comparison of the use of categories, and the use of report-writing conventions, enabled further analytic saturation of the production of the category 'troublemaker', and provided further confirmation of the important part location categories play in the warranting of the ascription, 'troublemaker'.

4. Finally, the *comparative analysis* of the category 'troublemaker' in another site – the radio interview – provided the opportunity to analyse the production of this socially significant category in another context – this time, the news interview, where the medium was talk. It was discovered that the conventions of 'reporting', with its evidential requirements, and the use of location categories, were again found to be critical in the generation of the category 'troublemaker'.

5. This inductive process led incrementally to the possibility of *generalization*: by analysing the production of the category 'troublemaker' in one sequence (a single case study), characteristics of its production then became observable in other sites, and distributional evidence for the systematic rules, which Sacks (1992a: 449) sought to establish for 'quotable' categories, became stronger.

In order to generalize the findings of a single case study, the analysis broadened its scope, and selected an example from another interactional site – the news interview, analysed in Part II. This analytic step creates the conditions for the application of CA methods to institutional settings. Analytic attention was focused specifically on the 'relevancies of categorization' and the 'procedural relevance of context' (Schegloff, 1991), to which the actors attend in the two different sites. The danger inherent in this kind of generalization is, however, as Schegloff (1991) warns us, in importing the researcher's own inferences based upon the institutional context into the analysis, and making claims that belong not to the inductive theory and practice of conversation analysis, but to the traditional concept of 'setting'. The validity of conversation analysis is undermined. It is, therefore, of utmost importance that the inferences made by the researcher are subject to scrutiny during the process of the analysis, and in its reporting. On this discipline, the validity of the method relies.

This observation then leads to the consideration of reliability, the companion of validity.

Reliability

In quantitative research, reliability is the cornerstone of validation. Reliability means replicability, and it is replication which underpins validity. Reliability is testable using widely used, sophisticated statistical methods. In the social sciences, the principle of replicability is seldom achievable in the same way. Does this, however, mean that social scientists are excluded, or excused, from considerations of disciplined method in the description of social 'facts'? Although it is a wide and varied enterprise, most qualitative researchers do in fact attend to issues of reliability, and have developed methods for testing the quality of their findings. I will not review those wider issues here, but will rather concentrate on how reliability is achieved in conversation analysis.

Important principles of reliability which are achievable in conversation analysis contribute to its robustness as a method. There are three: inter-rater reliability; accurate data collection and presentation; and selection of data.

In much research which involves coding, *inter-rater reliability* involves assigning categories, derived from theoretical constructs, and brought to bear on the data by the research process. Agreement about how to locate utterances, words and events within theory driven categories involves a certain kind of agreement (and often disagreement) about semantic meanings, shades of meaning, and so on. For conversation analysts, inter-rater agreement carries a different implication. For Sacks, inter-observer agreement is an integral part of the talk or text: the orientation of speakers/writers to hearers/readers is a continuous, analysable task. The research task is to make visible all the procedures employed by inter-actants in the achievement of this reliability. Like validity, analytic reliability is an extension of the interactional tasks faced by interactants: reliably making each turn accountable to the previous turn, and creating the conditions for the next. In order to be certain that all embedded procedures employed in the conduct of the talk or the form of the text are addressed, the analytic task is consequently most reliably achieved in discussion with others. These others may be fellow analysts, for whom the technical issues of analysis provide the main focus of attention; or may be ordinary language speakers who can offer a shared understanding of the 'common sense' hearing which underpins all conversation analysis. Both have perspectives to offer.

The *quality and reliability of transcription* also plays an important part in the reliability of the method, which depends entirely on naturally occurring data for its analytic credibility. This means that the tape- or video-recorded interaction should be of good enough quality to observe reliably details of interaction which should include intakes of breath, sighs, small, non-verbal sounds, and, in the case of video-recorded interaction, enough clarity to see how gestures and movements on the part of the interactants correspond with the talk. In the case of a text, it should be attributable, and available for inspection by the readers of the report. The use of the standard transcription system for conversation analysis, originally developed by Gail Jefferson (see Appendix A) is essential if you are working with sequential analysis at all. As we saw in the analysis of the Kennedy tapes in Part IV, the demonstration of the delicacy which attended the giving of advice by the President's political advisers involved both categorial and sequential features. The categorization analyst cannot ignore these details in the development of a full and convincing study.

The *selection of data* also plays an important part in the creation of an analysis which meets high standards of reliability. If the validity of conversation analysis depends on analytic saturation of the talk or text, then the selection of the talk or text should not seek to exclude possibilities which would affect the direction of the analysis. Remember that deviant case analysis is an important, and integral, feature of the method. The principle of selection of the text should, therefore, be inclusive with respect to the analytic task at hand.

If the researcher is seeking to explore a particular sequential or categorial feature, a limited sample of relevant data should be enough to get started. The results of this first analysis might then prompt him or her to seek further data which would provide the opportunity for an extended analysis. Reliability of the findings of an analysis depends on this search for a wider base, from which the variations in the phenomenon can be thoroughly examined. Throughout the Lectures, one can see Sacks starting with a single example of a phenomenon which interests him, developing a hypothesis about the features displayed, then turning to a wider data sample to test the hypothesis. When Schegloff (1968) analysed 500 opening sequences in telephone calls, he identified one deviant case. Analysis of this deviant case resulted in a modification of the hypothesis (Peräkylä, 1997). Finally, selection of data becomes critical in the application of CA to institutional analysis. An important issue in this kind of analysis is the breadth of data – which may be either, or both, text and talk – available to the researcher. The analysis remains inductively driven, but the scope for deepening the analysis rests with the richness of the available data, and the ability it affords to the analyst to move around the many ways in which institutions renew themselves through everyday practices.

Summary

In this chapter, I have reviewed some of the issues of reliability and validity as they affect any researcher contemplating the use of categorization analysis in one of the many applications which have been discussed in this book. Two important principles need to be taken into any work undertaken:

First, that the strength of categorization/conversation analysis lies in its fundamental principle that it is the receipt of an utterance/communication which provides for the proof procedures which validate the finding. That is the first task of the practising analyst, and in that sense, reliability and validity cannot be discussed separately from the process: they are an integral part of the analytic process.

Second, that methods are good for what they are good for – they are not intrinsically valuable. I love doing categorization analysis, and see in it endless richness. It is not, however, the key to understanding social being. It is a (very) useful tool. Validity rests on an appreciation of the limits of any analysis.

Recommended reading

Kirk, J. and Miller, M.L. (1986) *Reliability and validity in qualitative research*. London: Sage.
A general introduction to issues of reliability and validity in all qualitative research.

Peräkylä, A. (1997) 'Reliability and validity based on tapes and transcripts'. In D. Silverman (ed.), *Qualitative research: theory, method and practice*. London: Sage. This article provides detailed discussion of the principles and practice of reliability and validity in conversation analysis.

Seale, C. (1999) *The quality of qualitative data*. London: Sage.
A practical guide to issues of validity, reliability and method in qualitative research.

Silverman, D. (1993) *Interpreting qualitative data: methods for analysing talk, text and interaction*. London: Sage.
See Chapter 7 for a general introduction to issues of validity and reliability in qualitative research.

15

Working with an Extended Textual or Conversational Data: the Uses and Abuses of Computer-aided Analysis

CONTENTS

The problem of sustaining validity and reliability, and considerations of the quality and depth of the data lead to another topic, subject of much discussion among researchers in the qualitative tradition: how does the individual researcher, or research team, build and manage a database which is both relevant and sufficient to the analytic task? In this chapter, I turn to recent developments in the application of computers to the management and analysis of data.

Using computer-aided techniques in CA

Categorization analysis is, of course, a qualitative method. It is grounded in inductive reasoning, and focuses on the micro-processes of interaction, relying for its validity on the accretion of case examples. The new technology of the time – the portable tape-recorder – opened up a whole new domain of enquiry from the theoretical study of ordinary language by invented example, to the empirical study of naturally occurring talk. Sacks sampled tape-recorded data for particular examples; he also drew on a wide range of different kinds of text and talk to demonstrate that his findings were generalizable. In the 1960s and early 1970s – before the days of the personal computer – his data were gathered by hand-search methods and analysed in small samples. That tradition has generally characterized the development of CA. In all sciences, it is the advent of new technology which opens up new possibilities for analysis.

For example, to return to the theory of evolution, Darwin developed his theory of natural selection inductively through natural observational method over decades. It proved a powerful and enduring theory – but the causal mechanisms underpinning natural selection remained a mystery until two new technological developments enabled further enquiries. First, the invention of the microscope led to confirmation of the Mendelian hypothesis of the mechanism of inheritance within the genes, which now became visible (but notice that he built on already existing practical knowledge, gained by trial and error in the breeding of plants and animals). Later, the invention of X-ray crystallography enabled Crick and Watson to observe the interior structure of the gene, and start to form hypotheses about the underpinning physical mechanisms within them. The relationship between observation, generalization, practices and technology is complex, and can be applied to the development of the natural and the social sciences alike, as Sacks argued so elegantly.

Now – some 30 years into its development – a new generation of technologies is available to CA practitioners in the form of computer software. Two developments may have particularly beneficial consequences: first, the development over the last decade of software packages dedicated to the analysis of qualitative data. Second, in the coming decade, it may well be possible to reduce transcription time and costs with the development of increasingly sophisticated voice recognition software, presently in its early days of development. These developments mean that the size of datasets potentially available for analysis will increase dramatically. Will these developments bring more, better, different, or just too much analytic potential? The answer, I would argue, may be a bit of all four.

More

Generalizing from small data samples has already proved enormously productive in the generation of 'rules of application' which Sacks sought to demonstrate working on such a small text as 'The baby cried. The mommy picked it up'. Though he recognized that the 'machinery' which he used to analyse this little text was 'overbuilt', he justified it as providing more generalizable tools. His objective was to demonstrate the set of tools which would be potentially available as a procedure for any natural language speaker. However, as Jayyusi (1984) noted, the generation of a 'machinery' on so small a sample has meant that the machine was simply not adequate to the complexities of some of the work it might be asked to do. An example which she identified and did further work on was the case of 'disjunctive categorizations', discussed in Chapter 3. If the inductive argument from micro-studies has produced a rich result of findings of 'rules of application', it may now be time to test the extent to which those rules are applicable over a wide range of talk and texts. For example, contemporary studies now emerging are applying sequential analysis (Conversation Analysis) methods to different languages, seeking to establish which procedural rules are universal.

In Chapter 13, an application of CA methods to research institutional practices was discussed. A method of deriving 'categories in use' as a basis for validating the analysis of particular documents and incidents was generated. I used a hand counting method, appropriate to the data I was using, because the time which I would have taken to enter it into the computer was too great. Suppose, however, that I were using data which I already had on disc – say, the reports of a committee over the last five years; or the transcripts of 100 medical consultations which I could scan into a word processing package: then the same strategy might be employed electronically, saving on time, and potentially generating characteristics in the talk or text which would not be easy to spot using 'hand' methods. In these ways, rigour, and an increasingly strong claim for validity, can be achieved. Even some of the more sophisticated word processing functions can help to search large quantities of data and identify categories in use in a reliable and consistent way. Use of a qualitative analysis software package also offers the possibility of exporting the counting to a statistical package, and analysing the frequency of occurrences in a formal way which in some cases may support a qualitative finding and make the case for its validity.

In a study cited by Fielding and Lee (1998), a CA researcher using interview texts to study 'downgrading' talk sequences applied the following method:

- coding by type of discourse strategy (i.e., using the computer program to code segments of the text for the kind of discourse strategy under study);
- counting the frequencies of types of discourse within the interviews;
- selection of three from the set of types;
- checking for deviant cases where an identified discourse form was used to another purpose than that observed in other cases; and
- detailed conversation analysis of the three identified forms (done off-line).

The researcher commented:

> I managed to come out with three interesting phenomena from the data. One was how people downgrade their talk and make something less of an event than it was, and how people upgrade their talk and make something sound more

than it was, and the other area that came out was sensitive issues, where they are talking about sensitive topics. From that I was able to just pull out those examples to work on for more analysis. (quoted in Fielding and Lee, 1998: 146)

Better

Sacks, as we have seen, was concerned to stress that his method was not a departure from scientific rigour, but a logical extension of the principles of scientific method to include the critical study of the use of languaged procedures as a means of communicating and generating shared understanding. Validity, rigour and depth of analysis may be served by computer-aided methods, and where they are, the work of the researcher will not only be made easier, but more rewarding. These advantages should not be dismissed on the grounds of ideological principle held by some qualitative researchers, that computerization is quantification, and as such is inimical to qualitative analysis and insight.

Several issues relating to the quality of the analysis are relevant here:

- *Speed*: use of computer-aided text management enables searching wider datasets for particular examples in conjunction with
- *coding*: ensuring that all relevant data in a large sample are entered into the analysis, including deviant cases, would add to the force of the case for validity by showing that the phenomenon being analysed was not simply an 'interesting example' but demonstrably, a widely occurring phenomenon with consequences for the understanding of social action and coherence. Where it occurs, compared to where it does not, may be matters of interest to the researcher concerned to demonstrate the procedural relevance of the actions of speakers and hearers, writers and readers.
- *Simple counting and analysis of frequency* of occurrence over a large dataset, combined with the detailed analysis of strips of talk or text, can lend weight to such findings. For example, computers might be employed in an institutional study, searching consultations or court proceedings for particular kinds of exchange, and coding for particular phenomena – disjunctive categorizations, for example – which might then be compared in detail in the context of their occurrence for regular, and deviant, features and occurrences.
- *Deviant case analysis*: Computer-aided search techniques mean that deviant cases can be reliably retrieved and analysed in detail. Finding all deviant cases for analysis over a dataset would add to the force of the case for validity by analysis of deviant cases.

The computer data analysis package may be used not only for storage, sorting and retrieval of data, but for the actual analytic task. One researcher who has begun using computer software directly to increase analytic potential is Brian Torode, working in Dublin, with the software package 'Code-a-text' (Torode, 1998; Cartwright, 1998). Torode's application of coding to the analysis of a narrative sequence was described in Chapter 4. Torode has succeeded in demonstrating that computer analysis may add to the force of the analysis of even quite short strips of text and talk by enabling the researcher to demonstrate visually the deep nesting of dynamic elements in the talk which a hand analysis, or written description, might not be able to generate.

Silverman (1997b) argues for methodological pluralism in the development of qualitative research methods. Over the years, he has consistently argued that the apparent dichotomy between quantitative and qualitative methods is a spurious one, and that research methods, like tools, must be chosen accurately for the job they are meant to do. This means that even within the scope of one piece of research, quantitative methods may work hand in hand with qualitative methods to generate rich results. The issue is not purity, but utility. The task of the researcher is to design studies which make use of tools in a well constructed and justified way, and if computer programs can help, so much the better!

The advent of computer-aided techniques means that quantification can be accommodated within the CA enterprise in two ways: first, by increasing the quantity and range of data which can be examined in a single study; and second, by thus generating the kinds and numbers of instances which could then be subjected to generalization. Sacks worked from principles of a 'simplest systematics' in order to demonstrate the orderliness and regularity of situated interaction. His language reveals his intention: to produce a science of talk-in-action. His method was inductive: to work by case example until a large enough body of examples was available to generalize. We have now the means to generate a very large number of cases – through computerized search of large amounts of text – of particular kinds of interactional phenomena. This opens the possibility for the saturation (Glaser and Strauss, 1967) of data and for the development of comprehensive data treatment (ten Have, 1998) based on comparative analysis, to a level of reliability not possible by hand methods. For an example of this kind of strategy, see the study of conversational story-tellings from different cultures (already discussed in Part III) by Ervin-Tripp and Kuntay (1997). Using a large number of conversational narrative episodes, from different databases, they were able to demonstrate both variable and invariant features of conversational story-telling across cultures.

Different

If such a strategy might make certain domains of enquiry available to categorization analysis, it may also make categorization analysis look different. In my own study of a College of Further Education (Lepper 1994,

1995), I used quantification to identify what I termed, after Jayyusi, the 'relevant category environment'. At that time, I simply used a hand counting procedure. Had I been using a computerized searching technique, I might have developed a richer, and possibly more valid, picture of the categories-in-use. As it was, the analysis departed from classical studies in using a 'content analysis' technique to provide the evidential background for the 'relevancies of categorization' (Schegloff), and for the selection of particular texts for the analysis of interaction-in-context in that institution (the 'procedural relevancy of the context'). The principle could be applied to larger and wider institutional practices. An example which comes to mind might be the differing discursive practices over time in the same institution which might be studied using its records as the source. We glanced at such a record – *The Kennedy White House Tapes* – in Part IV. Hansard, the record of proceedings in the UK Parliament, comes to mind as another potential dataset.

The development of conversation analysis began with Sacks' painstaking analysis of examples from recorded talk and published texts which he came across. He speaks in the Lectures of returning to a single piece of data over months and even years, before seeing all of its elements. He wanted to develop a 'machinery' of conversational practices – that is, he sought to identify invariant features of talk-in-action. In order to do this, he began by studying any kind of situated talk which displayed features which might prove important. He began with local practices, building up a picture of a mechanism which was demonstrable through the analysis at hand. His concerns were 'emic' – that is, they concerned themselves with the analysis of local events and practical actions. This is still an important part of the project of conversation analysis, and some argue that it is all conversation analysts should concern themselves with.

However, there is another view, which proposes that now that we have a substantial, and growing, body of findings on universal features of talk, research may begin to build on that body of knowledge to generalize, extend and apply the findings within wider social domains. In a recent article, Heritage (1997) sets out a programme for such an enterprise. Subject to the caveats noted by Schegloff (see above), comparative analysis of institutional practices is now established technique. This development suggests to me a potential application which I would term, an 'ecology of conversational practices': the formal study of the ways in which, among the universal conversational features available to speakers and hearers, some are deployed in specific institutional settings, and not in others. As in the study of ecology (and faithful to Sacks' original conception), the perspective is one of systemic constraints. It involves exhaustively describing and comparing the ways in which the available conversational resources constrain speakers and hearers to create local and sustainable social environments. The existence of computer technologies such as hypertext links creates the opportunity for the CA researcher to cross the same data over and again, generating links at different levels, from original data to analytic formulations, thereby creating detailed maps of the local social ecology which it would be impossible to achieve by hand methods.

This kind of project would take categorization and conversation analysis into new territory, in which computerized analysis will surely play an important part in the management and analysis of data.

Too much

Of course it is also the case that the potential for data collection and analysis, given the potential magnitude of electronic data storage and processing, has grown exponentially. More and more naturally occurring data is available to the researcher on the internet. The rapidly growing capacity and speed of personal computers means that virtually unlimited processing power, once the preserve of 'main-frame' specialists, is potentially available to the ordinary researcher. Given all this potential, how can the individual researcher, or team, sort through what are relevant, valid and worthy data for study? Further, there is the issue of the ethical use of data which, by the nature of CA – naturally occurring talk and text – was not likely to have been collected for research purposes and therefore has not been formally 'donated' for the purposes of analysis. The use of tape-recorded data which Sacks took for granted in the 1960s would simply not be possible now. In California, where the original telephone helpline conversations which Sacks studied took place, the use of such data would now be against the law, in the absence of the specific consent of callers to the use of their conversations. In the next chapter, I will look at some of the ethical issues which must be taken into account by researchers.

For the purpose of this discussion, the dangers of using computer-based data management and analysis from the point of view of method are the main focus. These dangers are inherent in the potential benefits described in the previous sections:

- *Coding*: The use of computerized coding as an indexing device, enabling the CA researcher to store and retrieve similar, or different, conversational features from a large dataset, could lead the unwary away from attention to local rationalities, and towards treating codes as a means of defining what is 'really there'.
- *Generalization*: The attractions of being able to handle large amounts of data could seduce CA researchers away from the painstaking, detailed micro-analysis which underpins its validity, into spurious, premature or over-generalization.
- The attractions of technological capacities such as hypertext links to sustain comprehensive data treatment can draw attention away from the primary analytic task of CA. Development of the research

programme is then in danger of becoming technology led, rather than technology assisted.

These are serious concerns, which warrant the careful attention of those proposing to undertake any computer-aided research. Nevertheless, for those who feel they can work within the limits of what computer programs can offer, the potential benefits are still considerable.

Recommended reading

Fielding, N.G. and Lee, R.M. (1998) *Computer analysis and qualitative research.* London: Sage.
If you do decide to make use of computer-aided analysis, this text provides a thorough introduction to the advantages and problems encountered by researchers in applying computer analysis to qualitative research methods.

16

Ethics in Research

CONTENTS

As mentioned in the previous chapter, the freedom of use of data, since Sacks began his first analysis of telephone crisis centre recordings, has transformed. Sacks' use of those recordings would now be subject to the explicit consent of the caller. The data he used from a group psychotherapy session would require not only their specific consent, but probably also considerably more disguise of individual identities than Sacks provided. For CA researchers today, attention to the source of the data, and the explicit permission to use it, are important factors from a legal point of view. I would also argue that they are important factors from a good practice point of view. In this final chapter I will outline some of the ethical considerations which should be brought to bear on the collection and analysis of data. A sample consent form can be found in Appendix B.

Ethics

As researchers we are probably motivated by a wish to return something of value to society. Our analyses, however, even though they are, in the case of CA practice, based upon the rationalities of the speakers and hearers themselves, will surprise and possibly disturb them. As Sacks was at pains to point out, the mechanisms of talk are not available to everyday awareness, and the details of their interactional strategies may not necessarily come as good news to the interactants. Using naturally occurring data means that much data can be sought from the public domain, and is in no way subject to ethical considerations of privacy. Published records, public trials and hearings, broadcasts, newspaper texts – all provide a variety of different kinds of data, about the use of which no ethical dilemma should arise. Other studies undertaken by CA researchers are a different matter. The many studies of medical consultations, of which many are video-taped, require detailed consent, which is subject to legal constraint, as well as to issues of values.

An important distinction needs to be made here: ethics, or adherence to a body of rules, and values – the worth of a thing. The study of medical encounters provides a good example of the ways in which ethical issues impact on the activities of doctors and their patients, and anyone who attempts to study them. These in turn raise issues of values – the worth of an activity in relation to its intrinsic or contributory benefit to the individual. In some ways, ethics is the easier of the two considerations to tackle. So I will begin with some considerations which you ought to consider in collecting and analysing your data, if it comes from such a source.

The primary issue of concern to those involved in any medical interaction, or any similar interactional setting in which individual privacy is a concern, is the consent given by the patient, or subject, of an intervention. Whether it occurs within the medical concerns of the doctor–patient relationship (drug research, for example) or in the form of observing the interaction (a topic of much interest in CA research) – research is a form of intervention. Medical records, and research, are strictly controlled with a view to the protection of the privacy and dignity of the patient. Imposition of an external observer/intrusion should be given explicit consent. How this does or does not happen could well be an interesting topic for CA research – but it also applies to the research itself. What is the status of the patient's consent to be video-taped for the purpose of research?

Three important considerations apply – and they will also have an impact on the interaction which becomes the data:

- *Is the consent informed?* If so,
- *Is the consent voluntary?* For example, did the patient believe that treatment was contingent on consent?
- *Is the consent competent?* Suppose you are doing a study on the interactions between a delusional patient and his or her doctor. What is the status of the consent?

Today, you would not be given access to such data without the consideration of an ethics committee, and these judgements would not be yours alone to make. However, they bear consideration in selecting your project and attempting to collect your data. Data from public settings is much easier to obtain, but it would deprive the CA project of its full potential if issues of privacy and problems of data collection precluded the kind of study of 'intimate' interaction which the study of medical consultation, for example, enables.

Values

The second consideration which arises in the conduct of research in medical settings is that of the intrinsic, or contributory value of the research to the subject. Most medical research consent is obtained on the basis of contributory value – that is, the benefits of the research may not necessarily be returned directly to the subject, but may generally benefit a wider group of patients. An appeal is made not to the patient's immediate interests, but to the general good, and as such, an appeal is to the values of the individual subject. Social science, and in particular, qualitative research, has traditionally been very sensitive to such value, and, indeed, the tradition of 'action research' explicitly states its aim to return the value of its findings to the participants. Is it always as straightforward as that, however?

For example, in my study of the Further Education College, I was generously given access to 'intimate' documents – documents which were not produced for public consumption, but which were used by the members of the 'family' to go about their domestic business. My intention, and explicit promise, was to produce 'action research' – returning findings to the Principal and her staff which would enable staff and students to make the most of the 'learning environment' of the college. Starting from this premise, my first findings – the presence of the hierarchy of categorial relations named by its members, 'Family Tree' – proved an immense shock to the Principal, who thought she had committed 'team players'. She was unable to accept what I had found, and I was unable to help her make sense of it. This made me have to think through the value and ethical basis of my analysis, although the data was freely offered and no sense of betrayal of trust was really at issue. After much reflection, I had to conclude that the wish to return something directly of value may not be achievable, but that this does not constitute a violation of the principles of ethics and value in research. As researcher, you can only offer what you find. How it is received is not within your control. On the other hand, it does suggest that there is more to consider in the collection and analysis of data from 'intimate' settings, than the legal requirements of respect for privacy and consent. There is also the impact that your activities may have on subjects, and the balance that must be struck between your needs and interests, and theirs.

Summary

The growth of information storage and retrieval systems, and the massive capacity for 'surveillance' of individuals through such systems, has heightened concerns for the individual's rights to privacy and freedom from intrusion. Such debates occupy our media on a daily basis, and a complex politics of privacy has evolved out of those debates. The consequence has been the development of stringent laws governing the use of written documents and recorded information. However, in the same recent times, we have witnessed the release onto the world-wide web, of the tape-recording, obtained by deception and used without consent, of a private conversation between a White House aide and her friend. You can learn the law, and consider issues about value. In the end, however, it is your judgement which is needed to steer the course between the dangers and pleasures of the spirit of enquiry, and a sense of natural justice.

Recommended reading

Kimmel, A.J. (1996) *Ethical issues in behavioral research.* Oxford: Basil Blackwell. This book gives an overall introduction to ethical issues in research, and traces the interesting history of the development of ethical concern in the social and behavioural sciences.

Glossary

Analytic induction 'A technique used primarily by qualitative researchers to access commonalties across a number of cases and thereby clarify empirical categories and the concepts that are exemplified by the cases included in a category. It is a "double fitting" of ideas and evidence that focuses on similarities across a limited number of cases studied in depth' (Ragin, 1994: 183).

Category bound activities Action words which link 'subjects' and 'objects'. They are 'formulated, implicitly or explicitly, as conventionally accompanying some category' (Jayyusi, 1984: 36–7).

Category generated features Features of talk or text which are 'systematically produced through their tie to some category' (Jayyusi, 1984: 37).

Clusters (a) Categories . . . conventionally carry with them a cluster of expectable features – i.e. the constitutive trait . . . carries with it a cluster of related possible actions, traits, preferences, haunts, appearances, places times, etc. . . . The use of categorizations is not only descriptive of persons, but it is through and through an ascriptive matter. (b) This cluster is itself embedded in the logico-grammatical relationship between concepts (Jayyusi, 1984: 26–7).

Collection Sacks' term for the way in which categories-in-use are heard as belonging together. Sacks notes in the Lectures that the term, while borrowing some properties of the term 'set', does not implicate a theoretical or semantic grouping. The identification of a 'collection' must be warranted by the situated use of categories in the talk/text.

Consistency rule If a population of persons is being categorized, and a category from a membership categorization device has been used to characterize a first member of that population, then hear subsequent categorizations as coming from that device (thus providing for generalizability).

Context Sacks proposed a definition of context as 'something that is oriented to by

Members, and is not then simply a matter of . . . it happened at a certain time'. Categorization and conversation analysis seek to analyse the way in which context is constituted on a turn-by-turn basis.

Culture Sacks defines culture very precisely: 'A culture is an apparatus for generating recognizable actions: if the same procedures are used for generating as for depicting, that is perhaps as simple a solution to the problem of recognizability as is formulatable' (1992a: 226). In this way, he specifies culture as an observable, available to systematic investigation.

Discourse A widely used term covering studies from the analysis of language to the analysis of 'discursive practices' developed by Foucault. Conversation analysis is often grouped with other studies of discourse, but the empirical grounding of its methods distinguishes it from many other forms of discourse analysis.

Disjunctive categories Asymmetric category pairings which generate conflicting characterizations of the same person. For example, 'sick person/hypochondriac; policeman/thug' (Jayyusi, 1984: 132ff).

Disorderability Describes a sequence which can be taken apart and re-ordered without loss of coherence. Its converse, **non-disorderability**, describes a sequence which loses meaning and coherence if its components are rearranged.

Duplicative organization A collection of membership categories treated as a unit. When categorizing a population, potential members are then treated as a unit, not as countable individuals. When one category from that collection is used, then it will be inferred that any other category from that device can be used to construct an adequate description simply by virtue of occupying a position within that device.

Economy rule For any population of Members being categorized, whether the consistency rule, or combining rules, are being applied, it may be sufficient to apply only one category to each member.

Field 'Society as an object of inquiry is necessarily "theoretical" in the sense that, like a magnetic field, it is necessarily unperceivable. As such it cannot be identified independently of its effects; so that it cannot be known, only shown to exist. However, in this respect, it is no different from many objects of natural scientific inquiry.' (Bhaskar, 1989: 45).

Formal organization 'In contrast to the social organization that emerges whenever men are living together, there are organizations that have been deliberately established for a certain purpose. Since the distinctive characteristic of these organizations is that they have been formally established for the explicit purpose of achieving certain goals, the term "formal organizations" is used to designate them' (Blau and Scott, 1963: 5).

Frame Goffman defines his use of 'frame': 'definitions of a situation are built up in accordance with principles of organization which govern events – at least social ones – and our subjective involvement in these basic elements as I am able to identify them' (1986: 11). Goffman acknowledges the origins of his analysis of 'frames' in the work of Gregory Bateson (1972).

Indexical, indexicality The term used by Garfinkel to characterize the project of ethnomethodology: 'Members' accounts are reflexively and essentially tied for the rationality to the socially organized conditions of their use' (1967: 4). He proposed this basic condition of human sociality as a locus for social enquiry. It derives from the philosophical term: a type of expression whose semantic value is in part determined by features of the context of utterance, and hence may vary with that context. Among indexicals are the personal pronouns, such as 'I', 'you', 'he', 'she' and 'it'; demonstratives, such as 'this' and 'that'; temporal expressions, such as 'now', 'today', 'yesterday'; and locative expressions such as 'here', 'there', etc. (Audi, 1995).

Hierarchies of relevance When the talk produces disjunctions, or potential disagreements between speakers as to the relative values implicit in categorizations, recourse will be made to orders of precedence, which will be generated in accordance with local cultural practices; for example, 'Family Tree' provided a locally generated 'hierarchy of relevance' in the production and interpretation of categorizations in the 'Logbook' data (analysed in Part III).

Location categories 'For any location to which reference is made, there is a set of terms each of which, by a correspondence test, is a correct way to refer to it. On any actual occasion of use, however, not any member of the set is "right"' (Schegloff, 1972: 81).

'Member' and 'member' Sacks used this distinction to work at the difference between members (persons) who are speakers, and the occupants of categories, or Members, who are designated in the talk of members. This distinction is indicated in analytic texts by capitalizing, and/or placing in quotes, uses of names of categories as Members.

Membership Categorization Devices Sacks' definition is very precise: 'By the term categorization device we meant that collection of membership categories, containing at least a category, that may be applied to some population, containing at least one Member, so as to provide, by the use of some rule of application, for the pairing of at least a population member and a categorization device member. A device is then a collection plus rules of application' (1972b: 32).

Procedural relevance The orientation of the speakers and hearers to the relevancies at hand. These relevancies are not presupposed by the categorization analysis in terms of theoretical constructs, but demonstrated through analysis of the devices, with their relevant membership categories and category bound activities, implicated by the interactants in their talk.

Programmatic relevance If a pair of categories with the features of standardized relational pairs is relevant, then the non-incumbency of any of its pair positions is an observable, i.e., it can proposedly be a fact. Furthermore, various uses may be made of the facts of the presence or absence of persons to fill the potential pair positions. Jayyusi builds on this minimum condition of relevance in order to provide for situated relevance rich enough to account for the complex construction of what she terms the relevant category environment.

Pro-term A pro-term is an indexical term. Its referent, and hence its meaning, depends entirely on the function it plays within a sentence or utterance. Pro-terms include the personal pronouns, as well as indefinite locational adverbs ('there', 'here', 'before', 'after', for example) and indefinite prepositions. Verbs may also act as pro-terms where they are employed as actions, such as performatives (Austin, 1962) – for example, 'Look!'

Relevance Sacks' concept of categorization devices directly addresses the problem of relevance for speakers and hearers. He defines 'relevance' formally in terms of 'R' – pairs of categories – as the case where, 'if R is relevant, then the non-incumbency of any of its pair positions is an observable i.e., it can proposedly be a fact' (1972b: 38). For example, in his telephone helpline data, he showed that the 'search for help' involved exploring sets of related pairs, such that the giving of help would be an expectable, such as 'husband/wife', 'relative/relative', 'friend/friend'. In this way, Sacks provided, within the terms of CA, the minimum condition for the possibility of the construction of a social 'fact'.

Relevant category environment Speakers routinely orient to the relevancies of the talk by producing categorizations within devices, using the economy and the consistency rules. The relevant category environment is implicit until there is a disagreement about the relevance of a categorization. At this point there is recourse to repair, or to a 'hierarchy of relevance'. For categorization of data to be grounded in the 'relevant category environment', the researcher must demonstrate through his or her *saturation* of the text that all categorizations have been accounted for within the relevant devices.

Saturation The principle of inductive method that all relevant cases, including deviant cases, must be included in an analysis and explained within the working hypothesis, which must be revised until such time as all relevant cases are explained.

Sequential analysis Sacks demonstrated that conversation works in sequences. Without being able to identify sequences, we wouldn't be able to identify that a conversation was going on. Conversation analysis is the study of the orderly sequencing which underpins the procedural infrastructure of interaction.

Standardized Relational Pair A pairing of Members such that the relation between them constitutes a locus for rights and obligations. Examples abound: 'Husband'

and 'Wife', 'Mother' and 'Baby', 'Lecturer' and 'Student', and 'Doctor' and 'Patient'.

Topical coherence 'Speakers specifically place most of their utterances. Where, by "place", I mean they put them into such a position [that] what's just been happening provide[s] an obvious explanation for why this was said now (where, when they don't, a question could arise of why that now).' (Sacks, 1992b: 352)

Tying rules The means by which one part of a conversation is tied to another on a local basis.

Upshot the consequence of an action in which the agent's intentions played an important, but not determining, role.

Appendix A: Transcription Conventions

The glossary of transcript symbols given below is meant to explain the major conventions for rendering details of the vocal production of utterances in talk-in-interaction as these are used in most current CA publications. Most if not all of these have been developed by Gail Jefferson, but are now commonly used with minor individual variations. The glosses given below are mostly based on, and simplified from, the descriptions provided in Jefferson (1989: 193–6), at times using those in Heritage and Atkinson (1984), Psathas and Anderson (1990); see also Psathas (1995), ten Have and Psathas (1995). I have restricted the set given below to the ones most commonly used, omitting some of the subtleties provided by Jefferson.

Sequencing

[	A *single left bracket* indicates the point of overlap onset.
]	A *single right bracket* indicates the point at which an utterance or utterance-part terminates *vis-à-vis* another.
=	*Equal signs*, one at the end of one line and one at the beginning of a next, indicate no 'gap' between the two lines. This is often called *latching*.

Timed intervals

(0.0)	*Numbers in parentheses* indicate elapsed time in silence by tenth of seconds, so (7.1) is a pause of 7 seconds and one tenth of a second.
(.)	A *dot in parentheses* indicates a tiny 'gap' within or between utterances.

Characteristics of speech production

<u>word</u>	*Underscoring* indicates some form of stress, via pitch and/or amplitude; an alternative method is to print the stressed part in *italic*.
::	*Colons* indicate prolongation of the immediately prior sound. Multiple colons indicate a more prolonged sound.
-	A *dash* indicates a cut-off.
.,?¿	*Punctuation marks* are used to indicate characteristics of speech production, especially intonation; they are not referring to grammatical units.
.	A *period* indicates a stopping fall in tone.
,	A *comma* indicates a continuing intonation, like when you are reading items from a list.
?	A *question mark* indicates a rising intonation.
¿	The *combined question mark/comma* indicates stronger rise than a comma but weaker than a question mark.

	The absence of an utterance-final marker indicates some sort of 'indeterminate' contour.
↑ ↓	*Arrows* indicate marked shifts into higher or lower pitch in the utterance-part immediately following the arrow.
WORD	*Upper case* indicates especially loud sounds relative to the surrounding talk.
º	Utterances or utterance parts bracketed by *degree signs* are relatively quieter than the surrounding talk.
< >	*Right/left carets* bracketing an utterance or utterance-part indicate speeding up.
·hhh	A *dot-prefixed row of* hs indicates an inbreath. Without the dot, the *hs* indicate an outbreath.
w(h)ord	A parenthesized *h*, or a *row of* hs *within a word*, indicates breathiness, as in laughter, crying, etc.

Transcriber's doubts and comments

( )	*Empty parentheses* indicate the transcriber's inability to hear what was said. The length of the parenthesized space indicates the length of the untranscribed talk. In the speaker designation column, the empty parentheses indicate inability to identify a speaker.
(word)	*Parenthesized words* are especially dubious hearings or speaker identifications.
(( ))	*Double parentheses* contain transcriber's descriptions rather than, or in addition to, transcriptions.

Appendix B: Sample Consent Form

The following form was developed by Susan M. Ervin-Tripp, Psychology Department, University of California at Berkeley, and is reproduced here, with her consent, as an *example* of what could be included in such a form. It is used by the UCB Committee for the Protection of Human Subjects for all studies of language use.

****

Researcher name_____

LETTER OF CONSENT

PHOTOGRAPHIC, AUDIO, AND/OR VIDEO RECORDS RELEASE CONSENT FORM

As part of this project we have made a photographic, audio, and/or video recording of you while you participated in the research.
We would like you to indicate below what uses of these records you are willing to consent to. This is completely up to you. We will only use the records in ways that you agree to. In any use of these records, names will not be identified.

1. The records can be studied by the research team for use in the research project.

Photo _____ Audio _____ Video _____

[Please use initials]

2. The records can be shown to subjects in other experiments.

Photo _____ Audio _____ Video _____

[Please use initials]

3. The records can be used for scientific publications.

Photo _____ Audio _____ Video _____

[Please use initials]

4. The written transcript can be kept in an archive for other researchers.

Photo _____ Audio _____ Video _____

[Please use initials]

5. The records can be used by other researchers.

Photo _____ Audio _____ Video _____

[Please use initials]

6. The records can be shown at meetings of scientists interested in the study of _____

Photo _____ Audio _____ Video _____

[Please use initials]

7. The records can be shown in classrooms to students.

Photo _____ Audio _____ Video _____

[Please use initials]

8. The records can be shown in public presentations to non-scientific groups.

Photo _____ Audio _____ Video _____

[Please use initials]

9. The records can be used on television and radio.

Photo _____ Audio _____ Video _____

[Please use initials]

I have read the above description and give my consent for the use of the records as indicated above.

Date _____

Signature _____

Signature of Guardian, if Applicable _____

Native language(s)_____
Where native language learned (city or region)_____
Languages used on the tape_____
Where language(s) used on tape were learned _____
Age at which each language used on tape was learned _____
Education _____Occupation _____
Name _____ Age _____ Sex __

****

-=-

[put your name, affiliation and all relevant address information here]

-=-

References

Atkinson, J.M., Cuff, E.C. and Lee, J.R.E. (1978) 'The recommencement of a meeting as an interactional accomplishment'. In J. Schenkein (ed.), *Studies in the organization of conversational interaction*. New York: Academic Press.

Atkinson, J.M. and Heritage, J. (eds) (1984) *Structures of social action: studies in conversation analysis*. Cambridge: Cambridge University Press.

Audi, R. (1995) *Cambridge dictionary of philosophy*. Cambridge: Cambridge University Press.

Austin, J.L. (1961) *Philosophical papers*. Oxford: The Clarendon Press.

Austin, J.L. (1962) *How to do things with words*. Oxford: Oxford University Press.

Baker, C.D. (1984) 'The search for adultness: membership work in adolescent–adult talk', *Human Studies*, 7(3/4): 301–23.

Baker, C.D. (1997) 'Membership categorization and interview accounts'. In D. Silverman (ed.), *Qualitative research: theory, method, practice*. London: Sage.

Baker, C.D. and Freebody, P. (1987) 'Constituting the child in beginning school reading books', *British Journal of Sociology of Education*, 8(1): 55–74.

Bamberg, M. (ed.) (1997) 'Oral versions of personal experience: three generations of narrative analysis', *Journal of Narrative and Life History* (special edn), 7(1–4).

Baron-Cohen, S. (1992) 'The theory of mind hypothesis of autism: history and prospects of the idea', *The Psychologist: Bulletin of the British Psychological Association*, 5: 9–21.

Barthes, R. (1998) 'Rhetoric of the image'. In N. Mirzoeff (ed.), *The visual culture reader*. London and New York: Routledge.

Baruch, G. (1981) 'Moral tales: parents' stories of encounters with the health professions', *Sociology of Health and Illness*, 3(3): 275–96.

Bateson, G. (1972) *Steps to an ecology of mind*. New York: Ballantine Books.

Bennis, W.G. (1966) *Changing organizations: essays on the development and evolution of human organisation*. New York: McGraw Hill.

Berger, P. and Luckman, T. (1967) *The social construction of reality*. London: Allen Lane.

Bhaskar, R. (1979/1989) *The possibility of naturalism: A philosophical critique of the contemporary human sciences*. New York: Harvester Wheatsheaf.

Bittner, E. (1965) 'The concept of organization', *Social Research*, 32: 239–55.

Blau, P. and Scott, W. (1963) *Formal organizations: a comparative approach*. London: Routledge and Kegan Paul.

Boden, D. (1994) *The business of talk: organizations in action*. Cambridge: Polity Press.

Boden, D. and Zimmerman, D.H. (eds) (1991) *Talk and social structure: studies in ethnomethodology and conversation analysis*. Cambridge: Polity Press.

Bowlby, J. (1969/1982) *Attachment and loss: Vol I. Attachment*. New York: Basic Books.

Burchell, G., Gordon, C. and Miller, P. (eds) (1991) *The Foucault effect: studies in governmentality*. Hemel Hempstead: Harvester Wheatsheaf.

Burke, K. (1945) *A grammar of motive*. Berkeley: University of California Press.

Cartwright, A. (1998) *Code-a-text*. Sage software.

Cicourel, A. (1968) *The social organization of juvenile justice*. New York: John Wiley.

Clayman, S.E. (1992) 'Footing in the achievement of neutrality'. In P. Drew and J. Heritage (eds), *Talk at work: interaction in institutional settings*. Cambridge: Cambridge University Press.

Clegg, S. and Hardy, C. (eds) (1999) *Studying organization: theory and method*. London: Sage.

Collins, R. (1981) 'Microtranslation as a theory building strategy'. In K. Knorr-Cetina and A. Cicourel (eds), *Advances in social theory and methodology: toward an integration of micro- and macro-sociologies*. London: Routledge and Kegan Paul.

Coulter, J. (1979) *The social construction of mind: studies in ethnomethodology and linguistic philosophy*. Totowa, NJ: Rowan and Littlefield.

Coulter, J. (1989) *Mind in action*. Cambridge: Polity Press.

Cuff, E.C. (1993) *Problems of versions in everyday situations*. Washington DC: International Institute for Ethnomethodology and Conversation Analysis. University Press of America.

Culler, J. (1981) *The pursuit of signs*. London: Routledge and Kegan Paul.

Czarniawska, B. (1998) *A narrative approach to organization studies*. London: Sage.

Dalton, M. (1959) *Men who manage*. New York: John Wiley.

Dingwall, R. and Strong, P. (1985) 'The interactional study of organizations: a critique and reformulation', *Urban Life*, 14(2): 205–31.

Donald, M. (1991) *Origins of the modern mind: three stages in the evolution of culture and cognition*. Cambridge, MA: Harvard University Press.

Douglas, M. (1966) *Purity and danger*. London: Routledge.

Douglas, M. (1975) *Implicit meanings*. London: Routledge.

Drew, P. (1978) 'Accusations: the occasioned use of member's knowledge of "religious geography" in describing events', *Sociology*, 12: 1–22.

Drew, P. (1999) 'Therapy, counselling and survival through interpersonal connectedness: three studies of the social significance of discourse', *Journal of Contemporary Ethnography*, 25(3): 319–24.

Drew, P. and Heritage, J. (eds) (1992) *Talk at work: interaction in institutional settings*. Cambridge: Cambridge University Press.

Drew, P. and Wootton, A.J. (eds) (1988) *Erving Goffman: exploring the interaction order*. Cambridge: Polity Press.

Duranti, A. and Goodwin, C. (eds) (1992) *Rethinking context: language as an interactive phenomenon*. Cambridge: Cambridge University Press.

Edwards, D. (1997) *Discourse and cognition*. London: Sage.

Ervin-Tripp, S.M. and Kuntay, A. (1997) 'The occasioning and structuring of conversational stories'. In T. Givon (ed.), *Conversation: cognitive, communicative and social perspectives*. Amsterdam: John Benjamins Publishing Company.

Fielding, N.G. and Lee, R.M. (1998) *Computer analysis and qualitative research*. London: Sage.

Foucault, M. (1977) *Discipline and punish*. Harmondsworth: Penguin.

Foucault, M. (1991) 'Politics and the study of discourse'. In G. Burchell, C. Gordon and P. Miller (eds), *The Foucault effect: studies in governmentality*. Hemel Hempstead: Harvester Wheatsheaf.

Frith, U. (1991) *Autism and Asperger's Syndrome*. Cambridge: Cambridge University Press.

Garfinkel, H. (1967/1984) *Studies in ethnomethodology*. Cambridge: Polity Press.

Geertz, C. (1973) *The interpretation of cultures*. New York: Basic Books.

Givon, T. (1997) *Conversation: cognitive, communicative and social perspectives*. Amsterdam: John Benjamins Publishing Company.

Glaser, B.G. and Strauss, A.L. (1967) *The discovery of grounded theory: strategies for qualitative research*. Chicago IL: Aldine.

Goffman, E. (1974/1986) *Frame analysis: an essay on the organization of experience*. Boston: Northeastern University Press.

Goffman, E. (1981) *Forms of talk*. Oxford: Basil Blackwell.

Goodwin, C. (1980) 'Restarts, pauses and the achievement of mutual gaze at turn-beginning', *Sociological Inquiry*, 50: 272–302.

Goodwin, C. (1981) *Conversational organization: interaction between speakers and hearers*. London: Academic Press.

Goodwin, C. (1984) 'Notes on story structure and the organization of participation'. In J.M. Atkinson and J. Heritage (eds), *Structures of social action: studies of conversation analysis*. Cambridge: Cambridge University Press.

Goodwin, C. and Goodwin, M.H. (1992) 'Assessments and the construction of context'. In A. Duranti and C. Goodwin (eds), *Rethinking context: language as an interactive phenomenon*. Cambridge: Cambridge University Press.

Greatbatch, D. (1992) 'On the management of disagreement between news interviewees'. In P. Drew and J. Heritage (eds), *Talk at work: interaction in institutional settings*. Cambridge: Cambridge University Press.

Greatbatch, D. and Heritage, J. (1993) *The news interview: studies in the history and dynamics of a social form*. London: Sage.

Gregory, R. (1977) *Eye and brain*. London: Penguin.

Gumperz, J. and Hymes, D. (eds) (1972) *Directions in sociolinguistics*. New York: Holt, Rinehart and Winston.

Have, P. ten (1996/1998) 'Essential tensions in (semi)-open research interviews'. In Ethno/CA News Website: http://www.pscw.uva.nl/emca/index.htm

Have, P. ten (1998) *Doing conversation analysis: a practical guide*. London: Sage.

Have, P. ten and Psathas, G. (eds) (1995) *Situated order: studies in the social organization of talk and embodied activities*. Washington DC: University Press of America.

Heath, C. (1997) 'The analysis of face to face interaction using video'. In D. Silverman (ed.), *Qualitative Research: theory, method, practice*. London: Sage.

Heritage, J. and Atkinson, J.M. (eds) (1984) *Structures of social action: studies in conversation analysis*. Cambridge: Cambridge University Press.

Heritage, J. (1997) 'Conversation analysis and institutional talk: analysing data'. In D. Silverman (ed.), *Qualitative research: theory, method and practice*. London: Sage.

Heritage, J. and Sefi, S. (1992) 'Dilemmas of advice: aspects of the delivery and reception of advice in interaction between health visitors and first-time mothers'. In P. Drew and J. Heritage (eds), *Talk at work: interaction in institutional settings*. Cambridge: Cambridge University Press.

Hester, P. and Eglin, S. (1992) 'Category, predicate and task: the pragmatics of practical action', *Semiotica*, 88(3/4): 243–68.

Hester, P. and Eglin, S. (1996) *Culture in action*. Washington DC: International Institute for Ethnomethology and Conversation Analysis: University Press of America.

Hustler, D.E. and Payne, G.C.F. (1985) 'Ethnographic conversational analysis'. In R. Burgess (ed.), *Strategies of educational research: qualitative methods*. Brighton: Falmer Press.

Jayyusi, L. (1984) *Categorization and the moral order*. London: Routledge and Kegan Paul.

Jefferson, G. (1978) 'Sequential aspects of storytelling in conversation'. In J.N. Schenkein (ed.), *Studies in the organization of conversational interaction*. New York: Academic Press.

Jefferson, G. (1988) 'On the sequential organization of troubles talk in ordinary conversation', *Social Problems*, 35(4): 418–22.

Jefferson, G. (1989) 'Preliminary notes on a possible metric which provides for a "standard maximum" silence of approximately one second in conversation'. In

D. Roger and P. Bull (eds), *Conversation: an interdisciplinary perspective*. Clevedon: Multilingual Matters Publishers.

Jefferson, G. and Lee, J.R.E. (1981) 'The rejection of advice: managing the problematic convergence of a "troubles telling" and a "service encounter"', *Journal of Pragmatics*, 5(5): 399–422.

Jenks, C. (1995) *Visual culture*. London: Routledge.

Kimmel, A.J. (1996) *Ethical issues in behavioral research*. Oxford: Basil Blackwell.

Kirk, J. and Miller, M.L. (1986) *Reliability and validity in qualitative research*. London: Sage.

Knorr-Cetina, K. and Cicourel, A.V. (1981) *Advances in social theory and methodology: toward an integration of micro- and macro-sociologies*. London: Routledge and Kegan Paul.

Kuhn, T. (1970) *The structure of scientific revolutions* (2nd edn). Chicago: University of Chicago Press.

Labov, W. (1972) *Language in the inner city*. Oxford: Basil Blackwell.

Labov, W. and Waletsky, J. (1967) 'Narrative analysis'. In J. Helm (ed.), *Essays on the verbal and visual arts*. Seattle: University of Washington Press.

Lepper, G. (1994) *Making organizational trouble: an ethnomethological study of vocabularies of motive*. Unpublished PhD thesis. University of London Library.

Lepper, G. (1995) 'The uses of "formal organization" as an institutional resource', *Studies in Organizations, Cultures and Societies*, 1: 189–207.

Levinson, S.C. (1988) 'Putting linguistics on a proper footing: explorations in Goffman's concepts of participation'. In P. Drew and A.J. Wooton (eds), *Erving Goffman: exploring the interaction order*. Cambridge: Polity Press.

Levinson, S.C. (1992) 'Activity types and language'. In P. Drew and J. Heritage (eds), *Talk at work: interaction in institutional settings*. Cambridge: Cambridge University Press.

Linde, C. (1987) 'Explanatory systems in oral life stories'. In D. Holland and N. Quinn (eds), *Cultural models in language and thought*. Cambridge: Cambridge University Press.

Linde, C. (1993) *Life stories: the creation of coherence*. Oxford: Oxford University Press.

Lindstrom, L. (1992) 'Context contests: debatable truth statements on Tanna (Vanuatu)'. In A. Duranti and C. Goodwin (eds), *Rethinking context: language as an interactive phenomenon*. Cambridge: Cambridge University Press.

Lukes, S. (1986) *Power*. Oxford: Basil Blackwell.

McDermott, R.P. (1976) *Kids make sense: an ethnographic account of the interactional management of success and failure in one first-grade classroom*. Unpublished PhD dissertation. Stanford University Library.

McHoul, A.W. (1982) *Telling how texts talk: essays on reading and ethnomethodology*. London: Routledge and Kegan Paul.

McHoul, A.W. and Watson, D.R. (1984) 'Two axes for the analysis of "commonsense" and "formal" geographical knowledge and classroom talk', *British Journal of the Sociology of Education*, 5: 281–302.

McHugh, P. (1970) 'A common sense perception of deviance'. In H.I. Drietzl (ed.), *Recent sociology*, No. 2. 152–9.

MacKinlay, A. and Starkey, K. (eds) (1997) *Foucault, management and organization theory*. London: Sage.

Main, M. (1991) 'Metacognitive knowledge, metacognitive monitoring and singular (coherent) vs. multiple (incoherent) models of attachment: findings and directions for future research'. In P. Marris, J. Stevenson-Hinde and C. Parkes (eds), *Attachment across the life cycle*. New York: Routledge.

Main, M., Kaplan, N. and Cassidy, J. (1985) Security in infancy, childhood and adulthood: a move to the level of representation. In I. Bretherton and E. Waters (eds), *Growing points in attachment theory and research: Monograph of the Society for Researching Child Development*, 50(1–2): 66–104.

McLeod, J. (1997) *Narrative and psychotherapy*. London: Sage.

Mehan, H. (1979) *Learning lessons: social organization in the classroom*. Cambridge, MA: Harvard University Press.

Miller, E.G. and Rice, A.K. (1967) *Systems of organization: the control of task and sentient boundaries*. London: Tavistock Publications.

Miller, G. (1997) Building bridges: the possibility of analytic dialogue between ethnography, conversation analysis and Foucault. In D. Silverman (ed.), *Qualitative research: theory, method and practice*. London: Sage.

Mills, C.W. (1972) 'Situated actions and vocabularies of motive'. In *Power, politics and people: the collected essays of C. Wright Mills*. London: Oxford University.

Mirzoeff, N. (ed.) (1998) *The visual culture reader*. London and New York: Routledge.

Mitchell, W.T.J. (ed.) (1980) *On narrative*. Chicago, IL: University of Chicago Press.

Moerman, M. (1988) *Talking culture: ethnography and conversation analysis*. Philadelphia, PA: University of Philadelphia Press.

Moerman, M. and Sacks, H. (1971/1988) 'On "understanding" in the analysis of natural conversation'. In K. Nelson (1996) *Language in cognitive development*. Cambridge: Cambridge University Press.

Nelson, K. (1996) *Language in Cognitive Development: emergence of the mediated mind*. Cambridge: Cambridge University Press.

The New Shorter Oxford English Dictionary (1993).

Parker, I. (1999) *Deconstructing psychotherapy*. London: Sage.

Parsons, T. (1949) *The structure of social action*. Glencoe, IL: Free Press.

Payne, G.C.F. (1976) 'Making a lesson happen: an ethnomethodological analysis'. In M. Hammersley and P. Woods (eds), *The process of schooling*. London: Routledge and Kegan Paul.

Payne, G.C.F. and Hustler, D.E. (1980) 'Teaching the class: the practical management of a cohort'. In *The new sociology of education I, 1*.

Peräkylä, A. (1997) 'Reliability and validity based on tapes and transcripts'. In D. Silverman (ed.), *Qualitative research: theory, method and practice*. London: Sage.

Polkinghorne, D.E. (1988) *Narrative knowing and the human sciences*. Albany: State University of New York Press.

Psathas, G. (1995) Conversation analysis: the study of talk-in-interaction. Thousand Oaks, CA: Sage (Qualitative Research Methods 35).

Psathas, G. and Anderson, T. (1990) 'The "practices" of transcription in conversation analysis', *Semiotica*, 78: 75–99.

Ragin, C.C. (1994) *Constructing social research: the unity and diversity of method*. Thousand Oaks, CA: Pine Forge Press.

Riessman, C.K. (1993) *Narrative analysis*. Newbury Park, CA: Sage.

Ryave, A. (1978) 'On the achievement of a series of stories'. In J.N. Sheinkein (ed.), *Studies in the organization of conversation interaction*. New York: Academic Press.

Sacks, H. (1972a) 'On the analyzability of stories by children'. In R. Turner (ed.), *Ethnomethodology*. Harmondsworth, UK: Penguin Books.

Sacks, H. (1972b) 'An initial investigation of the usability of conversational data for doing sociology'. In D. Sudnow (ed.), *Studies in social interaction*. New York: Free Press.

Sacks, H. (1979) 'Hotrodder: a revolutionary category'. In G. Psathas (ed.), *Everyday language: studies in ethnomethodology*. New York: Earlbaum.

Sacks, H. (1984a) 'Notes on methodology'. In J.M. Atkinson and J. Heritage (eds), *Structures of social action: studies in conversation analysis*. Cambridge: Cambridge University Press.

Sacks, H. (1984b) 'On doing "being ordinary" '. In J.M. Atkinson and J. Heritage (eds), *Structures of social action: studies in conversation analysis*. Cambridge: Cambridge University Press.

Sacks, H. (1992a) *Lectures on conversation*, vol. I. Ed. G. Jefferson. Oxford: Basil Blackwell.

Sacks, H. (1992b) *Lectures on conversation*, vol. II. Ed. G. Jefferson. Oxford: Basil Blackwell.

Sacks, H., Schegloff, E.A. and Jefferson, G. (1974) 'A simplest systematics for the organization of turn-taking in conversation', *Language*, 50(4): 696–735.

Schafer, R. (1992) *Retelling a life: narrative and dialogue in psychoanalysis*. New York: Basic Books.

Schegloff, E.A. (1968) 'Sequencing in conversational openings', *American Anthropologist*, 70: 1075–95.

Schegloff, E.A. (1972) 'Notes on a conversational practice: formulating place'. In D. Sudnow (ed.), *Studies in social interaction*. New York: Free Press.

Schegloff, E.A. (1991) 'Reflections on talk and social structure'. In D. Boden and D.H. Zimmerman (eds), *Talk and social structure: studies in ethnomethodology and conversation analysis*. Cambridge: Polity Press.

Schegloff, E.A. (1992) 'In another context'. In A. Duranti and C. Goodwin (eds), *Rethinking context: language as an interactive phenomenon*. Cambridge: Cambridge University Press.

Schegloff, E.A. (1997) 'Whose text? Whose context?', *Discourse & Society*, 8(2): 165–87.

Schein, E.H. (1987) *The clinical perspective in fieldwork*. Newbury Park: Sage Publications.

Schenkein, J.N., (ed.) (1978) *Studies in the organization of conversational interaction*. New York: Academic Press.

Selznick, P. (1949/1966) *TVA and the grass roots: a study in the sociology of formal organization*. New York: Harper Row.

Sharrock, W.W. (1974) 'On owning knowledge'. In R. Turner (ed.), *Ethnomethodology*. Harmondsworth, UK: Penguin Books.

Seale, C. (1999) *The quality of qualitative research*. London: Sage.

Shiffrin, D. (1987) 'Discovering the context of an utterance', *Linguistics*, 25: 11–32.

Silverman, D. (1970) *The theory of organizations: a sociological framework*. London: Heinemann Educational Books.

Silverman, D. (1975) 'Accounts of organizations: organizational structures and the accounting process'. In J.B. McKinley (ed.), *Processing people*. New York: Holt, Rinehart and Winston.

Silverman, D. (1985) *Qualitative methodology and sociology: describing the social world*. Aldershot: Gower.

Silverman, D. (1993) *Interpreting qualitative data: methods for analysing talk, text and interaction*. London: Sage.

Silverman, D. (1997a) *Discourses of counselling*. London: Sage.

Silverman, D. (ed.) (1997b) *Qualitative research: theory, method and practice*. London: Sage.

Silverman, D. (1998) *Harvey Sacks and conversation analysis*. Key Contemporary Thinkers. Cambridge: Polity Press.

Silverman, D. and Jones, J. (1976) *Organizational work*. London: Cassell and Collier Macmillan.

Smith, D. (1978) 'K is mentally ill: the anatomy of a factual account', *Sociology*, 12: 23–53.

Spence, D. (1982) *Narrative truth and historical truth: meaning and interpretation in psychoanalysis*. New York: Norton.

Stern, D. et al. (1998) 'Non-interpretive mechanisms in psychoanalytic psychotherapy', *International Journal of Psychoanalysis*, 79: 903–18.

Strauss, A. (1978) *Negotiations: varieties, context, processes, and social order*. San Francisco: Jossey Bass.

Strauss, A., Schatzman, L., Bucher, R., Erlich, D. and Sobshin, M. (1964) *Psychiatric ideologies and institutions*. New York: Free Press.

Suchman, L. (1987) Plans and situated actions: the problem of human–machine interaction. Cambridge: Cambridge University Press.

Sudnow, D. (ed.) (1972) *Studies in social interaction.* New York: Free Press.

Torode, B. (1998) 'Narrative analysis using Code-a-text', *Qualitative Health Research,* 8(3): 414–32.

Trist, E.L. (1963) *Organisational choice: capabilities of groups at the coal face under changing technologies: the loss, rediscovery and transformation of a work tradition.* London: Tavistock Publications.

Vygotsky, L. (1962) *Thought and language.* Cambridge, MA: The MIT Press.

Watson, D.R. (1978) 'Categorization, authorization and blame negotiation in conversation', *Sociology,* 12: 105–13.

Watson, D.R. (1983) 'The presentation of victim and offender in discourse: the case of police interrogations and interviews'. *Victimology,* 8(1/2): 31–52.

Watson, D.R. (1987) 'Interdisciplinary considerations in the analysis of pro-terms'. In G. Button and J.R.E. Lee (eds), *Talk and social organization.* Clevedon: Multilingual Matters Publishers.

Watson, D.R. (1997) 'Ethnomethodology and textual analysis'. In D. Silverman (ed.), *Qualitative research: theory, method, practice.* London: Sage.

Weber, M. (1964) *The theory of social and economic organization.* New York: Free Press.

Wittgenstein, L. (1953/1968) *Philosophical investigations.* Oxford: Basil Blackwell.

Wittgenstein, L. (1969) *On certainty.* New York, Harper and Row.

Name index

Subject index